The State of Race

SUNY series in Multiethnic Literatures

Mary Jo Bona, editor

The State of Race

Asian/American Fiction
after World War II

Sze Wei Ang

Chua Mia Tee
Epic Poem of Malaya
1955
Oil on canvas, 112 × 153 cm
Collection of National Gallery Singapore

Published by State University of New York Press, Albany

© 2019 State University of New York

All rights reserved

No part of this book may be used or reproduced in any manner whatsoever without written permission. No part of this book may be stored in a retrieval system or transmitted in any form or by any means including electronic, electrostatic, magnetic tape, mechanical, photocopying, recording, or otherwise without the prior permission in writing of the publisher.

For information, contact State University of New York Press, Albany, NY
www.sunypress.edu

Library of Congress Cataloging-in-Publication Data

Names: Ang, Sze Wei, 1978– author.
Title: The state of race : Asian/American fiction after World War II / Sze Wei Ang.
Description: Albany : State University of New York Press, [2019] | Series: SUNY series in multiethnic literatures | Includes bibliographical references and index.
Identifiers: LCCN 2018035979 | ISBN 9781438475011 (hardcover : alk. paper) | ISBN 9781438475004 (pbk. : alk. paper) | ISBN 9781438475028 (ebook)
Subjects: LCSH: Race in literature. | Racism in literature. | Asians in literature. | American fiction—Asian American authors—History and criticism. | Malaysian fiction—History and criticism. | United States—Race relations. | Malaysia—Race relations.
Classification: LCC PN56.R16 A54 2019 | DDC 809/.933552—dc23
LC record available at https://lccn.loc.gov/2018035979

10 9 8 7 6 5 4 3 2 1

Contents

ACKNOWLEDGMENTS	vii
INTRODUCTION	1
CHAPTER ONE Tropes of Exemplarity: Morality as Racial Pedagogy	31
CHAPTER TWO Tropes of Degeneration: Morality and Political Efficacy	59
CHAPTER THREE Tropes of Insecurity: State Competition and Racial Anxiety	89
CHAPTER FOUR Tropes of Security: The Global American Dream	119
EPILOGUE	151
NOTES	155
WORKS CITED	173
INDEX	183

Acknowledgments

Early thoughts for this book surfaced at Cornell University under the guidance of Natalie Melas, Shelley Wong, Eric Tagliacozzo, and Laura Brown, and in conversation with others there, especially Nadine Attewell, Jo Chen, Jade Ferguson, Susan Hall, Yew-foong Hui, Janice Lim, Petrus Liu, and Sheetal Majithia. Françoise Lionnet and Shu-mei Shih modeled hospitality, conviviality, and intellectual rigor during the Mellon Postdoctoral Fellowship in the Humanities at UCLA. They drew into their orbit other amazing scholars; among them were Maya Boutaghou, Greg Cohen, Elizabeth Deloughrey, Alessandra Di Maio, Fatima El-Tayeb, Marcela Fuentes, Nouri Gana, Kirstie McClure, Sonali Pahwa, Sarah Valentine, and Travis Workman. Continued institutional and material support throughout the process has been crucial. The Research Grants Council of Hong Kong (Project Code HKU 740311H) and the Department of Comparative Literature in the Faculty of Arts at the University of Hong Kong made it possible to write the book. The Dean of the Arts Faculty, Derek Collins, and the department chair, Nicole Huang have been particularly supportive. Sections of chapter 1 appeared earlier in *CR: The New Centennial Review* 11, no. 3 (Winter 2011): 119–39. At the press, Rebecca Colesworthy offered timely, astute, and deft editorial guidance, and responses from anonymous readers drew out sometimes unexpected insights.

Along the way, I benefited from the generosity of others, both professional and personal. Kandice Chuh saw more fully the potential of the questions asked in this book long before I did. Jean Ma turned a chance encounter into a friendship. Timothy O'Leary deserves special thanks for always trying to do the right thing, and without his early enthusiasm the project might have turned out differently. David Pomfret provided thoughtful advice and unfailing good cheer at every turn when others might have flagged. Charles Schenking showed exceptional goodwill when he read the first draft in its entirety and then gave me the fortitude to keep going. William Corlett, Steven C. Dillon, Sanford Freedman, Carole Anne Taylor, and Anne B. Thompson were the best of teachers who became so much more than that. Friends who may not have always fully understood the nature of the work gave me the gifts of shelter, food, laughter, time, and patience. This incomplete list includes Mark and Jan Chandler, Katy Chan, Mabel Dunn, Fang Li Ping, Catherine Fobi, May Lam, Karen Leung, Paul Long, Rebecca Lovett and her family, Mika Kanda and her family, Carmen Man, Maggie Maurer-Fazio and her family, Lloyd and the Maxsons, Irene Ngiam, Emelia Ong, Ong Kian Ming, Sarah Potter, James and Soni Reese, Elaine Wong, Rebecca Yip, Isaac Wang, and Fifi Young. Yan Wong roped in her entire clan to show me relentless kindness, far beyond what I deserve, and for much longer than humanly possible. This book would not have been completed without my family who always wanted the best for me. Labor and love turned out to be not so very different after all.

Introduction

Race is not only local, it is global. While shaped by specific histories and parochialisms, racial tensions and the inequalities that fuel those tensions can give us a picture of how different parts of the world are connected. Racial tropes such as the "yellow peril," "model minority," "terrorist," "spy," "threat," or "contamination" have become commonplace in countries that otherwise do not share languages, cultures, religions, or histories. Stereotypes or variations of racist slogans such as "Go back where you came from!" and "This is *our* country!" turn up from Portland, Maine, to Portland, Oregon, and also across the Asia Pacific. How we talk about race, ironically, has become more similar in places and cultures still divided by significant political and cultural differences. The populist rage behind Donald Trump's surprise election victory in 2016 can even seem belated when compared to the rise of the far-right elsewhere: Boris Johnson and Theresa May in the UK, Marie Le Pen in France, Pauline Hansen in Australia, Xi Jinping in China, Narendra Modi in India, Hun Sen in Cambodia, Rodrigo Duterte in the Philippines, and Najib Razak in Malaysia.[1] Racism, unfortunately, is neither isolated nor original, but why?

The State of Race argues that some modes of racial thought are a transnational phenomenon because they emerge out of global as well as local histories.[2] Historical events that take place and have effects across national borders have shaped conceptions of race and its social meanings even when they first appear to be formed within particular cultures and contexts. The racial tropes I examine in this book may indeed have a presence everywhere in unexpectedly analogous and informal ways, but I want to suggest that the examples drawn from this study are global because they are first a part of global history. In other words, this book is primarily about how racial vocabularies have become more similar because national histories and cultures are formed in relation to transnational events, circumstances, and interests. The novels, short fiction, and cultural histories in the case studies of this book draw our attention to how racial tropes are similar across languages, borders, and time periods because they reflect the converging interests of each state as it is affected by the broader cultural phenomena that affect all states.[3] This book does not insist that racial formations everywhere are always alike. Rather, my interest here is in how hierarchies of value embodied in racial difference often reflect each state's interests as it cooperates and competes with other states, and the overlaps in various states' interests as they operate in a global system is what accounts for the overlaps in racial language. The social meanings of racial difference are determined in response to global and local formations.

Modes of racial thought in different countries can take on remarkably similar forms because the state is still central to our cultures and politics. As Françoise Lionnet and Shu-mei Shih have argued, we can neither do away with the state nor hold tightly to single nation frameworks in our analytical schemas: "Nation-states are alive as mechanisms of control and domination even when transnational corporations are supposed to have dissolved their boundaries. Minority cultural workers are transnational not because they transcend the national, but because their cultural orientations are by definition creolized in Glissant's sense" (9). In this book, the comparison of minor literatures helps us see that racism is resilient because it can be used to strengthen the political centrality of the state. This is not to say that racial formations are always identical. Differences in local expressions can in fact be valuable to the state precisely because race is flexible and adaptable to particular geopolitical conditions or historical periods. But while racial figurations need to be read within the national contexts where they circulate, they are not isolated from global flows. The model minority or invocations of the American Dream in the novels compared in this book demonstrate that the state mobilizes ideas about race to its own ends in response to events that take place across its borders.

But to understand how race is shaped by shared historical developments, we need to first understand the nation-state's effects on culture. Far from becoming outdated or obsolete, the nation-state has become more rather than less central to a globally-connected world after the end of World War II (WWII). Decolonization strengthened rather than weakened the world state system, and state sovereignty has to be understood in conjunction with its codependency on other states like it. Therefore, the cultural histories of state growth and development—especially in the second half of the twentieth century—presented in this book play two roles. First, the history of colonial and postcolonial state growth in Malaysia plays an important pedagogical role because it introduces a less widely known culture to readers unfamiliar with Southeast Asia. Second, these cultural histories demonstrate that to become modern in the wake of colonialism is to see one's self and history as part of a racial group that forms the basis of the nation. Racial thought is a symptom of the hidden connections that make up global culture. How we conceptualize race is part of an informal but consistent global racial system grounded in the expansion of state strength and capitalist logic.

Contrary to what seems intuitive, the end of colonialism did not lead to the end of Orientalist and colonial forms of thought.[4] Rather, the postcolonial state builds on colonial logic already embedded in the state infrastructures and institutions it inherited.[5] Colonialism may have created modern conceptions of race as biological and civilizational differences, but racial politics now confirms or negates the postcolonial state's ideas of what it takes to guarantee its success. Race formalizes state power even as it is formed by the state. As the fiction and the cultural histories in this book demonstrate, racism appears to be a social problem but it actually performs a necessary justification for state power as the state mediates inclusion and exclusion, both real and symbolic. But the racial tropes that appear as self-evident are, however, revealed to play more complex roles. Racial tropes are not only forms of representation; the literary examples in the chapters reveal that racial language is performative because it is morally prescriptive.

The State of Race returns our attention to the state because, on the one hand, the state plays a regulatory role in the transnational issues of national and international governance, migration, war, and trade. But, on the other hand, transnational events also shape how we think and talk about race because they first affect the nation-state. The state's influence over cultural life is neither static nor unchanging. National and global flows need to be understood as a form of relation where neither can maintain the upper hand, and where each potentially strengthens or weakens the other. Race matters in the accounting of nationalist attachments because it can either enhance or destabilize state legitimacy, and the state's relations to other states. Racial anxiety is therefore a symptom of how the state sees in a world where global power relations are unequal and precarious. But how is it that we come to adopt the state's insecurities as our own? By paying attention to local histories, especially to how the state develops or intervenes in racial discourse, this book uncovers surprising assumptions about how power, the state, and beliefs about race are connected.

Events in recent history such as WWII, decolonization, the Cold War, and globalization have not only failed to rid us racism, these political upheavals and social changes have actually intensified racial difference as visual and cultural markers of social identity. The collapse of colonialism, the Cold War, and economic and technological globalization introduced new challenges to state sovereignty, but individual states also respond by strengthening its borders and what those borders symbolize—the power to decide how human life is valued, at least within its own borders. Political events such as Brexit and Trump's "Muslim ban" are but two of the most recent instances of states reasserting their power in the age of globalization. The chapters that follow explain how in the wake of transnational historical developments, "race" has become even more authoritative in the organization of social life within the nation-state. The (global) American Dream embodies state desire from WWII onwards and it informs the figurations of the model minority and the terrorist spy in literary fiction and popular culture.

To that effect, this book draws on literatures and cultural histories from national and regional traditions not usually in conversation—the US and Malaysia in this case—to reveal how vastly different countries that on the surface do not have very much in common nonetheless share very similar ways of thinking about, and representing, racial difference.[6] The unlikely comparison of otherwise historically disjunct sites not connected by either direct colonial, economic, or military ties is a comparison not of equivalence, but of convergence. Key texts in these two different literary traditions converge in their use of the tropes of moral exemplarity or degeneration, and of state strength and weakness. Racial figures such as the model minority or the terrorist spy can be correlated to how the state sees, that is, how it sees itself as well as its subjects. Both ways of seeing are crucial to state power and legitimacy.

The aim of this comparison is not to resolve the historical differences between the literary traditions and canons of Asia and America, but to propose instead that despite real and tangible contrasts in the two sites, their overlapping figurations of Asian minorities are not accidental.[7] I do not mean to discount the influence languages and cultures has on racial formation, but I do want to propose that similarities as well as differences can be revelatory. Similarity and difference exist in a dynamic rather than fixed, binary, relation.[8]

While globalization is commonly thought to divide the world into winners and losers, countries on both sides of the purported divide actually share a common language of fear and anxiety about the racial Other inside as well as outside of state borders. This anxiety is now a part of global culture. In *The State of Race*, shared racial tropes are animated across historical periods, cultural particularities, and geopolitical ties because they are put in the service of strengthening state power in an interdependent world state system. Each novel and each cultural history is singular, and each is a product of its time and people. But seen together as part of a larger narrative about the world and its historical changes, they reveal how the state's interests—shaped by global flows—are embodied in racial language.

The dynamic relationship between similarity and difference may also be a feature or effect of globalization itself. As Anna Lowenhaupt Tsing argues, globalization is not an obvious story of how the strong always conquers the weak. The universal and the particular both play a role in generating our experiences of the global. The peripheries do not merely confirm what we already know about globalization—often consisting of knowledge and observations drawn through an imperial gaze—but rather, they require us to rethink our very definitions of how globalization works. Local expressions of the global encounter modify what we think about the "global," and these encounters reveal how interactions between the local and the global are sometimes contradictory, often messy, and that their outcomes are far from guaranteed. The comparison of the US and Malaysia in this book is only one of many potential global comparisons where both the "winners" and "losers," or the "strong" and the "weak" countries of globalization adopt similar racial language.

Malaysia, in particular, serves as an interesting counterpoint because the US neither colonized Malaysia the way it did Vietnam or the Philippines, nor intervened in overt or extended ways either militarily or economically as it did Indonesia and Laos. The similarities of racial language in both countries show us that while global connections are historical, they are not always linear or immediately visible. The fictions we tell about state power and legitimacy are produced out of diverse locations not necessarily connected by formal colonial or imperialist relations. Instead, racial tropes emerge out of the historical-materialist conditions of global events such as colonialism, WWII, and the Cold War. The tropes and the moral force behind them embody the uneven but certain growth of the world state system. And the integration of postcolonial, postwar states into the capitalist, world state system overwhelmingly shapes our uses of racial language. Some racial slurs do remain peculiar to certain cultures. For example, Malays sometimes refer to the Chinese as "pigs"—*Cina babi*—because the Chinese eat pork while the Malays who are Muslim consider pigs unclean or nonhalal. These differences in dietary habits do not appear as cultural differences in white US culture, and thus are not part of how Chinese Americans are racialized.

However, the more familiar racial marker, "slit-eyed" in English also appears in Malay as *sepet*. And while the quintessential Asian American stereotype of the "model minority" or "the yellow peril" is not translated into the Malay language, the figure of the overachieving Chinese or Indian Malaysian is nonetheless recognizable and common in local popular and political discourse. Chinese Malaysians are caricatured as *kiasu*, a slang word taken from Hokkien that is literally translated as "afraid to lose," and used to ridicule the Chinese as driven, unethical go-getters who outperform Malays in schools and business. "White rage" and the Malay "amok" (transliterated into English as "amuck") are different phrases that emerged out of different histories, but they both refer to moral outrage—and barely veiled threats—in a world where majorities perceive themselves as being "left behind" in their "own" country. Beliefs about innate, race-based aptitude motivate continued demands for the expulsion or deportation of minorities to secure the rights of the majority in the US and in Malaysia.

Given the recognizable overlaps in sentiment and semantics, what accounts for the analogous nature of racist imagery in countries that share neither a past colonial relationship, languages, religion, gender norms, nor cultural practices? *The State of Race* argues that the answer to this question lies in how race is a global problem because it is a problem of the nation-state in general, and not the American state in particular. National histories and fictions are discrete and local but they are part of a global story. While these racial stereotypes are varied in form, they describe similar kinds of tensions, sentiments, and anxieties about—and on the part of—the state under globalization. The comparison of minor racial formations, that is, not only within the context of white and nonwhite relations but also between nonwhite and nonwhite relations, shifts our theorizations of race within colonial and postcolonial studies. What we often take to be exceptional—in this case racism—is part of a much larger network of events and global shifts. In a previously unpublished essay, "India," W. E. B. Dubois's famous dictum, "The problem of the twentieth century is the problem of the color-line" emerges in an augmented form as "The problem of the Negroes thus remains a part of the worldwide clash of color. So, too, the problem of the Indians can never be simply a problem of autonomy in the British commonwealth of nations" (8).⁹ The problem of race is not limited to the national experiences of colonialism, slavery, or American segregation. Neither India's nor the US's problems with race can be understood only locally or solved by national independence. Race is a problem because it is not exceptional.

> They [Americans] do not want to solve [the problem of race], they do not want to understand it, they want simply to be done with it and hear the last of it. Of all possible attitudes this is the most dangerous, because it fails to realize the most significant fact of the opening century, viz.: The Negro problem in America is but a local phase of a world problem. (33)

We need to understand how race works in specific, local histories and cultures, but we also need to recognize that focusing only on specific national examples can create lacunae in our conceptions of state and culture. These blind spots can moreover preempt critiques of the state as the literary scholar, Ania Loomba, and the anthropologist, Yasuka Takezawa, have argued about India and Japan, respectively.

But what is the global story of race, and how can we think of race as a "world problem"? Race became a world problem with the advance of European colonialism that identified racial difference as a problem its civilizing mission could erase. But colonialism also created new social divisions that disrupted local cultures. In its drive toward epistemic certainty, colonialism's organization of human beings into racial groups posited race as both problem and solution. For example, racial identity became contentious in postcolonial Malaysia because the British guaranteed the rights and recognition of one race—the Malays—above and beyond those of other racial groups, including the *Orang Asli* or *Orang Asal* (literally translated as "true peoples" or "original peoples"), that is, the indigenous communities whose many different religions, customs, and languages are widely distinct from Islam and Malay *adat*. But neither the grouping of *Orang Asals* nor the Malays take into account native forms of social groups. And like American Indians, the indigeneity and prior claims of the *Orang Asal* have been relegated to the margins.

Colonial racial ideas not only continue after decolonization, they have flourished as part of dominant political discourse after the end of colonialism. Postcolonial belief in Malay supremacy is a legacy of colonial assumptions about racial difference and how racial difference should be best managed. But more importantly, race provides the cultural and ideological continuity that guarantees state legitimacy as postcolonial elites inherited the colonial state apparatus.

For example, under the British colonial regime, Chinese Malayans were deported "back" to China for crimes, poverty, and for holding the wrong political convictions, that is, communism, because the British assumed all Chinese belonged to China even if they were born in Malaya. Consequently, in their management of "bad" Chinese, the British actually created a structural necessity for the recognition of the "good" Chinese even if they did not call them "model minorities." Malayan-born Chinese had to perform as exemplary subjects or risk deportation to a land they barely knew. Today, conservative Malay politicians continue to exhort the Chinese to "balik Cina" or "balik Tongsan" when they pose a threat to supposed "Malay values." In other words, the Chinese who perform according to the Malay-dominated state expectations of "proper" or "desirable" racial behavior can stay, while those who do not, are free to "go back." Racist discourse thus transforms political disagreements into irrevocable racial and moral difference.

These epithets are rooted in British colonial logic and particular to the politics of inclusion and exclusion in Malaysia, but we hear similar sentiments in racist slogans in the US and other countries. "Go back to where you came from" is now part of a global culture of anxiety because these epithets reflect commonly held assumptions about the vitality of state power—usually as weak or threatened—under globalization. Racial tropes are global tropes because they are heavily invested in the sovereignty of the state and couched in a language of morality and rights that generate powerful attachments to the state. The "true" citizen can say "Go back to where you came from" to another person, and in so doing confirms his or her prior right to the state. Ironically, racism is seen as the political resolution to the social anxieties it provokes.

The State of Race contends that despite significant cultural, social, and political changes in the postwar period, cultural continuity runs from colonialism to globalization and it appears in the form of racial thought nurtured and protected by state power. The colonial state may have created and instituted modern notions of race in Southeast Asia, but it was the insecurities of young, postcolonial states in the Cold War period that turned ethnocentric fears and anxieties about the racial Other into an integral part of the ideologies of the newly independent states.[10] From Asia to Asian America, colonialist notions of racial difference as fundamental civilizational difference undergird representations of Asians and Asian Americans as efficient, industrious, and high achieving but also sly, dangerous, and untrustworthy. The contradictions in these racial stereotypes reflect the precarious positions of racial minorities often represented in relation to how "useful" they are as laborers, informants, or managers of other minorities in service to the state. Colonialism, Euro-American industrialization, and the need for cheap, indentured labor in Southeast Asia and the Americas first brought the Chinese and Indians to those new lands.

Colonialism's naturalization of race as a stable, unchanging category that posits cultural sameness, coherence, and homogeneity is taken up by postcolonial states in order to strengthen their own positions in the face of globalization's promises and its threats. Globalization, that is, the global flows, institutions, and processes that challenge the sovereignty of the state, has effects on how we think about racial difference because it has effects on the sovereignty of the state. The story of race as a global problem cannot be told without also telling the story of growing state power around the world driven by similar capitalist needs and geopolitical desires for increasing economic influence. European colonialism may have introduced modern ideas of racial difference to Southeast Asia through the setting up of the modern state, but national independence proved to be its incubator.[11]

"Nationalist" or primordialist ideas about racial identity are fundamentally tied to the world state system because as the cultural histories in this book demonstrate, globalization does not do away with the state so much as it refocuses state power on new global threats. The state's concerns around security and sovereignty are a reaction to globalization that serves to secure its own status within global economic, political, and cultural systems of influence that involve competing parties. The explosion of tribal nationalism or "populist" nationalism in the twenty-first century—a political push toward increasing the state's power to protect itself—around the world is an example of how states believe their sovereignty is under threat.

The postcolonial state therefore develops and protects its sovereignty on two levels that are often interrelated and interdependent, that is, in its actions as a political actor and as an economic actor on the world stage. In both its roles as political and economic actor, the state describes racial difference in a way that has the curious effect of framing race in moral language. Racial minorities have to "contribute" to the state—"model minorities"—and if they do not, they are traitors—"terrorist," "spy,"—or simply "disrespectful" or "ungrateful." Racial language has powerful effects on our social imagination because they not only presume to explain complex realities in an easily accessible manner, but because they inscribe racial minorities into moral narratives that have disciplinary functions. This moral language, however, takes the form of a morality that guarantees the health of the state above anything or anyone else.

Stereotypes such as the overachieving model minority or traitorous spy masquerading among true citizens organize racial identities into categories of either "good" or "bad" in ways that are useful to, first, the colonial state, and, now, the hypernationalist state in the late twentieth and early twenty-first centuries. Even "positive" racial stereotypes can mask complex relations. The myth of the model minority, for example, triangulates Asian American experience in black-and-white racial tensions in the US in a way that emphasizes Asian American alienness while simultaneously downplaying how race significantly shapes social experience. Racial language couched in moral language is moreover powerful because it explains and externalizes the alienation experienced in a world where economic and political insecurities have risen and look poised to continue to rise. The anxieties of being "left behind"—a strange but powerful use of apocalyptical, moral language—is the mark of being a subject of the state under globalization fearful of being marginalized in the new world order of global capital.

White nationalism in the US or Malay nationalism in Malaysia that claim a prior right to be in power argue that the US and Malaysia "belong" to whites and Malays. The state has the obligation to first secure the pursuit of happiness for racial majorities. Populist nationalism based on essentialist or "purist" notions of racial origin consequently harnesses moral language to make its claims for state sovereignty, and concerns about rights, protection, privileges, and victimization are presented as moral concerns that only the state has the ability to guarantee and protect. The state appears to be an effective bulwark against the threats symbolized by the immigrant or refugee because the state is able to take forceful, legal measures against "foreign" threats. Anxieties about race cannot be separated from anxieties about state power.

The following section of the introduction offers us a new postcolonial reading of racial thought as it developed from precolonial times, through European colonialism, to WWII, the Cold War, and finally, in the late twentieth and twenty-first centuries. Asian Americans and Malaysians have been racialized in different and uneven ways, and the next section retains their radical differences in the telling of their cultural histories. But both histories of racial subjection are a record of how the state exerts, defines, and enacts its political sovereignty in relation to racial difference as biological difference, and racial difference as civilizational difference. In mobilizing the two modes of defining racial difference, the state abrogates to itself the right to determine "good" and "bad" racial behavior in order to protect its sovereignty.

Read together, we also see how shared concepts of race within both national imaginaries have been informed by colonial notions of biology and culture, imperial relations between the putative East and West, and finally, also by the ideal roles of the modern nation-state in international and global politics. The conflation of race and morality in these two cultural histories shows us how race came to define state power in the wake of colonialism and in the face of globalization's future threats. Combined, both histories show us the contours of an informal system of race linked not by direct historical connections or geographical contiguity, but by shared anxieties around state power and how to secure it. The next section of the introduction offers broad overviews of how racial subjection is a function of state power.

State Power and Racial Categories

Colonial policies in British Malaya have been thought of as "benign" and successful compared to its more violent legacies in India, Burma, or British West Africa. But "benign" colonial policies have nonetheless had long lasting consequences that run even to the twenty-first century. For example, under the British, the major racial communities in Malaysia were segregated by the types of labor each group performed and where they took place. The Chinese were predominantly employed in as coolies in tin mines or were merchants in the cities; the Indians were laborers in the rubber plantations; and the Malays worked in rice-planting, agriculture or fishing. This division of labor that was the basis of British policy of divide and rule explains why as Malaya decolonized, it was left with economic and geographical racial segregation. As the primary form of social organization in late nineteenth century Malaya that has carried over throughout the twentieth century, British forms of racial management imparted an illusion of predictability and fixity during times of chaos, change, and historical transition. Colonialism introduced racial categories to mark cultural and linguistic distinctions, but these categories were also treated as stable and unchanging, and finally, as natural and rightful forms of political and social identity. But the belief that race first signifies biological difference and then cultural and linguistic difference is a piece of colonial fiction that organized and separated racial groups by temperament, dispositions, political beliefs, and "virtue." Today, brown bodies are still thought to be "lazier" and yellow bodies more "cunning" or "inscrutable" not only in the West, but also in the East. Race, consequently, is a distillation of the state's views of productive or desirable forms of behaviors that are thought to be fixed and uniform within each racial group.

"Racial language," or the language that colonialists used to describe the supposed behaviors, predispositions, and temperaments of the Malayan subjects laid the groundwork for racial stereotypes—the conniving Chinese, the lazy Malay, and the alcoholic Indian, for example—that still have emotive power and explicatory force. As they learned to recognize the racial categories that the colonizers introduced, natives started to see and speak of themselves and one another as raced subjects—separate and different on the basis of biology and moral disposition. Internalized racism involved not only seeing one's self as raced, but seeing other Asians as raced as well.

The British are moreover remembered as "benign" and successful colonizers because they set themselves in opposition to the Malayan communist army, whom they portrayed as "vicious" foreigners and spies of communist China. The history of the communist insurgency more fully elaborated in chapter 2 demonstrates that colonial success was achieved not primarily through military might, but by changing the terms in which we understand "good" and "evil." "Success" in colonial wars refers not only to actual, physical, or military victories, but also to how our language and conceptual categories about race and culture became infused with moral judgment.

To briefly summarize Malaya's early colonial history, the Portuguese and the Dutch colonized coastal areas of Malaya as early as 1511 because of their geographic importance to trading lines in the South China Seas. The port cities of Penang and Singapore came under British control in 1786 and 1819, and in 1826, they merged Penang, Singapore, and Melaka after the Dutch gave up Melaka in 1824. Known collectively as the Straits Settlement, these states fell under the jurisdiction of the British government in India. Most of the local Malay chiefs did not recognize this cessation of power to the British,[12] but it nonetheless established the beginning of British direct rule in Malaya via the Treaty of Pangkor, signed on January

20, 1874. Concurrent disputes in the Perak court over a royal succession, and also among the warring Chinese clans who worked Perak's very profitable tin mines, gave the British an opportunity to portray themselves as "peace keeper" or "mediator" within the Malay and Chinese factions. This perception of the white colonizer as "peace keeper" is foundational to how the modern Malaysian state sees itself as necessary to adjudicating between different racial groups.

The success of British direct rule and its Residential System was established under the aegis of the second British Resident, Sir Hugh Low, a diplomatic Malay scholar and naturalist who involved local Malay and Chinese leaders in his administration. Low and his successor, Sir Frank Swettenham, were both fluent in Malay, sympathetic to Malay customs, and engaged Malays in their administration, if only at the lower levels.[13] Local ruling elites began to cooperate with the British, and that consequently meant the colonizers could "govern a large country cheaply with a handful of Europeans" (Harper 19). However, the British limited Malay administration to areas with mostly Malay populations as the British did not trust them to govern the growing immigrant Chinese and Indian communities, thus imposing racial segregation in Malaya on social and administrative levels.[14] This strategy of divide and conquer later further allowed the British to keep the racial communities separate and at odds with one another, especially when anticolonial sentiments developed.

The term "Melayu" or Malay was not originally a racial term, but was rather first used to refer to the status of subjects of the Malaccan Kingdom,[15] and that of Palembang. Malays trace their civilization, sultanates, customs, and hierarchies specifically to the Malaccan Sultanate between the period of 1400 D and 1511 AD,[16] and Chinese and Indian traders had a long history of contact with Malay rulers beginning as early as the fifteenth century, although never at the levels between the years 1830 and 1930 when British Malaya received the highest influx of immigrants and migrant workers. Later, Chinese and European writings ascribed "Malay" to the other sultanates in the Malayan peninsula (Milner 51).

Ironically, this mythical "point of origin" in the Muslim Malay ethos—now the basis for national identity and ethnocentric politics—is the result of an intersection of transnational flows and cultural syncreticism intensified by the popularity of Malacca's harbor as a connection between India, China, Persia, Arabia, Java, and later, Europe. China was a powerful ally to and patron of the nascent kingdom and played an important role in recognizing Parameswara's position as ruler in 1405, who later paid a visit to the Chinese imperial court in 1411 as a form of tribute. The British themselves also played a part in creating and recognizing new sultanates as late as the nineteenth century, precisely so they could negotiate with local leaders and gain influence over those lands.[17]

However, historically, the "Malays" were not a distinct racial group. The founder of Malay civilization, Parameswara was a Hindu who converted to Islam and changed his name to Megat Iskandar Shah. However, Islam seems not to have taken a hold until 1446: "[. . .] when Indian Muslim merchants at Malacca organized a *coup d'état* and put on the throne a prince of the royal house whose mother was an Indian Muslim" (Gullick 39). Despite the prominence of Indian Muslims in precolonial Malayan history and origins, in the twentieth century, the racial group "*mamak*" are now considered "Indian" rather than "Malay."[18] As Judith Nagata points out, the offspring of mixed Muslim parents during the fifteenth century would have been considered full Malays, obliterating the fact that Malay royalty does not have a "pure" biological racial lineage (107–8).[19] "Malay identity" in precolonial times was further complicated by the various linguistic and cultural practices among the different ethnic groups that are now recognized as Malay, such as the Bugis, Achenese, Minangkabau, Javanese, Boyanese, and so on. Loyalty was not accorded on the basis of "race," but rather, was given to the sultan whose protection one fell under. Different groups had control of different sultanates. For example, the Minangkabau in Negeri Sembilan,[20] and the Bugis in Selangor, most of whom were in competition and antagonistic (Milner 14).

The Chinese settlers who immigrated to Malacca as a result of good relations between the two kingdoms intermarried with local Malays, and over time they lost command of their Chinese dialects and adopted Malay dress and customs, as well as European culture, but remained distinctly "Chinese." Called the Straits Chinese and also known as "Peranakan" or *Baba* and *Nyonya* Chinese, they sounded and acted like Malay but were nonetheless "Chinese."[21] These examples of precolonial notions of race and race relations as part of political and cultural systems contrasts with modern colonial notions of race as homogenous, unchanging, and stable. As a contemporary example of how the postcolonial state abrogates more power to itself now by imposing its own definitions of "race," today, non-Muslims who marry Malays are considered to *masuk Melayu* (become Malay) and are required by law to convert to Islam, take up a Muslim name, and their children are categorized as Muslim and Malay.[22]

Similarly, the Chinese were never a homogenous community. Defined primarily by their linguistic groups, the Chinese maintained distinct forms of "Chinese" identity because they retained political and cultural autonomy within their linguistic communities. Leadership among the different Chinese groups took the form of what was called a Kapitan system, led by the *Kapitan Cina*, usually the leader of a secret society, respected by his community as well as the Malay court.[23] Mostly from the southern Chinese provinces, these groups rarely intermixed, and certain groups such as the Hakka were often ridiculed by other communities because of their customs and language. They were further divided by occupational specializations.

> The Cantonese dominated mining and crafts, while the Hokkien and Teochew were agriculturists, small shopkeepers and boatmen. [. . .] Chinese of the same surname or clan but speaking different dialects also clung to their own dialect group. [. . .] When the Chinese migrants came to the Malay world, societies based on clan or dialect associations appeared to be an indispensable organization affording protection and assistance in an alien and often hostile environment. (Andaya 141)

Chinese laborers who arrived as indentured laborers were most often exploited by other Chinese and suffered appalling conditions onboard the ships that brought them to the tin mines of Malaya.

Precolonial Malays owed their loyalties not to an abstract idea of a singular Malay race, or a single sultan, but rather to their individual, respective sultanates in the different states. In his essay, Clive Kessler identifies as characteristic of Malay culture a political identity that has become conflated with "Malayness" and continues to have a hold on contemporary Malay group identity: "Malay society and culture, as they conceive of themselves, rest centrally upon a political condition: upon people having and being subjects of a *raja*, a ruler. The polity, a *kerajaan*, is not only a ruler's domain but his subjects' socio-cultural condition, that of having a raja" (139). In other words, the sultanate became a state-sanctioned marker of race in colonial Malaya, where racial identity became an important measure of one's place in colonial order. As long as the dignity and standing of the Malay Rulers remained intact, Malay identity was still secure in the face of all other modernizing flows brought about by British colonialism and the increase of immigrant communities. Anthony Milner likens the subsequent colonial dislocation of the relationship between ruler and commoner to "a type of psychological and spiritual suicide" (25).

The British successfully created the idea of the modern Malay by first uniting the competing sultanates. Individual sultans from the various sultanates were only first brought together at the first Federal Council or "Conference of the Rulers" in July 1897. As Frank Swettenham, the first British Resident, noted not without a little pride, the gathering of the Sultans was a success because it eventually led to the unification of the inland states on the peninsula.

> Never in the history of Malaya has any such assemblage been ever imagined. I doubt if anybody has ever heard of one Ruler of a State making a ceremonial visit to another; but to have been able to collect together in one place the Sultans of Perak, Selangor, Pahang and Negeri Sembilan is a feat that might have well been regarded as impossible. (As quoted in Chai 50)

Given the significance of the raja to Malay communal identity, the very act of bringing together the various heads of states from the different sultanates reified the colonial notion that all the brown peoples of Malaya were part of the same "race." The enterprising white colonialists were the first to "unite" the Malays, for whom racial unity today is the bulwark of racial identity and race-based political parties.

But while colonialism disrupted local communities and traditional cultural life, these histories are also a record of how local existing systems of exploitation, kinship, patronage, and social hierarchies were integrated with modern ideas of race. Traditional rulers colluded with the colonialists, and traditional hierarchies became the basis for new, modern hierarchies. Tan Malaka, one of the foremost Indonesian communist intellectuals of the early twentieth century, argued that native elites were complicit in colonial exploitation of the country, where indigenous systems of exploitation continued to exist in a dual economy alongside Western capitalism: "All of the social, political and economic traits of traditional society had been left undisturbed—had, indeed, been reinforced in political terms—by Dutch colonialism, while the capitalist economy thrived in a number of more or less completely separate enclaves" (Christie 39). This duality allowed native elites to assume power after decolonization and accounts for the continuation of colonial logic in the postcolonial state.[24]

The argument for the political and economic "rights" of the Malays today ties politics to economics in openly racial and religious discourse. Racial discrimination in favor of the Malays is the law of the land recognized by the British during decolonization and further entrenched in the 1960s and 1970s.[25] Pan-Islamics movements were popular among Malays, Indonesians, and others of the Islamic *umma*, including Arabs who were at first not included as "Malays."[26] These movements, aimed particularly at empowering nonelite Muslims to become more informed and educated both as Malays and as Muslims, were among the cultural factors that led to the interweaving of race and religion as modern Malay identity.[27] The end of colonialism left new postcolonial states with unwieldy new demographics, but the Cold War placed even greater challenges ahead of them. Developed more fully in the chapters of this book, the cultural history of the postcolonial state in the twentieth century exemplifies how the state looks outward as much as it looks inward in its drive to power. More importantly, it explains why state power in conjunction with the growth of capitalism has had such an overwhelming influence over the development of racial thought.

This relationship between race, state power, and capitalism as it unfolded in Southeast Asia was not isolated or limited to Southeast Asia. The US also has a long history of understanding or representing Asian Americans and Asians in relation to the labor they can perform within the larger goals of US state development, and their roles as laborers, workers, experts, or technocrats in the world economy. While different from Southeast Asian colonial history, the cultural histories Asian American literary critics, sociologists, and historians have produced paint a rich picture of the relationship between race and capitalism, and how trade relations and the geopolitical fight for dominance in the world economy have played important roles in shaping our beliefs about race through the Asian American experience. What appears as a common denominator in both histories is the emergence of racial tropes as moral tropes that secure state power driven by capitalist growth.

Modern relations between Asia and the US can be traced back to the late nineteenth and early twentieth century when the Asia Pacific appears as a possible new market for the expansion of US capital. Lisa Lowe, David Palumbo-Liu, Colleen Lye, and others also argue that the racial formation of Asian Americans is intimately tied to economic success in Asia and that success causes anxieties about the US economy. The racialization of Asian Americans from the nineteenth century to the twentieth century takes place within the context of American economic needs and Asian labor read through the prism of US Orientalist fantasies as well as its diplomatic relations with Asia. In other words, Asian American racial figures cannot be understood outside of the US state acting to protect both its economy as well as its polity from Asian immigrants. This history begins with the Nationality Act of 1790 that set aside Asians as "racially ineligible" for citizenship, and the Page Act enforced from 1875 to 1943 that banned Asian coolies from entering the US. While Asian American labor was crucial to the development of capital and the development of infrastructure such as its railroads, Asian bodies were deemed to be too threatening and unassimilable to the body politic.

The inclusion or the transformation of "Asians" into Americans at the turn of the century is made possible by imagining Asians as suitable laborers. However, Asian Americans were thought to be both desirable but also a threat to the United States. Asian Americans can supposedly "adapt Asia to America" and "transform America through the application of a 'Confucian' ethos" (Palumbo-Liu, 21), but they are also imagined to have an aptitude for economic development and thus might displace American workers. The production of the model-minority is made possible because of the correlations between Confucianism and Protestantism.[28] But Asian traditions believed to be Confucian practices, Palumbo-Liu shows, are really a product of the US imaginary.[29]

During this period, the Orientalist anchoring of the referent "Asiatic" to capitalism was further cemented by the geopolitical concerns that result from the need to open up and secure new markets for Western regimes. Colleen Lye's historicization of the representations of Asians or Asian Americans in the nineteenth century demonstrates that even while the US invented Japan and China as civilizational polar opposites, these oppositions were also collapsed to generate fear of an Asia that would overwhelm the US economically and demographically: "The 'yellow peril' articulates the numerical power of a 'Chinese' mass with a miraculous 'Japanese' developmental capacity" (Lye 17). The racialization of "Asia" was produced in the relations between US national identity and US relations with other nation-states. However, geopolitical lines were still changing, and Western countries began to fight for influence over China and access to its mythical, vast, untapped market as the colonization of Africa began to fall apart. The military presence of Russian in the region further complicated the politics of this time, and the British in particular played Japan against Russia's expansion into China. In the process, Russia was also racialized as "Oriental" on the basis of its "bureaucratic corruption" (23). China, Japan, and Russian were then seen to make up the "East" as opposed to the West.

The formation of "Asia," in this example, proves to be capitalism-driven geopolitics that is determined by so-called moral values assigned to particular races. Attacks against class or capitalism are similarly played out on the bodies of Asians as they appear in early-twentieth-century US literature. Lye goes on to argue that the figure of the "Asiatic," as represented in American naturalism, becomes legible through a reading of historical materialism where the figure of the Asiatic "embodies" the logic of capitalism. Subsequently, Asian American characters cannot but suffer violent fates in fictional works; they become the object that resolves the tensions and excesses of capitalism's effects in US culture. Asian bodies, or American bodies that resemble Asian ones, become the target of class critique because they stand in for capitalism itself.

That Asia is perceived to be both a challenge to and a part of US capitalism continues to structure US relationship to Asia in the late twentieth-century and early twenty-first century. Kandice Chuh and Karen Shimakawa point to "Pacific Rim" discourse as another form of closing the distance between Asia and the US, and that artificial contiguity allows for the imagining of an economic compatibility between the two polities.

> . . . the "meaning" of Asia responds to the exigencies governing US (inter)national self-fashioning at a given moment: "Asia" is the threatening rival to US technological dominance, the untapped natural and labor resource for US industry, the limitless consumer market for US goods and culture, the mysterious and feminized territory awaiting and in need of US military protection. (4)

While Chuh and Shimakawa describe US-Asia relations during more recent history, their descriptions confirms a continuity with early-twentieth-century US race-relations; racialization parallels economic needs. "Asia" and "Asians" are defined not only in relation to whiteness, but also to national and global economies.

The shifts in how Asians were beginning to be reimagined are paralleled by shifts in US immigration laws surrounding Asian immigrations that took place in the twentieth century. Racial restrictions on citizenship were removed in 1953, and were later followed by a general overhaul in 1965 that allowed Asian war brides, refugees, adoptees, and students into the country. These shifts in the mid-twentieth century, Madeleine Hsu argues, was a result of a confluence of historical exigencies such as the needs posed by Cold War international relations, such as the US's need for more allies during and after WWII. Soft diplomacy, civil war in China, and the Cold War played important roles in changing public perceptions about the earliest Asian immigrants to the US, the Chinese. Moreover, the emergence of Chinese luminaries in the 1930s, such as Pearl S. Buck, Chiang Kai-Shek, and his wife Song Meiling—an American-educated Methodist who was also close friends with Henry Luce, the famous publisher and China-born son of American missionaries—made Americans more sympathetic toward the Chinese. And finally, the unexpected predicament of high-profile and highly educated Chinese students and scholars who became stranded as refugees in the US as a result of Communist victory in China during the 1940s also informed debates on immigration reform in 1943.

Debates and appeals in support of the repeal of the Chinese Exclusion Act emphasized the "industrious," "law-abiding," "useful," "assimilable," and "upwardly mobile" natures of the Chinese, not to elevate the Chinese, but to change immigration laws so that they would receive similar privileges accorded to other racial groups (Hsu 99). It is at this time, Hsu argues, that we see a shift from the racial figuration of the Chinese as "yellow peril" to "model minority." Only Chinese immigrants with good educational backgrounds and the right kinds of cultural training were deemed fit to enter the US, and the admittance of these new "right" kinds of refugees became an important propaganda tool in the Cold War where immigration quotas and restrictions were deemed as an affront to other states because it was seen as an exercise or show of power.

Racial representations of Asians as laborers or subjects, or as synecdoche for capitalist social relations or capital itself, however, imbricate not only capitalist relations between nation-states but also the global political conditions under which capitalism evolved in the postwar period, that is, how states began to see race after the experience of WWII and the Cold War. Broader historical trends in the second half of the twentieth century indicate that the very nature of racist discourse and state attitudes toward racism especially began to go through a significant change as noted by historians and cultural critics such as Tak Fujitani and Rey Chow.

Fujitani, a historian of US-Japanese relations in the twentieth century, argues that World War II became a "global system of mutual emulation" because both the US and Japan had to disavow racism in order to mobilize racial minorities in their armies as well as allies in other parts of the world. Racism depends on both economic exploitation, but also on the cooperation of racial Others. Overt, or what Fujitani calls "vulgar" racism had to at least be veiled if either regime could be seen as legitimate. The US and Japan adopted an "inclusionary" attitude but also economically and politically utilitarian attitudes toward race that enfolded racial difference into "cosmopolitan" or liberal discourses. "Polite racism," however, was nonetheless still useful to the state in its management of racial bodies.

However, these cultural changes that the postwar period introduced are sustained because we have learned how to see from the perspective of the state.[30] To learn to see as a state is to first and foremost think of how to protect its political and economic standing against domestic and foreign threats. Racial minorities—especially the spy or the terrorist—the chapters of this book will argue, are a synecdoche for the double threat of fracture from within the state, and a challenge from outside of it.

To understand why race continues to be significant in the twenty-first century, we need to examine how the state's desire to safeguard its own sovereignty requires it to figure raced bodies as assets and liabilities. Global racial tropes that include both positive and negative tropes such as the model minority, the spy, the thug, and the lazy or the hypersexualized dark body organize extended and sometimes contradictory narratives of assimilability and difference. The presumed moral behavior, or lack thereof, of racial minorities reflects what the state wants from its subjects. This accounting of value is moral as well as economic and political, and reflects the state's own accounting of itself. Consequently, this book is about how the state's sovereignty is secured not only through the social management of actual, raced bodies, but also through influencing public discourse or popular narratives about global relations and the role the state plays in those relations. The racialization of different groups does not take place in isolation but in tandem and always in relation as a result of economic pressures felt locally and globally.

Consequently, in the broader historical trajectory of how Asia and America are read as capitalist subjects, actors, or objects, this book treats race as a product of how the state sees. The presence of racial tensions, ironically, offers the opportunity for states to demonstrate their strength even in the period of globalization where state power is thought to undergo "deterritorialization." Race, it seems, tends to upend commonly held beliefs about the cultural workings of the world. Arjun Appadurai in his ethnography of the cultures of globalization in the developing world identified what can be called the "reterritorialization" of state power as part of the modern state project. Globalization may pose new challenges to the state, but the state often reasserts its sovereignty in how it organizes racial difference.

> The great irony in much of this work is that it shows beyond a doubt that very often the creation of primordial sentiments, far from being an obstacle to the modernizing state, is close to the center of the project of the modern nation-state. Thus, many racial, religious, and cultural fundamentalisms are deliberately fostered by various nation-states, or parties within them, in their efforts to suppress internal dissent, to construct homogeneous subjects of the state, and to maximize the surveillance and control of the diverse populations under their control. (146)

More than twenty years later, the rise of the primacy of racial identification, which used to be recognized only in the "developing world" in the ethnographies of racial minorities, has now reared its head also in the "developed world." Conceptions of what "majorities" and "minorities" mean in cultural life play a crucial role in race relations, especially as globalization continues to shape and reshape the national and the global. What appeared to be symptomatic of "other" cultures is revealed to be part of a shared condition. When we look at how racial tropes have become more similar on a global level, "global culture" can be defined by the anxiety about the racial Other who now appears everywhere around the world.

The cultural histories of state development—often represented using the language of strength or weakness—consequently offers as a possible explanation for why anxieties over state sovereignty has continued to be a powerful ideological influence and why the state monopolizes our conversations about race in the early twenty-first century, as the US and other countries revive their own specific brands of cultural nationalisms and tribalisms. Ironically, even as each state reasserts its own brand of cultural nationalism, it does so within a moment in history where many other states feel compelled to make the same assertions, thus unconsciously illustrating how while national and transnational flows may sometimes work against one another, they are never uncoupled. In the operating logic of the world state system, global and national interests modulate one another, and at its center is the figure of the racial Other as a source of anxiety. Fear, for scholars such as Appadurai and Immanuel Wallerstein, is evidence of the state in crisis.

> For ordinary people, the single biggest and most immediate result of the decline of state legitimacy is fear—fear for their livelihoods, fear for their personal security, fear for their futures

and those of their children.... We can see the expressions of this fear in two obvious realities, of which the media regularly inform us: crime, and so-called ethnic conflict. (Wallerstein 51)

Wallerstein argues that "ethnic identity" is in essence a "political action," and that when the state cannot guarantee a "minimal level of fair play" (56), "mythmaking" becomes mobilized. Assertions of and debates over racial identity can then be used to amplify protests or dissension within the political structures of the state.[31] However, these assertions are often also a response to how the state mobilizes race. The cultural histories of race and their complex responses to, and interrelations with, state power come to light not only when we pay attention to historical facts but also to the artifice of narrative. The tools of literary analysis help us identify how narrative is instrumental to creating the assumptions we hold about race and tell us why racial thought retains so much explanatory power today. The political questions in this book were raised because they first came up in works of fiction in genres, including satire and utopian fiction, and because the formal innovations of fiction raise questions about how race becomes a socially meaningful category not primarily through mimesis but through the production of narrative effects. *The State of Race* further demonstrates that fiction can best destabilize or critique assumptions that race is a fixed category—often adopted by the state—precisely in its use of artifice. An attention to textual effects helps us see that the use of moral language used to describe race and the anxiety racial difference provokes has the uncanny effect of creating the illusion of order and certainty in this volatile mix of global and national interests. Moreover, if entire groups of people can be tied to "good" and "bad," or "right" and "wrong," then perhaps we have a way to understand, and therefore, regulate the world.

The novels discussed in the following chapters are read in relation to one another, not because they share linguistic, national, or geographical affinities. The breadth and scope of both traditions exceed the limitations of space and thematics of a single book that has as its central methodology a comparative analysis of racial figurations read as symptomatic of how the state sees.[32] Rather than offer representative histories of Asian American or Malaysian literary traditions, *The State of Race* draws on both traditions to demonstrate how different writers in different cultures after the end of WWII employ similar racial tropes in their work because they are responding to and critiquing racial tropes used by the state and repeated in popular culture. In other words, what unites the diverse set of fictional works is the suggestive possibility that the state continues to influence our ideas about race.

The Asian American and Malaysian novels included in this book were chosen because they mobilize similar plot structures of revelation or the discovery of "good" or "bad" racial minorities, and how the failure to do so is a cause for great concern. These fictions about state power on both sides of the Pacific uncover how the shared racial logics of moral exemplarity, moral degeneration, state weakness, and state strength are embedded in the cultural imaginaries of both states after WWII. Organized around the threat of separation either in the form of exile, deportation, or even death, the racial tropes in these novels situate sociality within precarious relations because of how the state sees its relative strength or weakness in the world. The act of "unmasking" racial minorities seems urgent and important because racial minorities are believed to be an implicit threat.

However, the novels included in this study have been chosen because they do not only repeat racial tropes or racial stereotypes, but also destabilize the state's normative views of culture and race as either self-evident, stable, or homogenous. The fictions that form the case studies in this book are fundamentally stories of uncovering or unmasking that is itself a play on how stereotypes appear to reveal the "truth" of racial difference, even as it does precisely the opposite. All the novels, in so far as they destabilize popular racial tropes, do so by playing on narrative reliability and unreliability: is the model minority who he or she claims to be? Will the American Dream come true? And to whom does this dream belong? If the American Dream is achieved, who guarantees its promises of upward mobility, safety, and security, and at what cost? Nothing is certain in the novels examined in the chapters that follow, and the anxieties produced in these fictions are set in opposition to state discourses on race and power that insist racial behavior is clearly discernible, clearly understood, and clearly predictable.

The culture of racial anxiety as one kind of global culture moreover requires that we reconsider methods of comparison and analysis. A comparison of locations and cultures as different as the US and Malaysia requires that we go beyond the limits of canon-formation based on nation or language as a point of comparison where equivalence can either be presumed or demanded. Neither linguistic, geographic, nor national affinities that have shaped our existing literary canons can explain why the US and Malaysia now share a vocabulary of racial anxiety. Instead, as Natalie Melas suggests, comparison as the comparison of equivalence might better be reformulated to include what she calls a "minimal incommensurability." A comparison that treats objects as part of a cultural taxonomy where each object is legible only when it is fungible reflects a colonialist logic where difference is resolved into categories of sameness in order for the objects to become comparable.

For example, the colonial logic that subsumes the many different "Malay" customs, languages, and beliefs into a singular "Malayness" that the colonial or postcolonial state adjudicates can appear in demands that "Asian American literature" and "Malaysian literature" have to be equivalent units before they can be called comparable. But by demanding categorical sameness, we risk organizing knowledge in an essentialist or homogenizing fashion, or placing geographical or historical limits on how we compare. Incommensurability, for Melas, begins with Foucault's notion of heterotopia and a "radical absence of common ground," developed through the Martinican writer, poet, and philosopher Éduoard Glissant's "poetics of relations," and finally as a rejection of capitalism's commodity fetishism, resists comparisons that unconsciously repeat either the colonial taxonomy or capitalism's commodification that renders everything equivalent according to its own laws of exchange (42). Further, Melas argues that postcolonial comparison retains incommensurability in order to decenter comparisons of equivalence that risk repeating imperialism's epistemic desire.

Cultural texts and cultural histories are specific and unique, but when seen in relation one to another, they present a picture of the world and the many unexpected connections that lie therein. As Shu-mei Shih argues, comparison is the axis of racialization not only in the way it interpellates raced subjects into social worlds through its imposition of dominant, white perspectives onto the raced subject, but also in the way that such a comparison establishes—and at times limits—spatial and historical associations between different parts of the world.

> If racialization is inherently comparative, a psychosocial and historical process, then we are working against the meaning of comparison as the arbitrary juxtaposition of two terms in difference and similarity, replacing it with comparison as the recognition and activation of relations that entail two or more terms. This second form of comparison brings submerged or displaced relationalities into view and reveals these relationalities as the starting point for a fuller understanding of racialization as comparative points. ("Comparative Racialization" 1350)

Both Melas and Shih argue for a rethinking of the politics of comparison because the decisions we make about how and what we compare can be tethered to capitalist or colonialist forms of thought that repeat and replicate unequal power structures the fields of postcolonial and ethnic studies have labored to overthrow.

Each novel discussed in the chapters that follow mobilize a familiar, shared symbolic language or racial stereotype, but their ends are singular and particular to the novels themselves. Figurations of the model minority or terrorist spy, or of weak and strong states, operate on different registers depending on the historical contexts in which the novels are set. And while the authors examined closely or referenced in the chapters can be read as part of both national canons, that is, made to "represent" their national cultures, *The State of Race* does not place such an expectation on the novels themselves.[33] In other words, this scrutiny of racial tropes is not mainly in the service of canon expansion, to ensure that we have a fuller understanding of those who make up racial communities, or to recognize the full experiences or the full humanity of racial minorities, although this book also furthers those endeavors. The main contribution of this book is to show how, when viewed through a transnational perspective, the cultural lives of racial tropes help us see that racial difference can be very useful to the nation-state, often in surprising ways.

I want to suggest that ethnic and minor literatures' political urgency can be found in their depictions of how race cannot be untangled from state power. Furthermore, these literatures trace state power as it developed across historical periods (time), and geographical histories (space) in response to global flows.[34] State power is coproduced by global flows, and it depends on integrating racial minorities into its image as a strong state. The comparison across historical periods and geographical histories helps us see that rather than geopolitical or linguistic ties, what connects us "globally" is our shared anxieties over state power and position within the world state system.

Through readings of twentieth- and twenty-first-century literature, each chapter in *The State of Race* foregrounds popular tropes about the desirability of undesirability of racial minorities in the eyes of the state. The first two chapters begin with the most well-known figures or racial difference: the model minority and the terrorist spy. The irony of figuring minorities as both positive and negative at the same time reveals that the burden is placed on racial minorities to always prove they do not have to be feared, that is, to always be fully legible within the state's economy of moral values. These contradictory tropes of race exemplify how positive and negative stereotypes are equally crucial to the symbolic system that organizes all racial minorities into a register of moral behaviors; the racial minority, however, does not stand to benefit from these social organizations or experiences.

The two novels that anchor the first half of the book may seem very different on the outset. *A Gesture Life* was written in the late twentieth century, and *And the Rain My Drink*, written in the middle of the twentieth century. The former focalizes Korean American assimilation into one of the most powerful capitalist countries and the latter, Chinese Malaysian assimilation into colonial society recovering from war. In the individual chapters, I elaborate on how moral language is crucial in each particular racial formation, but want to emphasize here that while they are drawn from two different moments of history and cultures, racial subjects in both novels come to see themselves through the eyes of the state.[35] Fiction draws our focus to how modern life is lived under state surveillance by showing us that these fears are first and most deeply felt by minor subjects whose lives potentially threaten the state's view of itself.

Both novels also uncover how the trope of the model minority is mobilized as a source of anxiety in the disciplining of racial minorities. The state of surveillance inculcates in racial minorities both the desire for assimilation, and a fear of the state that assimilates them. The two novels may diverge in their historical productions and in the literary conventions they deploy, but both texts converge in how they recast the model minority's legibility as a response to the state's own views of moral goodness and behavior, as well as why that legibility is crucial to the state in the first place. In both novels, the model minority is unreliable, and the authors' use of unreliability as narrative device underscores how racial anxiety is an effect of narrative itself.

Racial anxiety thus runs throughout the two novels, and the anxiety about the raced subject and the anxiety felt on the part of the raced subject are produced by the distended ways in which racial minorities are scrutinized. That the model minority is always an object of suspicion is concatenated to the threat of exclusion as morally sanctioned.[36] The risk of expulsion from the body politic—either legally or through social marginalization—is consequently arbitrary and justifiable, and it is the twinned experience of certainty and uncertainty that creates the effect of racial anxiety.

The State of Race turns from model minorities to model nations in the last two chapters to examine how race cannot be understood apart from the state's conceptions of its own authority and goals. If the first half of the book focuses on how the ideal racial subject is imagined, the second half of the book shifts to examine how the ideal state is imagined because the state's hopes and fears sustain racial anxiety. The tropes of the model minority and its other, the terrorist-spy, come into circulation because they are related to the state's visions of its positions of strength or weakness relative to other states operating in the world. Model minorities—and the spy or traitor—in these novels not only illustrate for us the moral nature of state discourse on race, but also show us how they are synecdoches of the state's own moral position as it asserts itself in relation to other states. Global racial tropes consequently tell stories of personhood as well as stories of social transitions. From model minorities to model nations, the state always looks both ways, inward and outward.

The second half of the book takes a historical turn to examine the ways in which, in the context of an uneven and unpredictable global economy, the postcolonial state mobilizes the languages of strength, weakness, hope, and fear to assert new, or to repurpose old, forms of ethnocentrism and race thinking. This section draws our attention to the intersections of cultural history and fiction to look at how ideal forms of state sovereignty and authority can determine the epistemic parameters within which figurations of race appear. Chapters 3 and 4 argue that the ethnic novel presents narratives of assimilation that are also narratives of integration into the capitalist world order because the need for racial assimilation in the nation parallels the state's need to become integrated into the world. Anxieties around state power materialize as anxieties around race, and it is the double anxiety felt on the part of racial subjects as well as the state that leads individuals to mistake the interests of the state for their own.

In chapter 3, the anxieties of the minor nation—embodied in tropes of insecurity—shape nationalist thought and the process by which the postcolonial state is formed vis-à-vis its relative position to what other states do to secure their sovereignty. This chapter pairs two Malaysian novels, Shaz Johar's *Sanctuaria*, written in Malay by a Malay Malaysian author, and Brian Gomez's *Devils Place*, written in English by a Tamil Malaysian author, as examples of how contemporary literature portrays the state's insecurities.[37] The development of state power within the capitalist world state system influences how we think of race and turn it into a source of anxiety because it now represents threats inside and outside the state's borders. The cultural histories presented in this chapter illustrate how "reterritorialization" and "deterritorialization" can inform the state's moral and political justifications of the stance it takes toward raced subjects.

Finally, chapter 4 traces how the (global) American Dream—embodied in tropes of security—concatenates race and social mobility to the state's own goals for the future, especially as capitalism seems to catapult us toward collective social disintegration and mass destruction. Racial temporality shifts from the past to the future, and the minority is imagined against possible threats they might pose in the future, especially in light of Asia's economic growth. Consequently, the anxiety that the state is becoming weaker in the face of natural, economic, and geopolitical threats afflicts world superpowers as much as the minor nation-states that fear losing out in a globalized world. As nationalist ideology, the American Dream and its global variants mobilize contradictory narratives of celebration and suffering, as well as narratives of exceptionalism and affinity. The two novels central to the final chapter, the Chinese American Gish Gen's *The Love Wife* and Chang-rae Lee's *On Such a Full Sea*, depict societies where racial minorities seem to have a safe and secured role in the state, but that safety and security reveal the state's tendency to dystopian forms of control so as to secure the American Dream. Narratives about race and national uplift such as the global "American Dream" shape race relations by inspiring hope as well as anxiety. Chang-rae Lee's works have been given slightly more attention in this book because of his prominence as a novelist who is read widely not only in Asian American literature, but also in Asia where his novels *A Gesture Life* and *The Surrendered* are set. *On Such a Full Sea*, which closes the analysis of the final chapter, is a particularly apt meditation on the dystopian future of the US after an environmental apocalypse destroys Asia was inspired by Lee's own travels in Asia.[38] The other novels treated in the chapters have also been chosen because they point to how the cultural effects of racial thought implicate global as well as national flows.

Comparing racial formations consequently reveals an emerging and uneven but converging global story of "value"—both economic and ethical—that has in its center new figurations of the "Asian." The confluence of racial anxieties, victim narratives, and a global "American Dream" in the imperial center and the postcolonial margins are symptoms of a growing global culture of anxiety. The differences in the cultural and racial formations in particular locations remain irresolvable, but racial anxieties nonetheless converge across genres and historical periods as tropes of moral exemplarity, that is, the moral exemplarity of singular subjects and also of the state. However, the individual chapters retain traces of these differences in the close readings, because each novel mobilizes these tropes to their own formal effects and narrative ends.

Finally, these works of fiction are but a few examples of how the moral tropes of race can be read not only as part of national traditions, but also as part of a global culture where similar racial symbols, figures, and language circulate because they are determined by the state and its needs. The different novels, each in its own way, seduce the reader into actually adopting the state's own perspective as it looks at the racial subject. And while each novel, short story, or film is unique, and each cultural history is particular, each intersects with a world history held in common. Read together, these works represent how globally shared anxieties around state power have produced moral tropes about race.

Chapter One

Tropes of Exemplarity

Morality as Racial Pedagogy

> It was during Sunny's absence that I finally awoke to this notion, that I was perfectly suited to my town, that I had steadily become, oddly and unofficially, its primary citizen, the living, breathing expression of what people here wanted—privacy and decorum and the quietude of hard-earned privilege.
>
> —Chang-rae Lee, *A Gesture Life*

For a novel about a model minority who achieves the American Dream, *A Gesture Life* has an unusual ending. Franklin Hata, or "Doc Hata" as he is affectionately known in his quiet town in Upstate New York, is one of the few racial minorities in his community. The novel begins when Hata is in his later years, after he has built himself a respectable and comfortable life there, only to give away all of his wealth and go into a self-imposed exile. The moment of acceptance and self-recognition that Hata experiences in the above passage comes almost three hundred pages into the novel, as Hata winds down the narration of his life. By this time in the novel's progression, his half-black, half-Korean adopted daughter, Sunny, has returned to the town with a young son in tow who is also part African American. But Hata will soon break the new and fragile reconciliation in his racially mixed family at the end of the novel just a hundred pages later. Close to the very end of his narration, we discover that much earlier in the narrative time of the novel, Hata had assisted in Sunny's first abortion, which he had insisted on despite her protests.

This passage raises many questions in the novel, but chief among them is the obvious question, "What is a model minority?," followed by the subsequent questions, "Why is the model minority significant?" and "What does it reveal about our cultural desires?" Ironically, Hata himself offers ambiguous answers to these questions. Focalized through first-person narration, Hata's recognition that he is a model minority is incipient, hesitant, and unsure at the end of the novel: "In truth I was beginning to understand my position after so many years . . ." (275). Hata offers no explanation of what the model minority looks like in his own estimation. Instead, his understanding of what a model minority is results from what he assumes others like about him, that is, his "popularity and high reputation." He believes that he has "oddly and unofficially" become the town's model minority—more by chance than by design—because he embodies a version of the American Dream come true, that is, ". . . what people here wanted—privacy and decorum and the quietude of hard-earned privilege." Hata is a model minority because he is polite, respectful of the law, keeps to himself, and because he is financially successful, he does not draw on the state's resources, and instead contributes to them. In his successful assimilation into middle-class American life, he symbolizes and confirms the vitality of the American Dream.

But the novel's narrative structure also builds on and disrupts the myth of the Asian American as model minority through its use of anachronism and flashbacks that reveal Hata's far less than exemplary past. The model minority, finally, is not who he claims to be. Lee's *A Gesture Life* does not merely present to us a model minority—other Asian American novels do this too—but it presents to us a model minority who is hidden from himself. Hata can only see himself as the state sees him, because the alternative would lead to complete psychic death. The reader discovers that the friendly sobriquet "Doc," given not because he is a doctor but because he owns a medical supply store, is really a grotesque and haunting reminder not only of the role he played in forcing Sunny to undergo an abortion but also how he acquired his medical expertise as a medic in a Japanese war camp. His role as a medic gives him access to the comfort women in the camp and enables his obsession with Kkutaeh, or K, a Korean comfort woman where he served. Hata's troubling relationships to female bodies as at once objects of sexual desire and paternalistic care—both equally strong desires that run through the past and present tenses of narration—are symbolic not only of gender relations in Asia and the US, but also of national and transnational tensions that are the result of WWII. In these postwar, transnational tensions, the model minority indexes particular historical exigencies of capitalism, racial difference, and immigration laws as they have played out in US national history as well as the US's relation to changing dynamics of war, gender, and racial difference in Asia.

However, Hata's exemplariness as model minority cannot be read apart from the unreliability of his narration, and his full and complete embrace of the model minority as a creation of the state. In this novel, the state plays a central role in how Hata relates to other races, both in wartime Japan and in his new American life; in both transhistorical and transnational contexts, Hata is legible only as the assimilated model minority. The first sentence of the novel, "People know me here," first seems to describe Bedley run as a warm and familiar place, but read in conjunction with the end of the novel where Hata's life—or lives—remain unknown and hidden from everyone he calls family and friends, the opening is ironic because "people" in fact do not know or understand him. Hata moreover remains hidden from himself.

Throughout the novel, Hata erases everything about his past as well about his "passing," that is, his racial identities either as Japanese or as Korean Japanese, and would rather be known only as a model "citizen." Hata's "passing" as model minority erases how race conditioned his past as a war soldier in Asia, but at the same time, this passing is possible only because he becomes legible in the US national imaginary as a model minority. Hata's refusal to acknowledge racial tensions and racial hierarchies in wartime Asia and postwar America nonetheless is evidence of the convolutions he has to go through to minimize the role race has played in his past and present experiences. This erasure, rather than his worldly "successes" is what makes Hata the consummate model minority; he embraces the state's desire to erase racial difference even as racial difference remains a crucial part of his social experiences. Hata is known and seen as a model minority, but it is that apparent awareness and celebration of his present life that allows his past to remain unknown, unseen, and suppressed.

A Gesture Life has an unusual ending for a novel centered on a model minority because Hata as model minority reveals the strangeness of the concept of moral exemplariness, especially when thought in relation to "citizen." Hata's exemplariness as citizen relies on the erasures of his past, of race, and finally, the erasure of social violence as part of the process of racial formation. In this, the novel reveals a distinctive relationship between the state and the model minority, where each confirms the other's purpose and place.

This chapter therefore argues that the model minority myth masks certain forms of social violence because it marshals moral or ethical narratives in the social disciplining of racial minorities. Discourses surrounding this myth shed light on why violence can be legitimately perpetrated and how the state's use of legitimate violence is also morally persuasive. An important part of how the state manages race and race relations, the language of morality in the process of racial subjection is a form of social discipline. The language of ethics or morality in US racial formations masks the implicit violence in social discipline. More significantly, race and racial discipline are built on moral values confirmed not only by social groups but also by the state. And finally, representations of the Asian American as model minorities normalize racial discipline as a moral right of the state and delineate the scope and shape of state power in its relation to racial minorities.

The mention of "morality" or "moral vision" can produce a great deal of anxiety, and for good reasons in a variety of ways. As Frederic Jameson and other critics have pointed out, "ethics" in its focus on the individual subject has been understood as hypocritical and self-serving, and distracts critics from theorizing about collective or political life. Ethics or morality can seem to be a desirable collective or individual goal, but it also often conjures up images of political control and repression. As Smaro Kambourelli cautions, the critical gesture of "turning to ethics" may not always be ethical in itself; assertions of the ethical may actually enact another form of violence, even as they announce themselves as critiques of violence (Kambourelli 937). We need to pay attention to how moral language potentially plays a part of the operation of power, and it is a role that literary critics help to play in their attention to modes of reading and how narratives work. Minorities have learned all too well that ethics has an unlikely but crucial relationship to how we live and work.

The negotiation of ethics or morality in public and social life is important precisely because race and morality are a part of political life. That ethics is not merely a matter of individual choice needs to be examined alongside other forms of subject formation. But racial minorities, and especially critics who work on minority, colonial, or postcolonial literatures, have an ambivalent relationship to ethics or morality in fiction because literature has a complex relationship to representation and verity, and what they mean for culture and politics. Literature cannot simply be read as examples of moral life, first, because as Robert Eaglestone has argued, such a reading of literature returns us to a mimetic approach to art where all readers are assumed to have identical responses to a reality that is unmediated by artwork. This is especially pertinent to minor and world literatures, which are far too often plagued by demands for, and claims of, "authenticity" where these demands inadvertently reduce all non-European literatures to the status of the empirical. Furthermore, even if such literature can be said to represent the "authentic" reality of racialized lives, they are at best representations of the alienation or violence that far too often delimits the lives of racial others. Ethnic literatures do not so much provide a model for responding to otherness as they reveal the complexities of the situations to which we should offer responses.

Postcolonial critics have pointed out that literature—and the novel form, in particular—has been used as a disciplinary tool under European colonialism. Literature as moral guidebook retains connotations and associations that make it suspect or that restricts the types of novels we can call "ethical."[1] That is to say, even literary works that can and do function as examples of ethics are either limited to certain kinds of literature, or when they do perform exemplarity, as Geoffrey Harpham points out, they do so to transform or reinterpret our interpretations of moral philosophy rather than assert or guarantee an urtext of ethics. Instead of reading literature for the purpose of discovering models of ethical behavior, my readings of the novels and films in this book, and especially in this chapter, highlight the moments when literature and film challenge the narratives of race that take for granted how moral language or race relations works, and point out how they organize our experiences of the world.

Morality in ethnic literature too often exists as failure or as absence. To insist that we need to be wary of moral language is to bear in mind that women and other minorities have historically been subjected to acts of ventriloquism and representation in public discourse that afforded them very little agency. In the past, racial minorities were not often given the opportunity to generate tropes or beliefs that adequately represented either their experiences or their desires, and instead were more often subjected to others' representations of their lives. Consequently, morality, to the raced subject, can often represent expectations imposed from the outside rather than something that comes from within them.

The figure of the model minority does not exist outside of the racial system that labels some minorities "good" or "bad," but rather helps to constitute that very system of racial difference and racial hierarchy that continues to have power over our cultural imaginaries because it offers us a way to organize the world.[3] While Asian Americans are frequently referred to as "model minorities," that is, as different and separate from other minorities,[2] the act of labeling some minorities and not others as "good" perpetuates the kind of systemic violence that affects all minorities. Morality as a trope of racial difference is important because it provides an immediate and accessible form of imagining one's self and one's self as part of a community, but as much as it signifies social belonging, it also signifies alienation and exclusion.

The link between morality and alienation is not limited to particular racial groups, of course, as class difference is often explained using moral language, which we will see more fully in the final chapter of the book. Class difference can also be couched in moral language and used to describe racial difference. Sociologists of the working class explain that changing labor markets in the second half of the twentieth century have left working men and women without the recourses or the hopes that were available to their grandparents, and consequently there is a parallel shift from seeing race predominantly as a result of biological difference to seeing race as the result of moral difference. In a time of economic instability, beliefs about "morality" and what one "deserves" or does not "deserve" generates social identity or social cohesion, and provides a language with which they can explain why some people succeed or fail in the new economy. Left behind by the economic changes of globalization, collective identities that are articulated as possessing particular moral values and not others provide a psychological bulwark against the unpredictability and insecurities of a more volatile and uncertain labor market:

> Most notably, social scientists have proposed the terms "symbolic racism," "subtle racism," "aversive racism," and "modern racism" to point out that racism now takes the following form: white Americans value individualism, self-reliance, a work ethic, obedience, and discipline, and they believe that blacks violate these values. Thus, they say that their racism is motivated not by a dislike of blacks but by a concern for key American values. (Lamont 72)

The racial Other poses a threat because they are seen as possessing different values that are ultimately at odds with "American values," and while we might disagree with their conclusion, the working-class subjects of Lamont's study—both white and black—identify racial difference by talking about the differences of "values" in their communities. Similarly, Jennifer Sherman argues that morality does not only dictate proper behavior, it also provides coping strategies to those living on the margins of the US economic market, especially in their relations to racial Others who are also subject to those same economic systems. "Race" is the result of how we think about moral norms and differences in so far as they are used to explain and organize the world as it shifts and changes, especially in response to the global economy.

Similarly, literary and cultural critics such as Chow, David Palumbo-Liu, and Waichee Dimock have identified a link between moral language and capitalism, and their influence on fiction and cultural politics. Engagement with the economic in our thinking about ethics and morality has remained central to scholars who increasingly seek to situate their work as a response to globalization where financial institutions, beliefs, and practices generate their own kind of rationality that then creates their own moral economy. The languages of economics and numbers are not accidental, and capitalist demands on labor and their subsequent effects on migration and transnational flows have become more central to our social lives and are reflected in all kinds of national literatures, including American and world literatures.

Following Foucault, Chow argues in *The Protestant Ethnic and the Spirit of Capitalism* that racism is not external to, but rather part of, the "systemic function" of capitalist society and is a part of biopower.[4] Capitalism and the injunction toward "good work" understood as labor have replaced religious experiences and provide the language and the imagery through which we justify suffering or duress under demanding conditions, and their opposites, worldly success and wealth. In his essay, "Rational and Irrational Choices: Form, Affect, and Ethics," Palumbo-Liu reads the literary against central ideas of rational-choice theory to articulate how certain narratives attain truth status, and consequently, how these narratives then have the power to illuminate certain actions as logical and ethical, and others as illogical and therefore null and void.

To use the language of what can or cannot be quantifiable also places limits and challenges on our imagination of social justice. In *Residues of Justice: Literature, Law, and Philosophy*, Dimock argues against the Kantian and Rawlsian conception of justice as foundational and self-evident, where justice as the primary ethical virtue interprets, fixes, and renders the world legible by its very act of adequation. For Dimock, the signifying field of justice in Enlightenment philosophy or nineteenth-century US law that draws from it depends on a commensurability that takes as its predominant figure of thought mathematical precision, represented most famously by the scales of justice. She contends that the very intelligibility of justice as a translation of incommensurable differences into like for like in law and philosophy proves also to be its own conceptual limits—limits that can only be addressed by the incommensurable in literature:

> Absolute and categoric in philosophy, negotiable and assignable in law, wayward and unsatisfactory in literature, justice, dispensed in different operative theaters, seems to carry different causal circumferences, different modes of evidence, and to yield up different styles of knowledge as well as different descriptive textures of the world. These conflicting images of justice call into question the self-evidence of that concept as well as its claim to being the axiomatic expression of human reason. (8)

"Justice" is a virtue that shape-shifts, depending on the disciplinary framework in which it is read, thus it appears to possess contradictory qualities and produces different effects when it draws from an assortment of textual sources, codes, and norms. Literature subtends and complicates moral philosophy because it reveals the unevenness of what seems to be a priori axioms and ideas.

But while economic rationalism cannot explain everything about the human experience, it nonetheless influences the way we think about ethics and morality, and the figure of the model minority reminds us that they are an important part of the cultural effects of racial thinking. Dimock's analysis of nineteenth-century laws, novels, and philosophical essays show that in a self-regulating equilibrium of pain and compensation, suffering is a measure of justice while Palumbo-Liu, on the other hand, focuses precisely on how affect is mobilized to produce ethical behavior, not as a corrective or deterrent to "bad behavior" but as the basis for the collective good of an imagined community not limited by national borders. Affect can perform in either a negative or positive capacity in Dimock's and Palumbo-Liu's conclusions, but they both begin from the premise that affect is always already enfolded within economic concerns and the units of analysis it generates.[5]

Stories or narratives are important to economic or rational concerns because it is in how we tell stories that we reveal our choices as not only logical but also "attractive," that is, our narratives about economic choices actually help us make those choices. "Rationality" may attempt to sideline or extenuate the ambivalence that emotions and affect bring to our experiences, but our choices also depend on affective attachments produced by narrative. Economic concerns that seem rational cannot exist independently from sentiment or emotion, and, in fact, sentiment and emotion play a large part in determining what narratives we find to be persuasive.

Questions about what makes a narrative morally persuasive are important because as the moral language in *A Gesture Life* demonstrates, claims of moral behavior especially as it is attributed to racial subjects do not only teach us how to think of what is just or unjust, they also teach us to think about race itself, and more precisely, how the emotion of anxiety shapes our narratives about race. The figure of the model minority describes race in terms of their value to capitalism and the nation-state because the myth of the model minority valorizes the moral exemplarity of liberal notions of the independent, self-choosing, and therefore self-sustaining individual. Only individuals who can succeed in and validate the capitalist economic model can be considered a "good" subject of the state, but this success can also create a sense of envy or anxiety in others, who would like to guarantee their own success in a competitive global economy.[6]

The Asian American as model minority is moreover enfolded into the national imaginary only when it strengthens the state's own power both as political actor (that is, when it exercises its right to exclude) and as economic agent (that is, when it safeguards its economic interests through selective immigration). Critics of *A Gesture Life* have focused primarily on how the novel's narrative looks at the Asian American's place within the national imaginary, but they do so in various ways. For example, Hamilton Carroll argues that the novel is a narrative of the failure of self-constitution as a national subject, and that the narrative of the failure of assimilation is undercut precisely by the gendered narratives of the novel's main female characters. This self-constitution as subject that is central to the form of the bildungsroman, Carroll argues, appears as an exceptional event because Hata is abstracted not as a citizen-subject but as a stereotype. However, Carroll also argues that this mis-abstraction, or the failure of Hata's constitution as citizen, is undercut precisely by Hata's relationship to the women he oppresses.

> Lee's novel, moreover, shows how Doc Hata's attempts to inaugurate his own nationally visible subjectivity are predicated on his abjection of K and Sunny and how—against Hata's will—a narrative that foregrounds the subordinated, marginalized position of female subjects displaces and overturns the masculine, cultural nationalism of his immigration story. (594)

The narration of Sunny's and Kkutaeh's subjection—especially at the hands of Hata and nested within his narrative—disables his claims of belonging to a nation-state, even if it is an assimilation-as-stereotype. Mark Jerng comments on Asian American subject formation via a reading of the becoming subject of the transnational adoptee—in this case, Sunny—as mediating and disrupting the rights claims and the position of victimization common to those seeking state recognition (53). This further complicates the narrative of assimilation because Hata and Sunny's relationship is not merely a transference of Hata and Kkutaeh's relationship, precisely because Sunny is familiar and unfamiliar—as a daughter with whom he shares no genetic ties—in the same way that Hata's and Kkutaeh's relationship both recognized and denied a shared kinship based on race. Young-oak Lee's reading of the novel as a phenomenology of diaspora, however, returns our attention to the experience of being a citizen under globalization through an inquiry that does not limit subject formation of the diasporic as antistate.

However, all these approaches once more obviate the centrality of the state and its discourses despite—or rather, because of—their otherwise very productive focus on psychoanalysis and the subject. Like Carroll, I also read the novel as foregrounding the imperialisms of Japan and the US, and that imperialism depends on exploiting gender and racial difference, but in his recasting of the "national" as traumatic history, the state itself disappears. It no longer plays a role in the recognition of minorities and renders the constitution of the subject to that which can be "individually" crafted: "Hata's inability to constitute his own identity through the attainment of citizenship and assimilation is addressed most readily in *A Gesture Life* through the trope of naming" (597). But to be incorporated into the national community is a fundamental condition of life: "For to exist at all, to be in civil society, is to be a citizen" (Lionnet 1507).[7]

This chapter asks us to critique how the state continues to play an overdetermined role in racial formation, especially in its legitimation of social violence. And it does so by questioning the symbolic politics of the state and the assumptions that become naturalized within the process of assimilation as model minorities. Race continues to matter because it continues to be an important function of the politics of the US state and elsewhere, and the continued assimilation of Asian Americans predominantly as model minorities requires that we understand how the state influences race relations. This returns us to the question of what a model minority is because a model minority, implicitly, is exemplary because he or she is a model citizen. Lee's *A Gesture Life* is a particularly apt example because it does not only depict what a model minority looks like but it does so by placing Asian Americans in relation to Asians, white Americans, and African Americans. Race relations in this diegetic world exceeds the white-nonwhite binary and points us toward a world where "race" requires navigating between not just one or two histories of race relations but between multiple national histories, both locally and globally.

The plot moves between the present time and the past, both in the US and in Southeast Asia during World War II, but it consistently revolves around the central character and narrator, Hata, who is Korean man but who passes for Japanese in wartime Japan and later, after he moves to the US. The first set of flashbacks in the novel detail the events of Hata's life when he was a medical officer in the Japanese army in Burma during WWII, especially when he falls in love with a Korean comfort woman named Kkutaeh who later reappears as a spectral form in his memories as "K." The second set of flashbacks revolves around Hata and his adopted daughter from Korea, Sunny, during her teenage years, approximately fifteen years before the present-time of the narration.

For Hata to secure a place in the national imaginary, he has to become the subject the state desires. On the outset, the model minority as ideal subject of the state looks like a successful and wealthy individual who also owns property, or in other words, someone who has achieved the American Dream. Moral exemplarity takes on the form of the racial minority as economic utility to the state; the model minority is successful on his or her own merits, and in the process confirms the state's own goodness. Hata's own conception of a meaningful life—the ideology of the assimilated—reflects how the model minority is figured as economic success in the political and civic landscape of the US, but this is a cultural belonging tenuously linked to his rights to own private property. Hata's "catalog" of photos is overwhelmingly important to him as a documentation of his American life, and for which he thinks justifies his place in the US. Hata stops himself from burning old photographs taken of his house for insurance files because they record and testify to Hata's growing wealth. Hata's store and his home, and the "good standing" he derives from his possession of them, define his life. Later, Hata describes the end of his life in Bedley Run as a commodity that has reached the end of its use value.

> ". . . more and more the time feels right to me, not so much from a financial viewpoint but from a sense of one's time in a place, and that time being close to done. It's not that I feel

> I've used up this house, this town, this part of the world, that I've gotten all I'm going to get, but more than this feeling I've come to expect, this happy blend of familiarity and homeyness and what must be belonging, is strangely beginning to disturb me." (21)

Hata's euphemistic explanation of his exile as resulting from the "sense of one's time in a place" refers to how he no longer fits into the racial landscape that he refuses to acknowledge in the course of the novel. Even though he says that "it is *not*" that he has "*used up*" the house or the town, this formulation of his home and community as a resource that can be "*used up*" reflects how he calibrates his world as being finite and how social relations—his friendships and relationships in that community—are reified as economic relations.

This conjuncture between race, economics, and morality in the model minority begins much earlier, not in the diegetic present of the novel but in one of the narrative's flashbacks or retroversions, when we are told that Hata is not ethnically Japanese, but a Korean Japanese who successfully passes as Japanese. Lee's novel complicates the model minority by depicting an unreliable model minority whose exemplarity is dependent on multiple subterfuges. As an ideal subject of the Japanese state, Hata's first racial performance foreshadows and prefigures his American life in significant ways. Lee's novel points us to how the very phenomenon of the model minority is transnational and not peculiar to the US, even if it has been most visible and central as an American cultural phenomenon. Model minorities exist in other cultures and histories as well and are often linked to assimilation and responding to the state's views of desirable behaviors and subject positions.

When he was a young boy, Hata's birth parents, Koreans in Japan, gave him up for adoption to a middle-class Japanese couple during the Japanese colonialism of Korea, and he adopted their last name. He effectively "became" Japanese and left his working-class Korean past behind him. However, the process of adoption transferred his attachments not to his adoptive parents, ironically, but to the state itself.

> This was when I first appreciated the comforts of real personhood, and its attendant secrets, among which is the harmonious relation between a self and his society. There is a mutualism that at its ideal is both powerful and liberating. For me, it was readily leaving the narrow existence of my family and our ghetto of

hide tanners and renderers. Most all of us were ethnic Koreans, though we spoke and lived as Japanese, if ones in twilight. (72)

Hata identifies as a mark of independence and adulthood the moment when he as an individual becomes aware of social life at large and the institutions that make social life possible. His relationship to the larger world that rescues him from his "narrow existence" and "ghetto" is immediately characterized as "harmonious," "powerful," and "liberating" when it was that larger world that is also responsible for relegating Korean Japanese to the margins of Japanese society.

The novel's plot development is thus centered on the gradual revelation of how Hata assimilates first to the Japanese state, and then to the American state. But this assimilation acknowledges that the state grants personhood at the cost of erasing some parts of his life (Hata's life as ethnic Korean) and building others up (Hata's life as Japanese). Hata's bildungsroman is consequently one of awakening that is also a process of erasure and selective blindness to how the state pretends racial minorities do not exist, or that they are insignificant. But this process of socialization—to Hata, it is one of individualization and adulthood—is part of the process of racialization. In other words, it is part of the process of recognizing not that race matters, but that race matters in particular ways to the state.

To assimilate or to pass as racially other is to adopt the state's view of how race matters and what races matter. When Hata says, "For me, *it* was readily leaving the narrow existence . . . ," he vaguely refers to the process of discovering that he is indeed a part of a larger society and that his place in it, as a Japanese, is one that is "powerful and liberating" as opposed to his place in it as an ethnic Korean in Japan. Hata only consciously recognizes himself as a person when he "becomes" Japanese, but in the process, he has to repress the means through which he becomes a subject of the state. Literally, Hata sees the state as life-giving because it enabled racial erasure and assimilation.

> I think of [my adoptive parents] most warmly as I do of my natural parents, but to neither would I ascribe the business of having reared me, for it seems clear that it was *the purposeful society* that did so, and really nothing and no one else. And I was more than grateful. And I knew even then as a boy of twelve how I should always give myself over to *its* vigilance, entrusting to *its* care everything I could know or ever hope for. (72–73, emphasis mine)

Hata does not define what or who provides "its vigilance" or "its care," but takes for granted that "it" will do so. Subject formation in part depends on the state's positive recognition but this recognition is also the premise and pretext of his own obligations and duties in return. This abstract institution is the "wholly other" and the singularity whom he recognizes and to whom he owes his allegiance for most of the novel. He surrenders to a fate determined by the abstract being of the state now anthropomorphized as an agent that acts and that has the right to require a response, particularly, a response of moral obligation.

The state's subjection and interpellation of racial minorities is part of the same process: the racial minority is interpellated as a subject, but freely chooses to do so because there are ontological rewards to that subjection. Anne Cheng's reading of Lee's novel problematizes the ethics of "passing" and assimilation, and she argues that the entrance into personhood is the ontological reward for assimilation (559). This reward is not an end in itself, however, but further generates other kinds of rewards and punishment that are part of the state's use of legitimate violence framed as ethical demands and moral obligation.

The state as actor determines Hata's personhood and subjectivity because it guarantees his rights and political recognition. Hata's primary attachment marked by feelings of "gratitude" and harmony are directed not to either set of parents, but to the state, and these feelings are also the passage to his moral obligations and duties. But Hata transfers his moral obligations and ethical relationships from people to the state because of his repressed anxieties over racially marked bodies, especially in relation to how raced bodies appear in the landscape of the US. For example, when he first discovers that the daughter he adopted from Korea is of mixed race, he becomes anxious and disturbed because he saw his adoption of Sunny as a way to cement his own position in American society through the symbolic reproduction of not only of the body but also of moral exemplarity: "I had wished to make my own family, and if by necessity the single-parent kind then at least one that would soon be well reputed and happily known, the Hatas of Bedley Run" (204). Sunny's mixed-race heritage—a sign that she was probably the unwanted offspring between a Korean woman and an African American soldier stationed in South Korea—and her later disobedience as a teenager disrupts Hata's own ideals of American family life and the idealized Asian body in American culture. Racial purity would also have signified moral purity.

Hata's experience of reading John Cheever's "The Swimmer," a story about a middle-class, white man who decides to swim cross-country through swimming pools in private backyards, only to finally return to his own home to find it locked up and deserted, not only reflects his frustration but also rewrites Cheever's rewriting of the American Dream. Early in the novel, Hata discovers a short story that Sunny had read for a class in high school and his subsequent fascination with the short-story interrupts his repression of the racial experience of being a model minority.

In the act of reading a canonical short-story about the failure of the American Dream, Hata's own anxieties come to the surface, and despite himself, he cannot help but note how differently the raced body appears in the American Dream. Hata imagines himself as the swimmer in the short story, but even in his mind, Hata cannot traverse the land and geography with the same freedom or ease as the character in the story. The restrictions he faces even in the act of reading further amplifies the dangers the swimmer might encounter, because this journey is made across private property. Cheever's swimmer does not swim through rivers, streams, lakes, or even dams, but rather private swimming pools built in suburban homes, and like Cheever's Neddy Merrill, Hata "if he could choose, might always go silent and unseen" (24).

But the quiet acknowledgment that "if he could choose" reminds us that Hata cannot choose, and that the raced body, model minority or not, cannot always go silent and unseen. Hata may own a pool and a backyard like the one Merrill swims through, but the raced body nonetheless appears in different ways on the map if it appears at all. Unlike Merrill, however, Hata's melancholic ruminations on the story converge not on what deliberate infractions of private property might mean but on how his own swimming body might appear as part of the semiotic chain that links bodies to America.

Even though Hata does not consciously note how he and Merrill experience and inhabit space differently, these racially conditioned experiences surface on the level of the narrative. Hata's unreliability as a narrator applies even to himself; he cannot help but betray his conscious mind. While Merrill not only conquers the trail of swimming pools by naming this "newly discovered river" after his wife, the pools that he swims through belong to his upper-middle-class friends. Hata, conversely, cannot name the swimming pools he wishes to traverse, because even when he imagines himself as the protagonist in his momentary fantasy, he remains trapped as a swimmer in his own pool. While the white swimmer trespasses on the private properties of others as he falls into financial ruin, the Asian American swimmer remains contained even in his daydreams. This rewriting critiques not only how the US as a nation-state is constituted, but also functions as sign of Hata's repressed desires regarding what he can or cannot possess, and how he can or cannot be represented within the US imaginary. The desire that he might always go silent and unseen betrays a general anxiety surrounding the Asian American body even when it is scripted as part of the American Dream.

The Asian American body as object of fear leads Hata to overemphasize moral exemplarity as a form of compensation for the threat yellow or brown bodies represent, and it finally ends in his self-exile. The raced body has to overperform moral goodness to seem less of a threat but in so doing, the social effects of race—a result of institutional inequality and social alienation—are taken on by racial minorities. In Hata's case, he places all responsibility for moral obligation on himself while simultaneously attributing everything good to the state and absolving the state of all culpability. The state is responsible only for the good things he experiences, and he or others like him are responsible for the bad.

Racial minorities are required to regulate emotions, both their own as well as those of others who might be afraid as a result of their encounters with raced bodies. In other words, model minorities are assimilated in so far as they recognize the affects—fear and anxiety—their racialized bodies generate, and act to preempt them. They are perfectly assimilated subjects of the state not only because they are high achievers, but because they recognize what their bodies mean and modulate their behaviors accordingly.

When Hata's nurse, Renny, who is South Asian insinuates that Hata puts up with, and glosses over, comments or actions that are far from "benign," Hata responds by assuming responsibility for any of the disquieting emotions that he feels as a result.

> It's true that at times I have felt somewhat uneasy in certain situations, though probably it was not anyone's fault but my own. You may not agree with this, Renny, but I've always believed that the predominant burden is mine, if it is a question of feeling at home in a place. Why should it be another's? How can it? So I do what is necessary in being complimentary, as a citizen and colleague and partner. This is almost never too onerous. If people say things, I try not to listen. In the end, I have learned I must make whatever peace and solace of my own. (135)

The racial minority secures his or her place in the nation-state by doing what they can do to ensure that they "feel at home," and as earlier passages demonstrate, "feeling at home," in Hata's unconscious use of language, occurs when one becomes economically successful and "tries not to listen." Within this frame of reference where the raced body is responsible for all emotions, Hata is compelled to be "complimentary," but it is not clear if Hata means instead to be "complementary," that is, to fit his life around those of others in order to make their lives complete.[8] *Complementary*, a word that first appeared in Ben Johnson's *Cynthia's Revels*, referred to courtiers who challenge one another in a duel of courtly compliments. If the semantic kinship between "compliment" and "complement" comes full circle etymologically, so does Hata in his conciliations. Hata is free with his compliments, but he might also unconsciously see himself as a complimentary presence in an America that he finally feels compelled to leave as an act of absolution.

Hata's anxieties over the raced body can be further understood through a reading of his anxieties over Sunny's and Kkutaeh's bodies. Hata's relationships to both women are very much gendered, but they are also raced bodies and they constitute the most intimate ways through which Hata sees other raced bodies, especially in their metonymic relation to "Asia." The process of abstraction that is part of what it means to be racialized—of being recognized but only as a model minority—is displaced into Hata's relationships with these two women.[9] As far as Hata is concerned, Kkutaeh and Sunny both enable and disrupt the symbolic appropriations of "Asianness" understood either as part of Asian and American civilizations.

When Hata's assimilation depends on the repression of both his memories and histories of the US—especially of his troubled relationship with his daughter—and also those of Asia, the process of assimilation is incumbent on Hata's repression of any kind of understanding of racism and its effects. Hata's conflation of Sunny and Kkutaeh is no simple conflation of Asia and Asian America,[10] but a repetition of race relations and racial ideas in Asia and America. Rather than confusion, Hata's attitudes toward both women draw disturbing connections between the two regions. In Hata's relationship to the two women the novel represents a far more egregious error than that of ignorance, it represents deep-seated patterns and attitudes toward race and women in the different countries, histories, cultures, and time periods. The women's positions relative to Hata's own position in the social hierarchy of relative value is both gendered and raced, and it is relative positions of power that determines how race or gender matters.

Neither one of the women's bodies or lives is narratively important, except in relation to Hata's own subjectivity—a subjectivity formed in relation to the state rather than to people—and the marginalization of the women is not so much the fault of the author as it is Hata's unreliable narration through whom we see all of the narrative action. Hata expects both Sunny's adoption, and the arrival of the comfort women in the war camp, to mark the "recommencement" of his days. The women are significant not for their own lives but for the emotions that they provoke in him.

> If someone had asked me then what I felt, I would have been unable to answer. But if I can speak for that young man now, if I can tell some part of the truth for him, I would say that he felt himself drawn to her, drawn to her very presence, which must finally leave even such a thing as beauty aside. He did not know it yet, but he hoped that if he could simply be near to her, near to her voice and to her body—if never even touching her—near, he thought, to her sleeping mind, he might somehow be found. (240)

Hata's passive construction of his past desires for Kkutaeh—to "be found," and not "to find"—disavows any agency in his coming-into-being. He places the burden of his personhood, literally, on Kkutaeh's silent and inert body. But what does this coming-into-being entail? Even though their racial and linguistic affinities are some of the primary reasons why Kkutaeh becomes so important to Hata, it becomes apparent when he ignores the other comfort women who are also Korean that Hata acknowledges or denies racial or linguistic identifications at will. Racial recognition is the privilege Hata takes onto himself in the hierarchy of male and female raced bodies. In these hierarchies of value, the dominant race (Japanese) and the dominant gender (male) chooses when to recognize race or ignore it.

Like his superior, Captain Ono, Hata moreover assigns Kkutaeh individuality and personhood insofar as she furthers the project of Japanese imperialism and insofar as the materiality of her body stands for the possibility of his own self-understanding. Hata's self-awareness and subjectivity, however, is linked to the Japanese state project. Both Hata and Captain Ono believed that Japanese imperialism in East and South East Asia would bring about a "Pan-Asian" prosperity. In order to do so, under Japanese imperialism and especially in Kkutaeh's situation, racial differences become erased but only selectively.

> What do you think the Home Ministry has been promoting all these years, but a Pan-Asian prosperity as captained by our people? . . . We must value ourselves however and wherever we appear, even in the scantest proportion. There can be no ignoring the divine spread of our strain. . . . I don't care about *her*. She is not of any consequence, except as a kind of rare vessel of us, to be observed and stewarded. (268)

Pan-Asian prosperity is balanced precariously on a racial hierarchy that the Japanese safeguard. Captain Ono and Hata had believed in the superiority of the Japanese and saw as their "mandate" the liberation of other Asian countries through colonialism—itself a mimicry of Western colonialism throughout the world and in Asia—in the service of progress. Japanese colonialism and "progress" then was a suitably moral one, and its moral goals miraculously transmuted and essentialized into racial bodies as we see in the examples of Kkutaeh and Hata. Kkutaeh, as an individual, was not important because she was Korean but because she possessed some recognizable "divine strain." Her body was assigned importance because it reflected Japanese racial superiority. The miracle of her survival and preferential treatment in the army camp, of course, is not a real miracle, but a transformation wrought by the state and its representatives, Captain Ono and Hata, who see her as being "more Japanese" than Korean.

In this novel, the double process of abstraction found in Hata's constant performance of model citizenship constructs race relations as a paradox of presence and nonpresence. Kkutaeh's body had become a racial object even as her true "race" was denied. Captain Ono insists that her bloodline was "the most pure Japanese" rather than Korean, and in rewriting her race from Korean to Japanese, performs the state's right and privilege to determine what race means, and who possesses what racial characteristics. And while Hata himself chooses to identify as Japanese rather than Korean, as a woman, Kkutaeh's choice is made on her behalf. Kkutaeh's moral obligation, like Hata's, is also to the state rather than to her sister or any of the other Korean comfort women, not by choice but as the textual effect of Hata's narration. Because of her gender and race, Kkutaeh is forced to serve as a prostitute in the Japanese war camp, but her beauty leads the men to consider her not only Japanese but "the most pure Japanese" in a double movement that objectifies even as it grants subjectivity, at least according to the logic of racial hierarchies where Japan is superior to all other Asian races (249). Japan's Pan-Asian project then was one that reasserted the

Japanese state's power even as it claimed a racial commonality across all Asian countries and cultures.

Later, the racial difference of Sunny's body reminds Hata of the humiliation he suffered during World War II as a Japanese soldier, but in the form of repressed memories. Hata's memories of his relationship with Kkutaeh, a Korean comfort woman in the Japanese army camp in Burma, are triggered when Hata sees Sunny in a sexual encounter at a party, years later. Like Kkutaeh's body, Sunny's body as symbolic of failure is overdetermined not only by racial formations in the US but also in Asia. To Hata, Sunny's "thick, wavy black hair and dark-hued skin" becomes a signifier of immorality and failure because he finds Sunny's birth to be the result of a "wanton encounter between a GI and a bar girl." Hata cannot bring himself to describe Sunny's father as "black" even though his careful descriptions of Sunny's body continues to focalize the narrative. Sunny's body bears the marks not merely of racial miscegenation, but also of imperialism where the GI is a signifier of US colonialism of Korea and the failure of Asian sovereignty and the failure of Japanese imperialism. As symbols of his desires—political and sexual—both women represent Hata's complex feelings about race, subjectivity, and political power, and they puzzle him because they do not see themselves in the same ethical relationships as he does, that is, as a model minority who from Sunny's point of view, ". . . [makes] a whole life out of gestures and politeness" (95). What Sunny does not see and Hata does not reveal, however, is that his life as model minority hides far more than her own teenage disobedience and troubles.

Kkutaeh's and Sunny's bodies become the canvases on which Hata's assumptions about the rightness of racial dominance and imperialism are played out. What Hata assumes to be gifts of love are actually acts of violence from the perspectives of the women. In the case of Kkutaeh, or "K" in Hata's present-day memories, he understands his penetration of her body as an act of love. Similarly, Hata "penetrated" Sunny's body by way of her abortion doctor, and by providing medical assistance in the surgical room. The abortion was an act of violence and of control not unlike that of actual rape. Hata's control over Sunny's body was an attempt to control what he thinks her body signifies. He views her body large with pregnancy as a sign, not of her failure, but of his own: "To remember that now makes me feel the way I should have felt, to brim at such a sight with sober pride and happiness, a grandparental glow, though then it was, I must recall, a most sickening vision to me, being the clearest picture of my defeats, familial and otherwise" (341). Hata exercises ownership over Sunny's body by killing the life within her, just as he had exercised ownership over Kkutaeh's body by refusing to take her life—at her request—in the Burmese camp. To do so would be to go against the wishes of the Japanese state that delivered these women as objects to satisfy their soldiers. Hata's moral obligation, finally, was to the state, and not to the woman he claims to love.

Another character in the novel, one of Hata's colleagues, makes a different kind of moral choice. The comfort women's arrival at the Burmese war camp changed the life of a young corporal who was obsessed by the few pornographic photos in his possession, but in an unexpected way. Soon after the girls' arrival, Corporal Endo pulled one of the girls—Kkutaeh's sister—aside and slit her throat. The girl's murder releases her from undergoing multiple and repeated daily rapes in the army camp and Corporal Endo himself was subsequently executed, not for murder, tellingly, but for treason: "He should be considered as guilty as any saboteur who had stolen or despoiled the camp's armament or rations" (189). The nameless girl's body was an object, inert and without agency, much like the tanks, tents, or a sack of rice, and only in her death does Kkutaeh's sister regain her singularity.

This gift of "life" is what Kkutaeh asks of Hata, a gift that Hata will not grant her even years after her physical death. Hata clings on to Kkutaeh as apparition in a curious case of the living haunting the dead.

> Though she sat down I couldn't feel any press of her weight, and once again, for a moment, I was almost sure she was a spectral body or ghost. But I am not a magical man, and never have been. I am unversed in the metaphysical, have long become estranged from it, and if this can be so, I believe the metaphysical is as much unversed in me. We have a historical pact. And as deeply as I wished she were some wondrous, ethereal presence, that I was being duly haunted, I knew that she was absolute, unquestionably real, a once-personhood come wholly into being. (286)

This ghostly being that Hata believes to be "unquestionably real," and whom Hata renames simply "K," becomes a part of his possessions and he refuses to let her "die," even when she asks him to—Hata refuses her freedom both in life and in death. When he refuses to kill Kkutaeh and thus refuses to release her from the prospect of multiple, repeated rapes every day, Hata acted with the law of the military camp, but in doing so he transgresses the ethical duty that, in this instance, demands the breaking of the law.

Hata recognizes only the call of the institution and ignores the call of the Other that demands death. Hata refuses to kill Kkutaeh when she asks him to, and keeps her alive to fulfill his sexual desires, and through the fulfillment of his sexual desires, his desire to belong to his platoon in what the soldiers took to be normal. Such desires are "lawful" in the Japanese army base, and indeed, Hata not only survives the war but later prospers—Hata's "responsible self" ultimately exists in relation to the Japanese state and he receives his rewards. Even after Hata leaves Japan for the US, the nation-state continues to be the transcendent, singular Other to whom he offers his sacrifices, sacrifices made on the basis of his belonging to the US national imaginary as a model minority. He sacrifices ethics in favor of the laws and morality that the military upholds and which stand for the nation-state in whose right it acts.

Lee's novel and his protagonist rewrite the model minority myth not merely to "reveal" that Asian Americans are "just like everyone else," but that ethical relationships and moral obligations have the potential to mask forms of social violence that are part of the political life of the state. Hata's exemplariness establishes ethical relationships with others only insofar as they further the state's project because Hata sees his primarily moral obligations as belonging to the state. Hata's history of abuse—first, the comfort women, and then, Sunny—substitutes "violence" with "right actions" because, first, as an agent of the state, and then, as legal guardian of a minor, he is given the power to police women's bodies and determine on their behalf behaviors that are acceptable or unacceptable, wanted or unwanted, as defined by their utility to the state. The language of ethics disciplines minorities by asking them to act in certain ways that erase the power relations between those of different races and genders because they erase the material conditions of racial and gender difference. The moral behavior of the model minority possess the power to erase the social structures on which the state's moral language is built.

Hata's own visibility as "model citizen" passes over his own racial difference even as he performs race as a "model minority" to remain within the national body. His own ethical choices as a model minority guarantee his place within the national imaginary, but it also reveals the violence with which the state interpellates him as subject-citizen. At the same time, the model minority is an ideal example of how social violence can be mystified because it assumes that the model minority takes his or her place in racial hierarchies with ease and as a matter of course, but there is nothing natural about the incorporation of the model minority into the nation. Even at its most obvious, the myth of the model minority, while appearing to describe one racial group, actually situates the racialization of Asian Americans in relation to other minority groups in the US that are less exemplary. Claims of ethics or morality—either as positive or negative examples—indicate how all minorities are imbricated within a larger discursive system about race and belonging.

However, the moralization of racial minorities has two goals: first, as we have seen above, it creates and maintains social order among and between racial groups; and, second, it guarantees the cohesion of the social formation as a whole. In other words, the moralization of the minor subject guarantees the state's wholeness and the state's moral position. René Girard's analysis of the mystification of social violence in *Job, the Victim of His People*, provides a useful model for thinking about the close relationship between social violence and justice as mutually implicated. And as Bonnie Honig argues, following Girard, we need to understand why social tensions continue to exist in our societies and how the trope of foreignness functions in our symbolic politics. Girard argues that most readers mistake Job's primary complaint as a complaint against God when Job's anger is directed against the people around him and the violence he experiences at their hands: "Violence is the true 'referent'; barely disguised in the threats of his friends and not disguised at all in Job's laments" (25). Job's friends' offer the explanation that his fall from fortune is divine retribution, and the assumption of Job's guilt transforms Job from idol—the object of desire—to scapegoat.

But this transformation of Job from exemplarity to dissolution is also part of the collective violence that remakes justice in its own image. The moral justification of Job's fall is also the moral justification for his banishment from society. Job provokes unanimous opposition and condemnation among those who know him, and it is the unanimity and agreement on what Job's fall means in this moral economy, Girard argues, that is both the goal and process in what he calls the "scapegoat mechanism." The common agreement on Job's degeneration ejects him from community at the same time that it legitimates the community's conception of what constitutes a just outcome. The goal of exile is not so much to achieve justice but rather to restore social unity and harmony. Social cohesion is the final use value of the scapegoat.

The social is formed by common agreement not only by determining who belongs, but also by determining what counts as "morality" and how those standards strengthen or threaten the community. To be just, or to be seen as just, is fundamental to any kind of community—however they might define it—but the scapegoat as sacrifice shows us how the object of this goal is finally social cohesion and social harmony. The victim or the sacrifice takes on the appearance of evil, and its ejection from the community thus restores peace and validates social bonds held in common.

> The system consists of whitening the community by blackening the scapegoat; to consolidate it, the belief in this mythic blackness must be strengthened. . . . The victim is expected to explain to his fellow-citizens all the evil that should in future be attributed to him. This facilitates everyone's adherence to the orthodoxy that is being developed. The strength of this adherence, in primitive societies, makes it possible to tie the final knot and make the scapegoat the principle of social unity, a god who is both harmful and beneficial. (*Job* 112)

The scapegoat is the sacrifice that restores harmony to the community. Social violence and alienation are explained and legitimated as morally just and appropriate because they are necessary to safeguard the wider community itself. Girard's unconscious choice of words—"whitening" and "blackening"—throws into relief how racial thinking has been historically imbricated with political thought, and vice versa even if implicitly.

Girard points out that most readers mistake Job's primary complaint for a complaint against God when Job actually directs his anger against his community and the violence he experiences at their hands: "Violence is the true 'referent'; barely disguised in the threats of his friends and not disguised at all in Job's laments" (25). Social violence is mystified precisely because the source of grievance or resentment is mystified and driven underground as in the case of Hata and Kkutaeh. Our ideas about "justice" reflects this mystification where social unity is the goal of the state when anxieties over disharmony or conflict—social protests, for example—are said to threaten the state's power or wholeness.

Furthermore, the concurrent processes of identification and alienation enable the process of victimization by which a victim is selected and expelled from the polis to save it. The scapegoat cannot be persecuted without due cause; it has to appear to "deserve" its fate. Job's fall evokes anxiety among his "friends" and peers because what happens to Job could very well happen to them. The process of identification is central here, and even as the position of victim is dependent on Job's equality and "likeness" to those of his "friends," it erases Job's individuality and makes him an example or model.

If Job's fall is the consequence of moral failure, then their own continued success is evidence of their difference from Job, and a confirmation of their own moral integrity. If Job admits to his degeneration, he affirms his friends' right to their wealth and reputation, and consequently, he also affirms their earlier envy and desire to be like him. For the scapegoat to reinforce the community's ties through its expulsion, it needs to not only be sufficiently different from other members of the community, it also needs to be sufficiently like them.

The model minority, in other words, has to conform to society's ideal of itself, but when it does conform to those ideals, it also becomes a threat that only expulsion can resolve. In *A Gesture Life*, scapegoating forces us to reexamine the relationship of race to violence and how ethics authorizes that relationship. Hata is what Girard calls a "perfect scapegoat" who believes, condones, and masks the violence of social processes that have as their goal the coherence and unity of the national imaginary. Scapegoating relies on several suppositions: first, the scapegoat is a part of the community and an *equal* to other members of the community; second, the scapegoat is an object of envy because of his good fortune; and third, the scapegoat acquiesces to his position as victim.

Hata as a model minority is both a part of Bedley Run—in this sense, he is their equal—even as he is alienated from it; his wealth and property are envied; and he never protests when others accuse him of cheating or when they make snide, racial comments in his presence. Hata cannot be allowed to become an exemplary property or business owner without also becoming the model citizen who at least looks integrated with the community, and who upholds the same values. If Hata is always seen as completely foreign to his community, his construction as "model minority" would be impossible. However, needless to say, model minorities can always lose this "privilege" of inclusion, and it is the threat of loss that disciplines them as US citizens.

At once part of and outside the national imaginary, Hata's liminal position sustains the boundaries of inside and outside that the state polices. Race itself is symbolic of social conflict, but how race as representation is constructed needs to be read within the larger frame of the state's role in such social conflicts.[11] Because the model minority is enfolded in the national imaginary only as long as he or she validates the nation-state and what it stands for, the racial minority as threat—Sunny's blackness or her pregnant body—must be ejected or erased so that the image and power of the state remains whole and uncontested. Ethical behavior or moral obligation confirms the subject's agency but also confirms the state's right to legitimate violence. However, such social processes of expulsion can hardly be undertaken overtly, not even by the state, without using the language of moral obligation.

Why should minorities be "good"? The racial formation of Asian Americans as model minorities reveals how central "good behavior" is in order to be incorporated into the national imaginary, and even then, only to be reminded that their place is precarious. Model minorities who do not assuage the feelings of anxiety the majority might have toward racial minorities will soon discover that they have a tenuous toehold in the nation. And if we, like Job's friends, often misread wealth and success as evidence of moral goodness, then how do we read Hata's deliberate actions that divest himself of the very things that have been central to his identity and personhood in the US? Hata's moral agency at the end of the novel is ambiguous because in his departure, he neither addresses what "disturbs" him nor does he explain what causes him to feel that his time in the town is "close to done" (21).

By choosing exile, Hata's fate at the end of the novel is that of the perpetual outsider, recognized and claimed by no one and who also recognizes and claims no one and no state. But in doing so, he also remains the perfect subject of the state whose self-exile does not restore justice; instead, his self-exile restores the state's social unity and social harmony. He is a scapegoat who acquiesces to the process of victimization and justifies his own scapegoating. Hata's fall in fortunes, finally, is a self-inflicted punishment and exile that leaves his community intact because he is the perfect state subject who confirms the state's views of race and morality.

By choosing exile, Hata acts as a choosing subject, but he finally cannot see or explain why exile is the solution to his uneasiness. Exile makes sense to him even if in an inchoate way, because for Hata, racial belonging is premised on the idea of moral goodness and to the very end, he adopts the perspective of the state: social cohesion rather than justice for or between individuals is the goal of his ethical relationships. In rewriting the myth of the model minority, the novel rewrites moral exemplariness as an indicator of state wholeness and power where difference is a threat to social uniformity and harmony. "Good" or "bad," especially as epitomized by "good" minorities and "bad" minorities, are part of the same racial system that has as its underlying logics and goals of protecting the state's sovereignty and economic good. Lee's novel, *A Gesture Life*, rewrites the myth of the model minority to reveal the inner life of an exemplary model minority, who is a model not merely because he is successful, but because he is successfully and wholly interpellated as a subject of a state. The model minority performs the function of confirming the state's own purpose and place as it organizes race relations. The threat of exclusion disciplines racial minorities and authorizes the relationship between state, race, and the performance of moral goodness.

The narrative of assimilation in late twentieth century US culture tells us what the model minority looks like and the model minority takes the form of the perfect capitalist actor who disrupts neither society's steady progression toward greater productivity and the accumulation of profit, nor the commodity fetishism that transforms human beings into their use value. Hata's self-exile in *A Gesture Life* reminds us that positive stereotypes reflect what the state values, and that in their demand for exemplarity, they erase the role of social violence in the disciplining of all racial minorities.

Moral exemplarity, moreover, regulates the "right" emotions felt by racial majorities and racial minorities to create emotional attachments that secure not individual personhood, but the wholeness of the social. Model minorities secure their place in the nation by securing others' emotional attachments to them, that of "not" anxiety. Lee's depiction of the model minority who has wholly embraced his subjection accentuates how race is described in moral terms in order that the raced subject can help prevent the anxiety of the majority that views bodies of color as potential threats. Simultaneously, racial behavior understood as moral behavior renders Asian American subjects anxious even when they are scripted as part of the American Dream because the scrutiny and the demands of state inclusion are arbitrary because they affect all racial minorities, and because they contain moral force.

The next chapter looks at how the myth of the model minority is not only a trope of racial inclusion or exclusion at work in the American cultural imaginary but that as a trope of state power, it comes to life in different cultural contexts, and at different historical moments. Neither time nor space erases the power or relevance of this trope because it is a sign of the state's investment in and dependence on cultural and symbolic spheres as it secures its sovereignty. The next chapter also shows that the trope of moral exemplarity does not exist in isolation; its circulation orbits the model minority's opposite, the figure of the terrorist or spy. In both Lee's and Han's novels, the model minority has a secret life or identity that reduces the racial minority to a constant state of anxiety in case of discovery. Hata is not a spy but has to hide how he was once an enemy soldier and lives with a repressed uneasiness that he will be discovered. Chapter 2 shifts our focus to how the global stereotype of the model minority is always implicitly paired with its negative, the terrorist-spy.

The hope that some racial minorities can be assimilated as exemplary minorities is accompanied by the anxiety that those same racial minorities may never be assimilated because their racial difference predisposes them to betrayal or deceit. Both beliefs are founded by the belief that race is first a sign of biological, and then, of moral or civilizational difference. The next chapter examines how moral attitudes toward race emerge not out of thin air but as the result of colonial forms of knowledge, and how colonial forms of knowledge later developed from WWII, through the Cold War, and decolonization. It is the climate of the Cold War and communist fears that intensifies and cements the earlier, colonial modern link between race and morality. Finally, anticommunist fears and sentiments in Asia proved to be intrinsic to the formative period that led the postcolonial state to adopt colonial ideas about race as their own. Lee's and Han's novels are published and set in very different historical contexts, but the overlaps in their portrayals of model minorities and terrorist spies are surprisingly similar because they are imbricated with state power and the state's ideas about race and how racial difference should be managed.

Chapter Two

Tropes of Degeneration
Morality and Political Efficacy

> Tyranny, oppression, moral degeneration, persecution and mass killing have always and everywhere started with the pollution of language, with making what is base and violent sound clean and decent ("the new order," "final solution," "temporary measures," "limited restrictions"), or else with using coarse and bestial language where it should have been humane and delicate ("parasites," "social insects," "political cancer," etc.). The writer ought to recognize that, whenever a human being is referred to as a parasite or a germ, there will follow, sooner or later, death squads and exterminations.
>
> —Amos Oz, "Integrity"

Han Suyin's novel, *And the Rain My Drink*, published in 1956, takes up two popular stereotypes of Chinese Malayans—the model minority and the communist spy—during the height of the Malayan communist insurgency that began in June 1948, and ended in December 2, 1989. The conflict took place over thirty years, long after Malaya gained its independence from the British in 1957.[1] For its time, *And the Rain My Drink*, a satire of the British colonial regime's response to Malayan communists—and possibly semiautobiographical because the author was then married to Leon Comber, a police officer in the Malayan federation—engaged with what would have been a taboo or controversial subject in the colony. The communist insurgency and the race riots of May 13, 1969, are the two most controversial but central periods in Malaysian history and the history of race relations. Often assumed to be ethnic minority Chinese in Malaysia,[2] communist terrorists or spies were feared because they are remembered for their participation in the only guerrilla war conducted in Malaysia after the end of WWII. Today, depictions of communism and communist soldiers are still among the most sensitive and policed content concerning national security and national history. For example, despite having been approved by the Malaysian Censorship Board, Lew Kit Wong's PG-13 film, *The New Village*, which portrays the communist's anticolonial contributions, was finally banned from the cinemas because of strident objections from the public to a movie that no one had even seen.[3] The film was vilified as "unpatriotic" despite getting through already conservative government censorship. More recently, an emotionally spare documentary about how Chinese families were affected by insurgency was also banned, presumably to avoid the kind of reaction Wong's film had earlier provoked even prior to screening.[4]

Half a century after the end of the Malayan Emergency, anger against "communists" continues to dictate what can or cannot be officially released in Malaysian cinemas. But what sustains the fear, anger, and vitriol directed against the communists? As laid out in the later sections in this chapter, the communists in Malaya held diverse beliefs about race, religion, and even about political structures and democracy. Communism in Malaysia either as political theory or social movement actually does not have a coherent and sustained ideological core when we look at the histories and the fiction about this period. What remains in this picture of communism is the violence, treachery, and the supposed animosity the communists, implicitly always Chinese, directed toward Malayan society as a whole.

There was truth to the portrayal of the communist as a fearsome figure because of the historical conditions of the war in which they found themselves. As guerrilla soldiers, they were forced to confront their political opponents in a brutal form of warfare in which they were ill-equipped to fight, and whose victories depended on their secrecy and surprise attacks from within the forests where the communists hid. They moreover had to count on aid and supplies from allies, friends, or kin who lived in villages. However, communism in Malaya and later, Malaysia, came to symbolize racial and civilizational difference in both the fictional and the historical depictions of the period. The communist soldier who fought heroically against the Japanese in WWII was transformed into an evil Chinese spy not long after the war ended. British representations of the Chinese communist turned their wartime ally to an internal enemy whose purported goal was the destruction of the Malayan state. This history is important because it played a formative role in the racialization of Chinese Malayans after the war, and because the anger against communism in Malaysia remains alive and delicate.

Han Suyin's novel represents the fear of the communist in ways that overlap with the historical accounts of the insurgency, and her work can be read for its fidelity to history. However, her depiction of the communist soldier as terrorist and spy is also a piece of satire. Han's novel offers a critique of this period of history not by offering an alternative representation of the communist to how they have been stereotyped, but by depicting the representations of the communists that would have been common at the time the novel was written. History intersects with fiction in this chapter, but the form of satire disrupts that history, not in the sense of calling into question history itself but precisely because it takes that history seriously, as absurd as it must have appeared to the author.

The main object of Han's ridicule is neither the communist soldier nor even the colonizers commonly thought of as the main actors in this period of history, but rather the stereotype of the communist soldier as terrorist. The novel relies on historical details in its settings, character development, and plot, but the novel's tensions and the emotions it evokes—fear, hilarity, and disbelief—are built on how it plays with assumptions about race from this period to dramatize how the categories of "good" and "bad" are fungible when they are used to describe racial minorities.

The novel's remarkable quality—and its success as a formally complex work of fiction—lies in how Han, the author, uses the assumptions that racial stereotypes provoke to structure the reader's own experience of belief and disbelief. Can we really know the racial Other? Han does not offer historical details to answer this question. Rather, it is the historicity of the stereotype as stereotype that grounds the emotional force of the novel. This question remains unanswered in Han's novel, and therein lies its power to disrupt the epistemic certainty that "race" appears to provide. No, we cannot really know the racial Other because no one—raced or not—can truly be known, and Han's novel refuses to answer a question that can never be answered in the first place.

The novel plays a game of deception with the reader when it leads us to believe we understand what the model minority or terrorist is "really" like, because the eponymous narrator of the novel assumes that she, too, understands what she sees. Narrative perspective appears to offer us "true" observations of history, especially through Suyin, the narrator. Calm, reasonable, and informed,

Suyin is perfectly reliable in the accuracy of her observations. However, the experience of reading the novel starts to become an unsettling experience when the narrator herself realizes that she cannot trust what she sees.

And the Rain My Drink portrays the busyness and confusion of a teeming, colorful, polyglot Malaya that is at the same time under siege, and follows the conflicts and confrontations among white colonizers, their native Malay and Chinese assistants, and the many other communities that make up the colony in the 1950s. The novel's settings range from the uncertain life of a communist camp in the forest, to rubber plantations, internment camps, mansions in the cities, and the luxurious parties thrown by wealthy Chinese traders. It presents the colonizers and the natives in their many shapes and forms from the wealthy Chinese merchants to the hardworking but worn out laborers, and also to the desperate and vicious Chinese communist. The narrative shifts from the first-person to an omniscient third-person narrator at certain points, but for the most part, it is framed by the narrator, Suyin, who works as a doctor in a local Malayan hospital and who employs Ah Mei as a lived-in maid.

The novel begins as Suyin meets one of the novel's main characters, Ah Mei, who is introduced as "Captured Enemy Personnel no. 234" at the police headquarters in the southern state of Johor, across the Straits from Singapore. Ah Mei has just been brought in to the station to make a formal request for the insect and leech bites on her arms and legs to be examined, and despite Suyin's diagnosis that the bites will fade with time, Ah Mei is to be rewarded for her services with a visit to the hospital under police escort because she has provided useful information on other communist soldiers.

Suyin and Ah Mei first appear as opposites and offer a sharp contrast in their status and position in Malayan society: Suyin is the model minority who is articulate, respectable, and a highly educated professional while Ah Mei, the recently "rehabilitated" terrorist, is uneducated, common-looking, and naive. In the same section, the narrator also describes Ah Mei as youthful and "extremely charming" with her "so smooth" face and "hands and feet very small." However, the narrator notes her petite Asian frame and childlike features not merely to reference Ah Mei's age—she is only twenty at the beginning of the novel—but because the narrative then goes on to note how the male officers in the room see her as sexually available because of her age, gender, size, and, unsurprisingly, because of the vulnerability of her status in colonial society.

Suyin's initial description of what she sees tells us that our narrator is sensitive and aware of how Ah Mei looks to others, even if she does not share those ways of seeing. The narrator's own personal view of Ah Mei comes across in more ambiguous ways, compared to the male colonial officers in the room: "Ah Mei and I look at each other. After a while I pull my mouth together again, guilty of so much secret mirth, and she turns her head but goes on smiling, gazing away and towards the window at the now gathered storm outside" (31). The narrator explains the context of their first exchange, which further builds up our trust in her acumen and understanding of the historical significance of the moment: "Ah Mei smiles, happily, for all of the treats which come to her because she is such an excellent informer on her previous comrades, going about in a comfortable police car is her chief pleasure" (32). The Chinese communist, now reformed and enlightened, is rewarded, but her childish pleasure in her rewards is also strangely pathetic. At this point in the narrative, Ah Mei is as different as she can be from the more cosmopolitan Suyin.

However, the narrator's assumptions about what Ah Mei wants and her condescending amusement at Ah Mei's childish pleasures soon dissipates, and by the end of the novel, the narrator can no longer think of Ah Mei as an innocent child who is barely grown. The early shared look and smile, "guilty of so much secret mirth," between the narrator and the terrorist becomes a potentially much more sinister exchange when Suyin, while never actually accused of being a communist, is later told that she, like other Chinese in Malaya, can always be suspected of being a communist. Suyin discovers that in the eyes of the state, she is not so very different from Ah Mei after all. Who, now, is the fool?

To the reader, the first, obvious comparison between Suyin and Ah Mei, that is, between the model minority and the terrorist-spy, turns out to be, more accurately, a schizophrenic comparison of Ah Mei the model minority to Ah Mei the terrorist-spy. Even though there is narrative tension in the contrast between Suyin's and Ah Mei's vastly different positions in colonial society and in the racial hierarchies of their social lives, the novel's emotional core lies in the belated realization—the narrator's and ours—that Ah Mei is simultaneously model minority and terrorist-spy, or the "model" spy. Suyin herself, the respectable doctor and model minority of the colonial state, later comes under suspicion as a possible communist. Who is the moral exemplar, and who is the possible spy?

The conjunction between the two stereotypes, usually read as opposites, destabilizes both stereotypes. Neither Suyin nor Ah Mei are ever free from suspicion in the novel because the Chinese body symbolizes both moral exemplarity and moral threat at the same time. The novel's depiction of the terrorist-spy as model minority takes seriously the racial stereotypes in circulation during the postwar period, but it also unmoors them in its satirical projection of both stereotypes onto the same Chinese body. The Chinese became objects of suspicion and fear not because they were merely one or the other, but because they were assumed to be equally capable of masquerading as one or the other. After the end of WWII and the Cold War, the communist as terrorist continues to evoke fear because it retains its wartime symbolism of the racial minority who can never be fully known and therefore never fully trusted.

It is precisely the ability of the state to project contradictory meanings onto the raced body that makes racial stereotypes a part of state power. Han's fusing of the two stereotypes in the character of Ah Mei draws our attention to how racial hierarchy in the colonial state overlapped with moral order, and also how these overlaps between race and morality fell within the purview of the colonial state and the judgments it makes about security, law, and social order. Racial minorities could not determine for themselves who they were; it was the colonial state that assigned to them the labels of moral exemplarity or degeneration. The contradictory assumptions about race or our expectations about what race means as part of our symbolic life appear more clearly in fiction rather than in history or the law.

However, the history of this period also explains why race became so necessary to securing colonial power in the postwar period. Han relied on historical events and details that would have been commonly known to her readers at the time, and this history explains why the racial stereotypes of model minority or terrorist emerged as a result of the historical-materialist conditions of the period. But these histories are also put into the service of a different cultural narrative, that is, of racial identity as moral identity.

Racial anxiety about who is or is not "communist" taught colonial and postcolonial Malayans to see new enemies now assumed to be hidden in plain sight: enemies can be identified by the color of their skin and the shape of their eyes. Racial anxiety describes the process of learning to see oneself as raced, but also to see the racial Other as part of a reward system that the state oversees: racial minorities are either deserving of reward (model minority) or punishment (terrorist-spy). This reward system builds on colonialist notions of race, biology, and cultural traits, and it uses the conflation of race and morality to further the colonial state project. Moreover, the fight against Malayan communists created laws and policies that drew on moral language to strengthen state power. Negative stereotypes, like positive stereotypes such as the model minority, are the cultural expressions of state interests and the historical conditions of state power. Fiction, on the other hand, mobilizes those stereotypes in order to draw our attention to the intimate relationship between racial stereotypes and the ideologies of the state.

Postcolonial Malaysian fiction and film are not limited to themes of national history, war, or race. Writers and directors also explore many other themes on other important social questions such as poverty, urban and rural life, our relationship to nature, changing gender relations, and myths and tradition. However, the Japanese occupation and the communist insurgency remain important to the national cultural imaginary and these histories appear in works produced by Chinese Malaysians and also the work of prominent Malay authors and filmmakers. The Malay Malaysian national laureate A. Samad Said's novel, *Salina*, first published in 1961, features a female protagonist who undergoes poverty, hardship, and sexual assault as a result of the communist insurgency. In Pak Samad's most famous novel, moral dissolution in the postwar period was not the result of racial or civilizational difference, but the consequence of war and the disruptions that follow. *Salina* follows the travails of a young Malay girl, Nahidah, after her abusive father falls in battle during the insurgency. Given the colonial state's insistence that the communist threat was also a racial threat, Pak Samad's novel is remarkable for the fact that it did not attribute Nahidah's suffering to the Chinese communists.

> *Waktu British kembali ke Malaya kehidupan orang-orang di Singapura banyak yang berubah: ada yang dengan tiba-tiba menjadi kaya, dan ada pula yang dengan tiba-tiba menjadi miskin. Dan dalam waktu BMA (British Military Administration) orang serba tidak tentu arah, tidak tahu masa depan mereka. . . . Ayah Nahidah sendiri kurang beruntung. . . . Kemudian, entah mengapa, bertukar pula fikirannya untuk menjadi sojar.*

> When the British returned to Malaya, the lives of Singaporeans [the novel was written before Singapore separated from Malaya] changed a great deal: some became very wealthy all of a sudden, and some became poor all of a sudden. And during the BMA (British Military Administration) people were lost and did not know what their future would look like. . . . Nahidah's father himself was a little unlucky. . . . Then, no one understands why, he changed his mind and became a soldier. (Translation mine, 137)

The narrative voice describes Nahidah's father's poverty as something that was equal parts fate and equal parts the consequence of what life was like under the BMA, and portrays her father as one who is, if not foolish, at least unwise and certainly irresponsible when he decides to become a soldier. As a result of his choice, he dies in the war against the communists and his two children, Nahidah and her brother Mansur, are left in the indifferent care of their stepmother. As a result of his death, Nahidah is preyed on by older men in the Malay village where she lives and out of financial necessity works as a waitress in a restaurant. Her work exposes her to further unwanted male attention and casts suspicions on her moral purity.[5]

Written by one of the most respected Malay writers of the twentieth century, *Salina* resists the racial stereotyping that would have assigned "good" and "evil" to the various racial groups that Han describes in British colonial society. His novel goes on to attribute the dangers Nahidah experiences as a result of the process of modernization and corruption that the Malay community experienced after the end of WWII.

> "*Semua orang dah pandai makan suap, semua orang dah pandai* black market; *pendeknya semua orang cari jalan untuk lekas kaya. Tak tau lagi? Dunia sekarang ni ginilah. Orang kejarkan duit! . . . Sapa kata orang tak berani? Untuk dapaatkan duit orang berani membunuh sekarang ni," kata Abdul Fakar seolaholah dialah seorang yang baik.*
>
> "Everyone understands how to be corrupt, everyone knows about the black market; to cut the story short, everyone wants the fast track to wealth. Don't you know? That's how the world is now. People chase after money! . . . . Who says people can't find the courage? People are brave to kill enough for money now," said Abdul Fakar as if he was a good man. (Translation mine, 225)

Seen from outside the colonial state's perspective, moral degeneration was not so much a result of racial difference as it was the all-too-familiar consequence of a corrupt state governing during a time of social transition and widespread poverty. Moreover, while racial stereotypes describe the Chinese as money-loving and vicious, *Salina* overturns those assumptions. The Malay women in Naridah's village face danger—not from unknown outsiders but from those who live within their community and who are in the position to take advantage of those weakest and most vulnerable among them. Moral threat exists not in particular racial groups, but in a social world that leaves a few "*tiba-tiba kaya*" ("suddenly rich") and others "*tiba-tiba miskin*" ("suddenly poor") across all racial groups.

The independent filmmaker and publisher Amir Muhammad's (2016) now banned documentary, *Lelaki Komunis Terakhir*, or *The Last Communist* (the official English title leaves out the male gender that the Malay title denotes) includes interviews with former Malay and Chinese communist soldiers and leaders now living in Thailand, and shows how the movement was not only demonized but decidedly "Sinicized."[6] Malay involvement in the communist movement and in cultural works about this historical period have become invisible because it falls outside of official state narratives about "good" and "bad" subjects. The censorship of postwar Malaysian fiction demonstrates that the politics around what can be said or what must be excised from the nation's history and literary or filmic traditions because of their *moral relevance* are part of the discretionary power that the colonial state, and also the postcolonial Malaysian state, allocates to itself.[7] The state does not take a neutral moral position when it comes to racial subjects.

The Chinese Malaysian writer Shih-Li Kow's melancholic short story, "Precious Things," published in 2008, exemplifies how racial anxiety permeates the mundane and the ordinary even decades after the communist insurgency has come to a close. The narrator, a young woman, stumbles into an antique store in Melaka on a rainy day that she first mistakes to be a tiny museum, but she quickly discovers that the objects are for sale and she is introduced to each item. During the awkward tour, the proprietor asks her bewildered visitor to keep track of the worth of all the items in store one item at a time as she narrates how those everyday objects were used by her family and their servants. The narrator finally decides to buy an expensive, little wooden box that the proprietor claims was made by one of the servants as a token of his love for the young lady of the house. But as soon as she steps out of the store, she discovers a grimy sticker at the bottom of the box that says, "Made in China." The narrator's disillusionment is a reflection of our anxiety about "authenticity," but this belief in authenticity is tied to the threat of being duped and also a reminder of the threat of deportation: Chinese Malayans are not who they say they are, and that they should go back to China where they "really" belong.

The short story provokes anxiety because it is historically plausible. However, the story plays on notions of "authenticity" and "plausibility" through its references to racial stereotypes and the physical and psychological features usually associated with "Chineseness." The story provides no historical documentations; rather, the anxiety it provokes is based on the assumption that we understand what "Chinese" racial identity symbolizes in Malaysia. Race stands in for "history." It is not historical accuracy that is at stake in this short story, but the social significance of how race appears as an always already legible epistemic category because it also appears as a moral category.

During the strange tour that makes up the diegesis of the short story, the tour guide presents to the narrator what seems to be yet another ordinary household item that makes up the store's goods: "She showed me a faded photograph of a slender girl in *samfoo* who was her sister who had been suspected of being a communist and sent back to China, and died of tuberculosis before she was married. This was tagged at seventy-five ringgit" (81).[8] We discover that the girl in the photograph is Chinese, not through descriptions of her skin color, eye shapes, or facial bone structure, but through the narrator's descriptions of the cultural traits and political beliefs usually assigned to the Chinese. She wears a particular kind of dress or costume usually worn by lower-middle-class Chinese women, she was susceptible to a particular type of disease, and she was suspected of being a communist.

More chillingly, we also know that the proprietor is Chinese because of how she behaves. That the seller feels nothing for the fate of the girl in the photograph is a play on the stereotype of the Chinese as crafty money-grubbers who put value profit above all other ties. At the end of the story, the narrator feels foolish for paying too much to an unscrupulous shopkeeper who is cunning and deceptive because she is Chinese. But who is the real fool in this story? If the picture is real, the proprietor must be a fool because she sells everything her family owns to strangers for small sums. But if the picture is fake, the narrator is gullible for believing in a lie. In this little play about racial anxiety surrounding authenticity and history, no one wins, and everyone has been made a fool.

This short story about racial anxiety demonstrates an unusual effect of racism on how we interpret what is before our eyes. It destabilizes our assumptions about the world by both asserting that our ideas about race fixes the world for us, but at the same time, that nothing can be fully certain because the racial Other, ultimately, can never be trusted. Guilt or innocence can never truly be proven, and the anxiety surrounding race can never be resolved. Fiction in this instance replicates the effects of racial anxiety.

The reader cannot be sure of the slender girl's identity, or if she did eventually die of tuberculosis. Nonetheless, the narrative tension of the story relies not merely on uncertainty but also on the certainty that this was a part of actual history. The exchange value of an old photograph of an unknown girl lies in the possibility that the girl who is "suspected of being a communist and sent back to China" could—and must—very well have existed. Suspicion as well as historical plausibility are now interwoven into the very fabric of the narrative that leads the narrator to buy the photograph because racial anxiety teaches us to be extra vigilant where the Chinese are concerned.

The next section of the chapter turns briefly to how race was thought of in moral terms in Malaya during the mid-twentieth century, and how this effectively created an aura of suspicion around racial minorities during the communist insurgency. The material history of the communist matters, but so does the history of how race has come to assume symbolic significance. The significance of global racial tropes lies in the conjuncture of both material and symbolic considerations.

The historical sections of this chapter serve two functions. First, they provide a lesser-known colonial history to readers new to Southeast Asia; and second, they explain the material history of racial formation in Malaysia, and how the material history of modern race became a moral narrative. Modern notions of race were foundational to the colonial state's strategy of "divide and conquer" and proved to be effective not only because the different communities were segregated by industry and geography and thus could not effectively organize against the colonizer, but also because they began to see other racial groups as competitors for the state's resources and protection. Eventually, these conflicts that first emerged as a result of modern state rule, could only then be adjudicated by the state itself.

But the state does not only manage racial difference, it needs racial difference to guarantee its own power and the social contract of the nation. This social contract in Malaysia adjudicates the redistribution of resources through the state's race-based economic policies as well as the moral justifications for them. Charles Mills's notion of the "racial contract" and global liberalism helps us understand how the ideology of a free market and free individuals—the condition under which the postcolonial state finds itself in the second half of the twentieth century—has become one of the most important tropes of freedom and progress. Social contract theory in the tradition of Locke and Kant, and the contemporaneous form given it by Rawls, begins with the premise that all individuals are morally equal and that the state is impartial in its adjudication and apportionment of rights. A just polity is therefore the polity that protects the rights of the individuals within it.

However, this history and conception of liberalism begins with a faulty premise, because equality in the state of nature cannot be assumed since the West was founded on slavery, genocide, and indentured labor. Racial normativity, where the racial majority retains its privileges and power because it is invisible, erases precisely the conditions of its own production in order to assert and maintain universalizing claims. The postcolonial state that does not recognize its inheritance of colonial structure repeats the same erasures. Furthermore, the moral code of the racial contract reflects the colonial state's interests in guaranteeing "loyalty" and good behavior on the part of the colonized so that the colonial state continues to legitimize their right to rule.

The histories of racial divides and the contributions of racial minorities are erased from the demands and claims of rights, justice, individual freedom, and obligations to the state as if they never existed. As epistemic construct, the racial contract refers to the ways in which racial majorities and minorities—in the context of the US, white and nonwhite persons—belong to different classes to which differential privileges accrue according to racial lines. In order to maintain these privileges, what Mills calls "structured blindnesses and opacities" are needed to sustain political, moral and epistemological contracts between racial majorities and minorities (19). Both the US and Malaysia are founded not only on the labor of different racial groups, but also on the desire to erase these histories and to turn the story of nationhood into one where only whites or majority Malays played important roles.

Moral Narratives of Race

The state's fear of the racial minority presented as moral fear emerges most clearly in colonial narratives after WWII ended and the British returned to Malaya. Ironically, racial fear manifested as moral fear was not first directed against the communist terrorist, but against the native elites who had cooperated with the Japanese. In *Red Star over Malaya*, Boon Kheng Cheah relates a strange moment that appears in the colonial archives. The military report written soon after Japan's surrender in 1945 records British confusion when confronted with what seemed to them to be an example of native audacity, and the encounter raises interesting questions about the relation between morality and race. Submitted by Deputy Chief Civil Affairs Officer Brigadier H. C. Willan, the report is a part of the British military administration's investigations and interviews to determine the Malayan sultan's past relationships to the Japanese.

To sum up, Col. Hay [the Senior CAO for Johor] and myself came away with the impression that the Sultan [of Pahang] was delighted that the British had come back, and that he had disliked the Japanese intensely. He appeared to have no guilty conscience when the question of collaboration with the Japanese was mentioned. He was undoubtedly satisfied with the setting up of the BMA. (As quoted in Cheah 268)

The sultans who did not actively collaborate with the Japanese were deemed "good" sultans and received recognition from the British administration, while the sultans who were considered collaborators lost their positions to another member of their royal family. Moreover, the British officers were surprised that the sultan showed no remorse over having collaborated with the Japanese during the war. Presumably, according to the British colonialists who retreated under the cover of night, Malayans should have still remained loyal to the British even after they had been abandoned.[9]

Power, the colonizers demonstrate, lies with those in the position to pass moral judgment on others. This notion of good and bad subjects in turn justifies the return of British colonialism after the departure of the Japanese in a secular logic where "good" or "bad" is both the decision of the colonial state that also confirms state power. The colonizers are never under moral scrutiny, it seems, while the colonized never escapes it. That the British can judge the sultans as either being "good" or "bad" raises the question of whose right it is to make such judgments, especially when the British evacuated Malaya before the Japanese established a beachhead. Furthermore, the comparison between the British and the Japanese transforms the British into "good" colonizers and erases the British's own record of murder and theft in light of the cruelties of the Japanese occupation.[10] "Good" and "bad" colonialism was mobilized to justify British recolonization of Malaya after the war, and postwar colonialism also would not have survived without colonial ideas of race that linked skin color to civilizational values and traits. The return of British colonialism was cast as not only legitimate but desirable to the local population because the British did not abuse their power "excessively" compared to the Japanese,[11] and the British further encouraged this view during the communist insurgency, thus transforming their wartime allies, the communists, into Malaya's new public enemy.[12]

The conflation of "Chineseness" with communism, that is, the conflation of race with political affiliation, began during WWII and the anti-Japanese resistance.[13] When the Japanese arrived in Malaya in 1941, they continued the practice of divide and conquer with the aid of local collaborators from all major racial groups. The members of the Malayan People's Anti-Japanese Army (MPAJA) were also drawn from all races, but the MPAJA was dominated by the Chinese while most Japanese collaborators were Malay, and the resentments against both groups later led to further postwar racial animosities.[14] The British historian Noel Barber and Frederick Spencer Chapman, a key member of Force 136 who trained communist soldiers during WWII, recognized that the communist resistance was at the frontlines of the fight against the Japanese. Upon their return at the end of WWII, the British decorated key communist leaders for their contribution in the battle against the Japanese during WWII, including Chin Peng, the last leader of the Malayan Communist Party (MCP). But soon after, the communists who became suspicious of British intentions for Malaya and who agitated for decolonization, were declared to be traitors to Malaya.[15] This denunciation would take the form of a major propaganda war as well as military operations.[16]

In the war between the British and the communists, the British were widely credited with winning the war by winning the ideological war in Malaya, but this war for the "hearts and minds" of the Malayan people would also have devastating and long-lasting effects because it conflated race and moral behavior. "Communism" became synonymous with the Chinese, even though not all communists were Chinese, and not all Chinese were communists because Chin Peng became the face of the MCP.[17] By giving the MCP a "Chinese" face, the British transformed political contestations over colonial rule into a contestation over racial identity and racial inclusion. Even after the end of the communist insurgency in 1989, Chin Peng was never allowed back into the country, and his family's request to have him interred in Malaysia after his death in 2013 was rejected by the state.

The figure of the communist became a useful racial trope that described not only Chinese Malayans' political positions or national identity, but also their moral values or lack thereof; Malaya needed to be protected from the threat the Chinese posed. Secrecy was necessary to the communist movement because of unequal power relations between the communists and the colonizers but military action on both sides depended on secrecy and espionage. The head of the MCP during the war, Lai Tek, was a double spy who was an informant for the British and the Japanese at the same time, and betrayed his fellow communists for personal gain. But this secrecy, while keeping the communist movement alive well into the 1980s, also meant that it had little success in explaining its side of history. Manned, funded, and supported by local communities without the military and administrative backing of a full colonial regime as the British were, the communists were literally poor peasants and young men and women, most of whom had entered the movement during the resistance against the Japanese and had collaborated with Britain's Force 136.

During the war itself, the poor availability and quality of communications technology in the communist camps hampered coordinated military action taken by various platoons spread throughout the peninsula. Their attacks were often sporadic and uncoordinated within Malaya, and there is no evidence that the MCP received timely or sustained communications from either China or the Soviet Union. As the leader of the MCP, Chin often heard about communist victories or failures only when they were reported in the colonial newspapers or radio announcements. Ironically, he learned of High Commissioner Henry Gurney's assassination by a communist regiment only a day after the fact, on a Radio Malaya news broadcast (Chin 289).[18] Despite their lack of resources, the communists were still the most powerful anticolonial group in Malaya during the postwar period so long as they could move and act without detection by their enemies who had superior technology, arms, and forces. Unsurprisingly, writers and filmmakers have been fascinated by the general climate of dread and anxiety of this period, and adopted the motifs of espionage or undercover agents at war.[19]

British war propaganda portrayed communists as cruel and merciless, especially toward their own soldiers if they were suspected of having doubts or second thoughts, but the British also downplayed the role they played in fostering that same ruthlessness among the communists.[20] By offering exorbitant rewards for the capture or murder of known communist leaders and actively recruiting and developing spies and double agents within the communist army, the British sowed dissension in the communist camps. To the communists, allowing a British spy or double agent in their ranks resulted in exposing the entire camp to British troops.

> Outsiders didn't see and didn't understand; they looked upon it simply as a murder of a human being. But they didn't know why the person was condemned to death. This was the reality of the armed struggle—we didn't just have to kill our obvious enemies, but were also forced to kill the enemies in our midst. Our own warriors would accuse us of wrongdoing for plotting with enemy agents if we didn't. (Rashid 55)

The spy, in other words, was as much feared by the communists as the British. By working for the British, the former communist soldiers turned spies posed a real threat to the already isolated and malnourished troops in the jungle camps.[21] Consequently, spies or traitors were summarily treated as enemies guilty of treason.[22]

While much more work needs to be done on the kinds of racial thinking adopted within the MCP, the leaders' own views about race were certainly more liberal than those held by the British colonialists, and even some of the early national leaders of Malaya.[23] For example, rather than condemn early Malay-Japanese collaborators for being traitors, Chin Peng, Abdullah CD, and Rashid Maidin saw collaborations between Malay anticolonial groups such as the Parti Kebangsaan Melayu Malaya (PKMM) and the Japanese as utilitarian and not so different from the collaboration between the CPM and the British Force 136 during the Japanese occupation.[24] Both groups had as their objectives Malayan national independence but had merely decided to achieve their goals by different means (Abdullah 58, and Chin 132).

The diversity of the key leaders' journeys to and within the party indicates a heterogeneity of beliefs and dispositions that the label "communist" belies. The political journeys and beliefs held by the communists were not always uniform or consistent, as the memoirs written by various leaders of the MCP attest, and the MCP was often receptive to other groups or individuals, as long as they shared the goal of national independence. C. F. Yong argues that communism was introduced to Malaya not by the Chinese communist party, but by anarchist Chinese who were utopian in their vision for a society free from authority, and without imperialism or the need for military action.[25] Their early leaders came from the more radical sections of the Kuomintang in Malaya (Yong 639).[26]

Leaders of the MCP boasted of their connections and solidarity with other members around the world, but on close examination, they held different religious beliefs and political positions even within the party. More curiously, their ideas about government also lacked ideological consistency, and this possibly accounted for their failure to establish stronger ties around the region. Rashid Maidin, for example, argues that the structure of the CPM was a "centralized democracy," and later confesses to respecting the conservative and often authoritarian former Prime Minister Tun Dr. Mahathir Mohamad for his "anti-imperialist spirit" and the role he played in developing the country's economy through the 1980s (Rashid 93). Religion seems to have held no significance to Chin Peng, but on the other hand, Abdullah CD and Rashid Maidin were as dedicated to the Islamic faith as they were to anticolonialism and economic justice. One of the key leaders in the MCP, Abdullah CD was also involved in other anticolonial groups such as the PKMM who had first collaborated with the Japanese before later supporting the MCP in the fight against the British.[27] He was first a part of the Young Malays Union, or Kesatuan Melayu Muda (KMM), before joining the Malayan People's Anti-Japanese Alliance during the war, and later, the MCP. Other members of the communist movement, like Chin Peng, came to the party through their support of and involvement in union work at local and British tin mines or rubber plantations. Despite the differences of positions and personal journeys among the leaders of the MCP, as a whole, the communists came to symbolize the disintegration of social, institutional, and moral order in Malaya. Only the British army stood between Malayans and the moral bankruptcy of communism.

In a telling passage regarding the British administrator's decision to focus their attention on propaganda rather than engage the communists in a protracted firefight, the British saw the war as an exercise in shaping and defining "correct" political desire. The colonized had to be taught to want the right kind of government.

> [Gurney and Thompson] knew that arms alone could never win a guerrilla war but that political stability *was* a major key to victory—that normal workaday government had to function, to make decisions, had to be *seen* to function; otherwise there would be no hope for the millions of bemused, bewildered bystanders caught up in the turmoil of a war of terror. And without hope, without belief in government, the only alternative would be Communism. (Barber 64)

Colonialism during this period recast what constituted "normal," "functional," and desirable daily life and who could guarantee it, but Malayans of that period were not being asked to choose between democracy and communism. Instead, they were asked to choose between communism and "government," that is, the colonial government. This is a crucial shift in rhetoric that continues in postcolonial political discourse where, until the elections of March 2018, the opposition was not seen as a legitimate force or option within the local political system. The political choice open to colonized Malayans was not a choice between democracy or authoritarianism, or even between capitalism and communism, but rather between a government that works and one that does not.

At the end of the Baling Talks, the MCP offered to end the war and surrender their arms if they were to be recognized as a legitimate political party, as fully participating citizens of Malaya, and for the British to grant Malaya national independence (Chin 370). But driven by the knowledge that they were in reality weaker at the bargaining table, Chin Peng and other party representatives also decided that they would accept the right to establish a political party ". . . which, specifically, would not be termed a communist party" (371),[28] and that they would accept those conditions if none of the communists would be treated as prisoners and punished. Central to communist demands in the Baling talks were the demands for basic, humane treatment of those who had served in the anticolonial struggle, and for a fair and equal chance to organize, defend, and present one political view among other political views in an independent democracy. However, representatives of the British colonial administration and the representatives from UMNO and MCA, Tunku Abdul Rahman and Dato Tan Cheng Lock, rejected those stipulations.

The breakdown of the Baling Talks reinforced the notion that the state decides for its people what make up "acceptable" political systems or parties; one is judged good or bad in relation to the desires and beliefs of the colonial state. The contest of political ideologies that was the emergency was a contest between who could define and provide "normality," a battle that the British eventually won because they won the war over who could define "right" or "wrong," and "good" or "bad." Social behavior is catachresis for political belief in this colonial chiaroscuro where one is judged "good" or "bad" only in relation to the state.

But colonial ideas of "good" or "right" included "benign colonial policies" such as coerced deportations, a British colonial policy that sent communists or merely suspected communists "back" to China regardless of whether or not they were born or had family in China. This policy reinforced the belief that regardless of birthplace, all Chinese Malayans "belong" to China, and it has continued to appear in contemporary racial thought and racist slogans as "*balik Cina.*"[29] This normalization of a psychically violent colonial act that scripts Malayan-born Chinese as always "from China" produces powerful emotions around Chinese Malaysian presence today.[30] While Chinese Malaysians can no longer be deported if they hold political views different from the state's, they continue to be subjected to regular, public exhortations to leave, especially when they hold political views different from Malay-supremacist political parties.

"Benign colonialism" included institutionalized segregation and incarceration within the colonial state, or what in Han's novel, is called "preventive detention" (88). Euphemistically called "New Villages," the British uprooted and incarcerated whole Chinese communities in internment camps surrounded by fences, barbed wire, and guards to prevent them from providing food or medical supplies to communist soldiers in the forests. Half a million of these "villagers" were placed under curfew and forced to give up their farms and livestock in their cramped new quarters.[31] By imprisoning Chinese communities in these camps, the British cut off food and medical supplies to the jungles but the British further argued that the communists were responsible for the creation of those camps: innocent Chinese would not be imprisoned if their fellow Chinese did not toe the colonial line.[32] The internment camps taught all Malayans, and not just Chinese Malayans, that freedom and democracy were created by incarcerating everyone who might pose a danger to the state, and the security laws created during this time are still used for the same purposes today. In some cases, "returning" to China was the only way to escape detention or to allow family members to reunite as Han dramatizes in her novel.

Consequently, the portrayal of the communist as terrorist increases anxiety on the part of racial minorities because it reminds them that their place in the body politic is a precarious one and that inclusion in the nation-state depends on having the "right" beliefs and the "right" kinds of actions that follow from them. But even then, as Han's novel demonstrates, the raced subject never fully escapes suspicion. Neither the narrator nor one of the main protagonists of the novel, Ah Mei, are fully trusted or "reliable" even when they both perform their jobs well.[33] But while these definitions of good behavior and the stereotypes of racial character first began circulating during the colonial period, they continue to have emotive power today; the figure of the communist plays a large part in regulating ideas about good and bad citizenship. WWII and the postwar period continue to hold an equivocal place in the national cultural imaginary because they serve as the grounds for both national inclusion and also for exclusion.

After the war, the British argued that Chinese and Indian communities that were previously seen as transient should be rewarded because Malay elites had welcomed and cooperated with the Japanese occupiers.[34] This ultimately tied notions of rights to race, and race to the performance of "proper" or "right" values. The British first attempted to "reward" Chinese and Indian involvement and bloodshed in fighting the Japanese by granting them citizenship under the proposed, but ultimately, failed Malayan Union (Andaya 254).[35] In the same period, laws were enacted to police the nascent presses, mostly to control Islamic or Chinese revolutionary influences within the country. This censorship possibly accounts for the construction of a stronger sense of national identity as opposed to identification with the transnational Islamic *umma* or a Chinese diasporic identity.[36] However, Malays continued to hold a privileged position within the new nation-state because they argued—and still argue—that Malaya was the land of the Malays.[37] Malay supremacist narratives of victimization, often encoded in the official state narrative, frames Malay experience today as the experience of those victimized by the anti-Muslim West, as well as Chinese and Indian minorities in Malaysia who are innately "predisposed" to success in a globalized world.

On the one hand, the postcolonial state controls how race affects social life by deploying narratives of rewards and punishments that explain why members of some racial groups would succeed and be included in a new, independent state. But on the other hand, the violence of the emergency and the propaganda generated during the communist insurgency was also used to stereotype the Chinese as traitors and terrorists who should be deported to China for the safety of all Malayans. Paradoxically, the same trope of exemplary behavior that was used to include the Chinese was also used to contend that Malays need preferential treatment in the new state, because without such protections they would be "victimized" by the more enterprising Chinese and Indians already "unfairly" predisposed to business and industry.[38] Both positive and negative racial stereotypes were mobilized to argue for inclusion of minorities and also preferential treatment for one race above others.

The sometimes contradictory narratives that represent inclusion into the national imaginary nonetheless effectively enable the state to reinforce the ideas, first, that racial difference is natural and unchanging, and, second, that the state is the best or only possible arbiter between the different racial groups. But the state itself plays a role in creating racial tensions that it then adjudicates. Postcolonial feelings of subjection are produced through the feeling of fear and anxiety, especially of the racial Other. The stereotype of the communist as terrorist-spy functions as an expansive trope that signifies irresolvable racial difference, foreignness, betrayal, and moral incompatibility that only the state can manage.

Malaysian fiction written, directed, or produced by racial minorities and their allies in general embody a heightened awareness of how members of all racial groups are racialized.[39] This history of racial formation, and especially of how the state moralizes race, therefore fills an important gap in national and cultural history because contemporary novels that invoke communism such Tash Aw's *The Harmony Silk Factory* and Twan Eng Tan's *Garden of Evening Mists* use national history not only as background and motif, but also because their use of national history is sometimes selective. They may allude to certain historical references and narratives but ignore others.

At the end of his novel, for example, Tan cites interviews with an English planter who lived in Malaya during the Emergency at the end of *The Garden of Evening Mists*, but ignores other historical works and memoirs about that period. The author makes a claim for historicity when he lists in the author's notes not only his personal interviews with an English planter who lived through the violence of that war but also historical accounts written by British historians. At the top of Tan's list, Barber's orientalist *War of the Running Dogs*[40] consistently valorizes and celebrates the white colonialist administrators and generals as individuals and officers who were superior to the natives who worked for them, even as he details how their successes depended on the groundwork accomplished by local Malays, Chinese, and Indians who worked as soldiers, undercover spies, and police officers in the British administration. The selectivity of the history that their novels reference and portray reflect how Malaysian writers and directors either consciously or unconsciously work within the restrictions of state censorship and official discourses around the communist insurgency, and how they continue to labor under racial anxieties and ideologies even in the absence of real or actual legal action.

In other words, Aw's and Tan's novels and their fictional worlds sometimes overcompensate for certain stereotypes and biases about the Chinese in Malaysia. The communist characters in Tan's novel are two-dimensional and are more like props that lend color to the setting and plot: they are depicted only as angry, violent, uncompassionate, vengeful, and irrational. The novel repeats colonial descriptions of Malayan communists and sets them in opposition to the "rational" and "self-controlled" anglicized Chinese Malayans who cooperate with or work for the colonial government. He repeats the stereotypes of the model minority and the terrorist-spy in an antagonistic relationship that is finally resolved in favor of the model minority.[41]

Han's novel, on the other hand, recognizes those very same stereotypes and presents them to us in an ironic manner that forces us to confront how these stereotypes are rooted in a deeply conflicted history. Readers of Han's novel never truly find out if they—like Han's eponymous narrator—fully understand the communist characters in the novel. The subaltern rarely speaks. All these works, despite their differences, illuminate how Chinese and Chinese Malaysian writers are hyperaware of racial stereotypes. The racial minority is constantly under surveillance not merely because they might break the law, but because they are believed to be morally suspect and consequently must always perform legibility.

Han critiques the demand for racial legibility by taking both representations of the Chinese as either model minority or terrorist seriously even as she satirizes them. On the one hand, Ah Mei, a "rehabilitated" communist, is precisely the kind of subject the British wanted to create during the emergency: a former communist who has seen the error of her ways and who has returned to where she "belongs." She has now been rehabilitated into exemplariness and obedience to the colonial empire. But, on the other hand, the model minority's exemplarity is what makes her so grotesque because it draws our attention to how the raced body can never be trusted, even when it appears to say and do the right things. Han's novel plays with narrative secrets not only as a trope or motif, but also as plot development, and the protagonist at the center of the novel is a model minority—Ah Mei, not the narrator—who is also strange, angry, and possesses repulsive traits. Rather than the narrator, Han's protagonist, Ah Mei, connects the other minor stories in the novel because she is the possible link—but again, nothing is ever certain about Ah Mei and everything is conjecture—to the other communists and communist spies, and thus holds the many different parts of the novel together.

Like Ah Mei, the Chinese men and women depicted living in the hospitals, servants' quarters, or the internment camps are always shown "grinning" and laughing, but also as cunning and self-serving because their expressions of happiness are described in the narration as masking their true emotions. Ah Mei is especially threatening to the narrator precisely because she excels at what she is asked to do even when she lives in Su Yin's home as a reformed and conscientious worker, because as it turns out, she has become the consummate informer who cannot stop telling tales about those around her. She tells tales on not only her fellow communist soldiers, but also of what she sees in her new home with Suyin; it is as if the model informer can no longer stop spying on others.

Because Ah Mei carries out what she has been asked to do too well, she overturns our assumptions of what it means to be part of the social. The narrator comes to realize that human relationships are intimate because they are not always on public display. Privacy is crucial to the social, and without privacy none of us can form meaningful social ties. However, the state requires that Ah Mei reveals publically what is done in private so that she can receive recognition and protection from the state.

Paradoxically, her indiscriminate openness then renders her unintelligible to the narrator who cannot see her as a human being, but rather only as "the communist informer." The assumption of inscrutability, secrecy, and unintelligibility affects not only Ah Mei, but all Chinese who are communists or presumed to be communists in this novel. The synecdochical relation between political position, reliability, and the yellow body—contiguity as political sympathy justified the incarceration of hundreds of Chinese villages in mid-twentieth century Malaya—is personified in Han's depiction of a model reformed communist spy. Which Chinese person can be trusted?

On the one hand, the sight of the raced body evokes anxiety, but on the other hand, it is racial minorities who have to live in perpetual anxiety because they are always threatened with exile ("*balik Cina*") or hyperpolicing (model spy). Racial anxiety, while it first seems to identify how certain bodies are signs of danger and violence, actually refers to how racial minorities are expected to always respond to—and assuage—others' fears. The narrator fears Ah Mei even at the end of the novel because Ah Mei's motives for informing on the communist movement are never clear to her: "I remember precisely the first occasion when I became uneasy concerning Ah Mei. There is no name for this tremulous imperfection of doubt which one refuses at inception, nor can I define in words that quality in Ah Mei's voice, the precise gesture, which gave birth to this unease in myself" (232). Suyin first comes to be wary of Ah Mei when she watches Ah Mei converse with a psychologist who notices how she occasionally speaks in the first person, and at other times in the third person. But it is not Ah Mei's confusing—not necessarily confused—use of the different forms of address that disturbs Suyin after all.

What renders Suyin silent in Ah Mei's presence is precisely Ah Mei's own volubility and her exemplary performance of the role she has been asked to assume. The cognitive dissonance of informing on one's companions has given way to a constant performance of tale-telling not only in the interrogation rooms, but also in Suyin's home. Suyin is uneasy because she cannot tell when or how she is interpellated as subject in this state of emergency where servility is the mark of a good subject; Suyin too, is Chinese, and despite her privileged status as doctor in a colonial government hospital, she is under suspicion. Ah Mei's performance of exemplarity as rehabilitated informant is threatening because it interpellates even Suyin, the Anglophone

Chinese doctor, as a raced subject who should also be kept under surveillance because no Chinese body can escape racialization.

In an early episode in the novel, Suyin watches as an official from the Ministry of Information coaches a young orphan girl rescued from a communist camp, as she tells her story and sings revolutionary songs. When the official wrongly identifies an anti-Japanese song as a communist song—the communist army was at the forefront of the war against Japan after the British evacuated—Suyin corrects him, but is then corrected herself:

> 'Yes, I know,' replied Jimmy. 'But many things which were not communist have become communist now . . . in fact it is so difficult sometimes . . . but not for you,' he added, his brow clearing. 'Not for you or me . . . we are positively not communists.' He meant to make me feel more secure, above suspicion, in these suspicious days when all liberalism is suspect which is not tainted with servile acquiescence, but instead I felt suddenly a traitor, and nothing else. (224–25)

If objects, customs, art, history, and of course, people, can "become communist" in retrospect and after the fact, then who or what becomes communist in the future is similarly indeterminate. The plasticity of the category "communist" across time is moreover enabled by the role that other Chinese also play in the policing of their fellow Chinese.

Throughout the novel, Chinese Malayans play significant roles in the search for, interrogation, and arrest of the communists. Historically, they played key roles in the investigative process, formulation of propaganda, and in undercover work because they possessed not only the language skills and cultural knowledge that white and Malay officers did not, but also because they could pass as communists. But while "passing"—here, passing is the performance of moral goodness in the eyes of the state rather than hiding racial identity—allows Chinese Malayans to perform the kind of labor that the white colonialists need, it does not guarantee their own freedom from suspicion and in fact opens them up to suspicion. The Chinese Malayan colonial subject therefore has to work aggressively to preempt such misrecognitions where one's loyalty to the colonizer can come under question. The character Jimmy Lo's insistence that "they" are above suspicion ironically only reminds Suyin the narrator that she is still under surveillance and mistakes on her part could lead to closer scrutiny if she had not been in a position of privilege.

Of the Chinese Malayans who were incarcerated on the basis of suspicion, their innocence and moral exemplarity in the internment camps are determined by their performance of subservience. During a tour of the internment camp, Quo Boon, the wealthy businessman asks Commandant Hinchcliffe how he ranks the individual detainees according to their communist leanings. Detainees are categorized as black, gray, or white in the camp where black is the color that marks the most ardent communist supporters, and white, those who are closest to being rehabilitated from communism: "What other measures have I got but the measure of their good behavior, their servility when I walk among them through the camp? And isn't good behavior the standard in any prison?" (Han 93). "Good behavior" is defined as the recognition and respect of power, authority, and hierarchy. Moral language in this instance resolves racial anxiety produced by the sight of raced bodies, but it does so at the expense of the incarcerated raced bodies. This spectacle of disciplining potentially dangerous Chinese bodies displayed to other wealthy Chinese Malayans reaffirms their own exemplariness, but it is a spectacle that also serves as a warning of what could happen to them. The model minority can easily fall from privilege to disfavor.

In Han's novel, the classification of "traitor" first seems to give clarity to a political situation full of uncertainties, only to fail at the end of the novel because they create the illusion that we can identify good or evil by looking at the color of someone's skin. Moral tropes offer the illusion of clarity especially during times of chaos, and it purports to clarify the world not only for white colonizers who have to organize a polyglot and multiracial society, but sometimes, also to the colonized themselves. The stereotype of Chinese as traitor is created not merely out of arbitrary signs of phenotypical difference or even by the practice of particular customs, but through the violent act of betrayal that was encouraged by the colonial regime. One of Han's characters identified only as the "General," but most likely based on the real historical figure, General Gerald Templer,[42] explains how colonizers are responsible for inculcating the "right" kinds of loyalties in Chinese Malayans: "These youngsters haven't got any *Loyalty* to this country. We want to teach them loyalty. . . . Freedom and democracy. All pull together. We want to teach these youngsters that" (293). But in order to do so, they need to betray others who are like them.

The betrayal of one's community, however, is read as "good" moral action in the moral universe of the colonial world because it signals a higher commitment to the state. An important comical and bathic minor character, Big Dog Tsou, finds himself to be unintentionally rehabilitated despite his initial intentions to work as an undercover informer for the communists in the internment camp. He entered the camp fully committed to gathering information on behalf of the communists, but while in the camp, decides to work for the colonial government to secure his own freedom and liberty by informing on his former comrades. However, Big Dog Tsou is later rearrested and executed when a different communist informer who was captured also identifies him as a key communist in his village (205). Ah Mei, Big Dog Tsou and the other communist who betrayed him must prove their loyalty to their new country by betraying others of their own race in this farce, and in so doing, successfully perform racial behavior determined for them by "benign" colonial policies.

Consequently, the cycle of suspicion and violence runs throughout the entire novel, and the narrator's insecurities and anxieties are never fully resolved. Han's novel concludes with a wedding, when Ah Mei finally marries Ah Tong, another "surrendered" former communist in a ceremony where half the guests are white and native police officers. But ironic to the end, the wedding comes on the heels of yet another series of misunderstandings where Suyin and two other constables discover that she was a high-ranking member of the MCP. They rearrest her only to release her after a few days because even those who work for the colonial state can no longer tell who is telling the truth and what secrets are real secrets. The communist characters in the novel remain all surface, light, and illusion to the end. The constant demand for secrecy destabilizes the state's own attempts to assimilate her life to its narrative of national integration, but it also represents the complexity of the demands placed on the raced subject who is aware that he or she needs to be legible to others at all times. To be seen is to be reduced to an object of fear and to be subjected to fear, that is, the fear of either being too good or not good enough.

Racial anxiety thus plays on our anxieties about the racial Other by telling us that there is a reason to be afraid, and also that the object of fear is already legible if we only knew how to read the signs. If the prewar colonial period set the ground for understanding race in ways that made it easy to recognize, organize, and therefore govern the colonized, the postwar colonial era produced the kind of racial anxiety that made racial thinking a natural and necessary ideological given. Stereotypes remind racial minorities that their place in the nation-state is a precarious one, where inclusion depends on having the "right" beliefs and the "right" kinds of actions.

This chapter reads Han Suyin's *And the Rain My Drink* as a satire of colonial fictions about race by interweaving two major stereotypes of Chinese Malaysians, that of the model minority and the communist spy in the novel's central tensions. The trope of the terrorist-spy draws our attention to how the threat of expulsion therefore requires racial minorities to be exceptionally and incontrovertibly legible. Suyin the narrator and Ah Mei the reformed communist both have to prove their racial—and moral—legibility to the state. The racial minority always has to perform overt moral goodness to assuage the state's fears, and even then, may yet come under suspicion. Neither the model minority nor the terrorist exists in isolation and both are equally important to the state project.

But the novel's deployment of both stereotypes require us to ask how the cultural history of why stereotypes came to be important in Malaysian colonial history, and why these stereotypes were central to postwar twentieth-century fiction such as Han Suyin's novel. Colonial stereotypes depict the Chinese in the 1950s during the communist emergency in diametrically opposite ways, and it is these contradictions that create a sense of anxiety around the raced body as always legible but never legible enough. The model minority could turn out to be the model spy.

Opposing and contradictory racial stereotypes thus create a sense of anxiety about the racial Other, and anxiety on the part of the racial Other. Both kinds of anxiety justify the state role and significance in social and cultural life that are now irremediably racially mixed. The belief that racial minorities pose a grave threat to social order are most commonly expressed in the stereotyping of racial minorities as traitors, spies, parasites, thugs, criminals, rapists, "illegals," or as invaders plays an important but different role in the process of racial subjection as compared to the myth of the model minority. These beliefs about racial behavior—that certain racial groups are not only predisposed to crime, but to certain types of crime depending on their race—appear everywhere in politics, culture, and society, and frame minorities as detrimental to the state and to social order. Cold War politics in the form of anticommunism and the war against the communist insurgency is as much the writing of national and racial fictions as it is about the political contestations for influence, power, and territory.

The production and the policing of contemporary fiction moreover serves as a record of how the state has a stake in monitoring cultural and artistic productions, and reactions to contemporary Malaysian film and literature records the social attitudes toward key historical events and give us a rich picture of how the colonial anxieties that surrounded race, state, and nation during colonial times have continued to be relevant to postcolonial Malaysia.[44] Late colonialism and the climate of the Cold War produced a form of racial anxiety that depended on contradictory ideas that the racial Other is at once always legible but never fully known, but the postcolonial state adopted for its own.

In summary, postcolonial racial anxiety did not begin with decolonization, and it has a long history rooted in colonial epistemology and bureaucracy. But in the postwar period, racial anxiety gave the colonizers a reason to continue governing peoples that were beginning to want to govern themselves. The history of Malayan decolonization was the history of its colonialists, that is, the British and the local elites they supported, and it is simultaneously a history of the naturalization of race as fixed cultural differences and the belief that one race—the Malays—had the right to rule.[43] The suppression of the cultural history of how race became imbricated with moral narratives in this chapter explains why racial tensions have not disappeared in the aftermath of WWII and the communist insurgency, and why they take the form that they do.

Colonial and postcolonial feelings of subjection are produced in large part through the emotions of fear and anxiety, and while stereotypes, racial tropes, and cultural myths often increase anxiety directed toward the racial Other, this general sense of anxiety in turn is experienced on the part of racial minorities as a form of policing, both as individuals and as a social group. After the war, racial anxiety taught the colonized to see new enemies when the Japanese left. Now, they see new enemies who are hidden in plain sight among them.

Racial stereotypes and colonial beliefs about race create racial anxiety on the level of culture, but the next two chapters will elaborate on how racial anxiety is part of the political condition of the world state system in general after decolonization and continued into the Cold War and beyond. In fact, rather than disrupt colonial representations of racial difference as moral difference, decolonization and the Cold War actually intensified the link between race and moral character through the revival of civilization discourse and the tropes of state security and insecurity. The next chapter examines how the state's moral vision about racial behaviors is informed by its perceptions of weakness or strength according to its own needs, especially when the state sees itself in relation to other states.

Racial anxieties embodied in stereotypes are a cultural expression of state interests, but it is also a symptom of how we learn to see like a state and particularly as a state in competition with other states. After WWII and decolonization, feelings of weakness or the fear of being victimized are directed toward those the state sees as new "imperialists" outside its borders, and also toward racial minorities within its borders who symbolize alienness because of the color of their skin, the languages they use, the religious beliefs they hold, or the customs they practiced. The postcolonial state in the era of globalization learns to see in two directions at once: outward, and inward. The state learns to see itself as a state that faces threats from outside its borders as well as within its borders, and racial anxiety is the symptom of the state caught up in globalization's contradictory demands that the state performs its strength even when it perceives itself as weak. The state's insecurities is, in other words, a cultural effect of the postcolonial state's development after WWII.

Chapter 3

Tropes of Insecurity

State Competition and Racial Anxieties

NO SELF-HELP BOOK CAN BE COMPLETE WITHOUT taking into account our relationship with the state. For if there were a cosmic list of things that unite us, reader and writer, visible as it scrolled up and into the distance, like the introduction to some epic science-fiction film, then shining brightly on that list would be the fact that we exist in a financial universe that is subject to massive gravitational pulls from the states. States tug at us. States bend us. And tirelessly, states seek to determine our orbits.

—Mohsin Hamid, *How to Get Filthy Rich in Rising Asia*

Mohd. Aswan Md. Johar's *Sanctuaria* begins in medias res when Mus or Musliha, a Malay-Muslim woman, finds herself lost and disoriented outside a *surau*, the neighborhood prayer room, and Pak Maarof,[1] the caretaker, who mistakes her for a man, rescues her and offers her shelter.[2] Written in 2014 under his pen name "Shaz Johar," the novelist's fifth novel is set outside a rural village in Malaysia, where various members of a multiracial cult group finally escape as the cult slowly disintegrates. Shaz loosely modeled the novel's plot on the Jim Jones cult that committed mass suicide in 1978. Shaz's dystopian "sang-tua-ria"—Mus receives a lesson on how to pronounce the name of the secret commune before she recovers her memory (22)—presents itself as a successful utopian alternative to the oppressive and authoritarian Malaysian state. But its opening does not first focus on ideal, perfect society, or space. Instead, the novel turns our attention to who is or is not the ideal or "good" and, therefore trustworthy, subject. The description of the utopian state is preceded by the description of the state's utopian subject. Mus's disorientation, her ambiguous gender identity, and her dissimulation about her gender when we first encounter her raises questions about the reliability of her account. Why does she look like a man, and why does she pass as a man? Does she have drug habits, and are the two related? And finally, can we trust Mus and what she says about Sancturia?

The novel's play on religious and mainstream fears over gender roles—a woman who does not look or act like a woman, and whose very speech is suspect—draws our attention to how moral position and credibility are determined in large part by one's conformity to expected racial, gender, and religious roles. These roles, moreover, are usually predetermined by generally held cultural beliefs, and as we will see in this chapter, beliefs about right and wrong actions can be influenced either formally or informally by the state. The more we learn about the commune, the more we are confronted by how our beliefs about reliability or unreliability are shaped by the state. In our own suspicions of who Mus is or claims to be, we are for a moment seeing like the state. We discover as we read that good, bad, reliable, or unreliable racial behavior is influenced by the state's own preconceptions about desirable or undesirable behavior. In Shaz Johar's parable about state power, the state's needs or anxieties, in other words, inform commonly held beliefs about moral right and wrong.[3] Race does not exist on its own as an independent thing with its own life, and is often concatenated to state power.

Shaz's fictional utopia would be striking to readers familiar with Malaysian society and its politics because he depicts a postracial utopia that attracts not only faithful Malay Muslims, but also Hindus, agnostics, and atheists from among the Chinese- and Indian-Malaysians. Sancturia's utopia is a place where the traditional divisions of race, religion, language, gender, or sexuality no longer preclude entry or belonging, and at first it succeeds even beyond its founders' imagination. The leader of the commune, Arif bin Saad, uses a traditional title that puns on his name in a way that elevates his status. "*Yang Arif*" means "the Wise one," and the appellation "Yang," which is part of traditional Malay titles, usually refers to leaders of or royalty within the community. The honorifics "*Yang Berhormat*" or "*Yang Amat Berhormat*" are used for political dignitaries, and "*Yang Di-Pertuan Agong*" is used for the monarch. Arif's pretensions to nobility set him apart as an equal to state dignitaries outside of their commune, and make his commune akin to his private sultanate. While this might sound odd initially, this practice actually mirrors precolonial Malayan governing structures, where what is now known as Malaysia used to consist of separate and competing sultanates. Yang Arif passes as a wise sultan who could have flourished if not for the interruption of colonial rule, but in this new rewriting of the postcolonial Malaysian state, he invokes a precolonial right to rule as a Malay male. Portrayed as an alternative to the real state—that we find out is also simultaneously its ally and competitor—Sanctuaria represents "good" nationalism, that is, the belief that a strong or "good" state can resolve the deep disagreements of race or religion and the primordial sentiments they inspire. As a fictional postracial utopia, Sanctuaria is set against the real state's failures to provide a strong or good enough vision that can unite its citizens.

Shaz's novel fundamentally warns us against not only the possible failures of the state to unite its diverse body of citizens, but also against how anxieties over the state's weakness or strength can lead to greater state control. The commune's foundational moral ideals about the openness of borders and postracial inclusiveness are finally undermined by the state's need to protect itself. But it is the state's obsession with its perceptions of itself as threatened instead of its earlier original ideals that eventually leads to its self-destruction. In so doing, the novel directs our attention to how social difference is welcome when the state can draw symbolic value from it, but that difference ultimately cannot be tolerated if it eventually threatens state power itself. *Sanctuaria*'s importance as a parable of state power consequently lies not in its utopian portrayal of the desires for postracial harmony but in its portrayals of the state's desires to protect its power, and the role race plays in the process.

Sanctuaria's postracial vision initially defines it as a community, but these values are revealed to perform the more crucial function of securing the state against dissent because racial inclusivity allows the commune's leaders to legitimize ideological control and submission to the larger project. However, the commune grows to become increasingly authoritarian and finally surpasses even the real state it tries to replace.

> "Dulu semua orang boleh keluar-masuk, yang keluar boleh bawak kenalan lain masuk, bawa fahaman baru, yang suka dengan fahaman dan cara hidup Sanctuaria bawa pulak orang lain. Macam tu lah pusing-pusing, makin lama makin ramai. Tapi bila dah tak terurus, Yang Arif dengan Charmaine mula buat undang-undang. Tak ada siapapun yang dibenarkan keluar. Hidup dan mati kekal kat sini." . . .

"Yang sesat mati dalam kesesatan. Macam tu lah lebih kurang bunyi tajuk paper satu Malaysia lepas dia orang semua jumpa mayat-mayat bergelimpangan kat sini nanti." O ketawa lagi.

"Before, people were free to leave and enter, and those who left were allowed to bring in people they knew or new knowledge while people who liked Sanctuaria's values and lifestyle could bring others too. That's how things evolved until we grew bigger and bigger. But when things became disorderly, *Yang Arif* and Charmaine started to create laws. No one was allowed to leave. Life and death took place here." . . .

"Those who were fooled died as fools. That's more or less what a paper on 1Malaysia would say after they find the bodies scattered here." O laughed again. (Translation mine, 221)

As O, one of the strongmen of the commune explains, Sanctuaria was first set up as a free clinic and welfare center that offered shelter to those who had been rejected by wider society. The commune was formed out of the desire to create a safe space of "transgression" and freedom where its inhabitants were free to "act out" or adopt behaviors that go beyond the normative bounds of either tradition, race, or religion. They are free to *"keluar-masuk"* (come and go) in Sanctuaria when, in the larger state of Malaysia outside the diegesis of the novel, entry to the institutional space of the state, family, and places of worship is governed either by official policies or cultural norms that revolve around race, gender, sexuality, and religion.

The freedom of physical mobility they experience in Sanctuaria is furthermore exceeded by the dizzying freedom of thought that the commune encouraged. *"Fahaman baru"* raises red flags in a Malaysian culture where taxpayer-funded bodies such as *Jabatan Agama Islam Selangor* (JAIS)[4] and *Jabatan Kemajuan Islam Malaysia* (JAKIM)[5] set down and enforce guidelines for living in accordance with Muslim values, and who at times, presume to speak even above the sultans who are the heads of Islam according to the constitution.[6] This freedom that O describes explains why Sanctuaria initially grew in numbers, *"yang suka dengan fahaman dan cara hidup Sanctuaria bawa pulak orang lain"* ("people who liked Sanctuaria's values and lifestyle could bring others too"). We are not told what kinds of new knowledge or philosophies were brought to Sanctuaria, only that the people who agreed with their philosophies and lifestyles entered the commune and brought others along with them.

The interracial marriage between its leaders, Arif and Charmaine, symbolizes the possibilities the commune holds for racial reconciliation, freedom, and inclusivity, but what attracted people to the commune was the shared moral language of, and the desires for, unrestricted freedom and inclusivity. But by the time the reader is introduced to Sanctuaria, the commune has become an authoritarian state with "laws" that police every aspect of social life within the commune's self-defined borders. What began as a rejection of the state ends as an attempt to amplify the biopolitical powers of the state to include the control over life and death. Sanctuaria's attempt to escape the state returns us to the nightmare of ever greater forms of state violence.

O, who first comes across as a sympathetic and therefore reliable narrator, attributes Sanctuaria's eventual failure to Arif's miscalculations. In O's opinion, Arif is too open and too inclusive, especially toward his Chinese Malaysian wife, Charmaine, whom O calls the "mastermind" of the machinations that turned the commune dystopian (220). But while O is otherwise kind to those trying to escape and his critiques of the commune are compelling, his explanation of the commune's failures is the result of resorting to common gender and racial stereotypes, rather than seeing Arif's violent and ultimately self-serving responses to difference and dissent for what they are. When Arif realizes that they have failed and face either imprisonment or even capital punishment, Arif orders Charmaine to kill as many of their followers as she can, including their children, and finally, he shoots her and then himself (279, 283). O moreover depicts the female characters in the novel as either helpless victims or in the case of Charmaine, manipulative and murderous. When O describes Charmaine as the "mastermind," he absolves Arif of all culpability and portrays him instead as innocent and a victim of Chinese, feminine wiles. The stereotype of the smart and capable but ultimately untrustworthy and destructive Chinese thus remains untroubled in O's description of what derailed Sanctuaria's early utopian goals.

But what O also misses in his analysis is that Arif's decision to protect what he thought needed protection, that is, the commune's "weaknesses" was what eventually caused Sanctuaria's destruction. Sanctuaria began to fall apart because it saw itself as under threat—because it was "*tak terurus*"—and consequently acted like a state under threat, and doing so led the commune to implode. Sanctuaria's laws and borders, O notes, were a response to what the founders saw as "*tak terurus*," literally translated as "not in alignment" or "not ordered." What caused the disorder in Sanctuaria's utopian project of freedom? O does not offer an explanation in this passage, and we can only surmise from other parts of the novel that as their numbers grew, ideological alignment became at once necessary and also impossible. Holding together utopia turned out to require the use of force as well as rhetoric, "*mulut manis*," literally translated as "sweet mouth," though it is a metaphor that more accurately denotes deceptive persuasion (220). O's troubling analysis of Sanctuaria's eventual collapse is mistaken, not merely because he repeats racist and gendered views when he misattributes the causes behind Sanctuaria's eventual implosion to innate racial and gendered differences—personified in the wily Chinese wife—and repeats yet again the racial narrative that difference is an internal threat to the state.

Sanctuaria finally falls because it effectively acts as a state without limits. In the process of describing its combustion, the novel lays bare the state's desires: to secure its own wholeness. Arif's and Charmaine's overambitious goals may contribute to the failure of the commune, but other sections in the novel also point us to how the nature of the state requires it to accrue power to itself at increasing rates because it fears becoming a weak state. The ideal of shared values—threatened by difference, that is, that which is *tak terurus*—leads them to become increasingly tyrannical and savage in their responses to opposition because they had come to see difference as a threat to state power. The state has to protect the state above all else. *Sanctuaria* is not a utopian novel about how racial inclusivity is possible as an ideal of the nation-state, but about how the state sees itself under threat, and racial and social difference pose threats to its composition and integrity.

Sanctuaria was successful not because it escaped detection, existing as an autarchy in its own private space apart from the world, but because it successfully colluded with the actual state even on the outset. As an alternative to the state, Sanctuaria nonetheless needed to be supported by other states that afford it recognition even if, as in this case, that recognition is informal and hidden. As the commune's residents grow increasingly restive and some of its members like Mus confirm the villagers' suspicions that Sanctuaria was a troubled place, we learn that Sanctuaria had evaded the state's censure because they had bribed the local police officers and the *Tengku*, one of the princes of the state (272). Even though Sanctuaria first presents itself as a competitor and substitute for the state, it cannot protect itself and instead depends on states outside of itself for protection. While the actual state did not officially recognize the commune, they feigned ignorance and allowed it to flourish until that collusion threatens its own legitimacy. Sanctuaria's final ruin takes place when these representatives of the official state can no longer risk public criticism of their own moral positions relative to the commune's actions.

Sanctuaria's allegorical treatment of the state's insecurities is not ahistorical or peculiar to the writer, but reflects the cultural effects of the Malaysian postcolonial state and the historical conditions of the Cold War that produced the relation between the state and racial difference. As chapters 1 and 2 demonstrate, racial stereotypes embody the state's ideological anxieties, and how they are shaped by particular historical turns. Sanctuaria's failures in the novel refract the state's anxieties, that is, how the state can view itself as weak and under threat. These threats appear from within the state boundaries (for example, O's beliefs that racial and gender difference symbolize that which is *yang* "*tak terurus*," or that which is not aligned) as well as from without its boundaries (for example, the need for other states' recognition, even if, or perhaps because, they exist as partners and as competitors).

In this chapter, tropes about race or about the relative weakness or strength of the state are neither random nor arbitrary but are a response to the historical conditions in which they appear. In the case of Southeast Asia, decolonization and the Cold War created new forms of anxiety now inflected by interstate relations. *Sanctuaria,* along with other works of fiction that are parables of the state, highlight for us how the state sees itself in binary terms, that is, as either strong or weak and always relative to other states. Race, influenced by local and global relations, plays a particularly fraught cultural role. The language of moral exemplarity or degeneration and of strength or weakness teaches us to see how the state corrals narratives about racial difference to tell stories about state power and legitimacy. The next section of the chapter provides an overview of how global developments in Southeast Asia influenced the Malaysian state's own use of racial and moral discourse in describing threats to its sovereignty as internal as well as external threats. In the postwar, postcolonial history of Southeast Asia, the state confirms its power through the trope of weakness, often deployed in response to threats from other states that racial minorities represent. Colonial racial divisions in the region created the image of the racial enemy across the border that, in the postcolonial period, became conflated with the enemy within.

When the anthropologist James Scott began looking at the role the modern state plays in agrarian culture, the modern state first appeared as if hostile and opposed to traditional and nomadic communities. But he discovered that rather than going on an offensive against its people, the state was in actual fact attempting to keep track of them. Scott argues, following

Foucault, that the desire for knowledge led to the creation of new technologies of surveillance and control because modern governmentality needed to generate new knowledge in order to use its peoples and resources. In the process, however, these new practices and institutions that helped the state keep count of what it saw as its resources, began to change the lives they were designed to monitor. The state's synoptic view not only represents or describes social life as they came into the purview of the state, it creates the objects and subjects in its naming of them. Modern, rational citizens begin to also conceive of their identities as part of the modern nation-state *because* they see themselves through the eyes of the state, and adopted the same languages, concepts, and categories to describe themselves as subjects of the state.

To be a racial subject is to learn to see oneself through the eyes of the state, and to experience anxiety as a racial subject is fundamental to being a state subject in the postwar, globalized world order. Racial anxiety, in other words, is a symptom of seeing like a state. But the state's concerns over sovereignty do not only revolve around its anxious counting of people and resources, they are also directed outward toward other states. Race may inform our ideas about who belongs in the nation, but our ideas about race are no less informed by the other forces that shape those very borders. Transnational flows, regional alliances, and ethnic unrest have played similarly important roles in the development of governmentality in postcolonial Malaysia and Southeast Asia. The history of regionalism is at the same time the history of nation-building, because each state guards its borders so that it can guard its economic standing against its neighbors who are allies as well as competitors.

This chapter in particular draws on the postwar cultural history of the state to show that racial tropes are not only the result of the state acting out its sovereignty within its own borders, but also as a result of how the state is constituted in relation to other states. State legitimacy does not appear only from within the nation-state, as if it were somehow isolated from the rest of the world. Instead, the state legitimates its power, often most brutally enacted against minorities within its borders, formed in relation to other states. The state's anxieties about its neighbors as well as its anxieties about minorities in turn create racial anxiety felt on the part of racial subjects, and these relations appear most clearly in the fictions that the state tells about itself, as well as the fictions that are now being told about the state.

Southeast Asian Postwar Insecurities

After WWII ended, the postcolonial, Malaysian state, like other newly decolonized nations in Southeast Asia, found that it was neither secure nor stable, and conversely, it faced new, daunting challenges as a result of first, the Cold War tensions, then the globalization of financial and technological systems, and later the war on terror after 9/11. These events have driven the postcolonial state—especially a Muslim-majority state like Malaysia that sees itself as a minor, more vulnerable country in the shadow of other Western or even Asian countries—to accrue greater power to itself. The state's relation to global flows matters because the recognition of and integration into the world state system plays a role in shaping the postcolonial state and its racial projects.

"Thadun," a Burmese short-story about modern governmentality published in 1995, and Brexit, a referendum that signaled a rejection of globalization in June 2016, are two unlikely parables of state anxiety in the late twentieth and early twenty-first centuries. But in their disjuncture, they show us how cultural nationalism is not merely symptomatic of globalization's failures; cultural nationalism is formative to how the state constructs narratives about itself and its position in the world. In the theater of world politics, Brexit took the world by surprise, including even those who voted to leave the European Union. As a referendum that was ostensibly about economic uncertainty and the UK's future, Brexit was simultaneously a vote on what a strong state looks like and what it should do. Those who voted to leave attributed the loss of jobs, increasing economic uncertainties, and the lack of opportunities to the growth of immigration. Voters also perceived the UK's growing weakness in the face of the EU's growing strength as reason to pull out of the EU.[7] To leave, Brexiters argued, is to return the state to its rightful place and role in organizing social life.

The average voter, however, may not have realized that the picture of "strength" may not be obvious in a world connected by interdependent markets, economies, and political alliances.

> "Sovereignty is relative," said Christophe Crombez, a Belgian economist and specialist in European Union politics at the Europe Center of Stanford University. "Even the United States has to abide by World Trade Organization rules and other treaties. If you really wanted to be completely sovereign, you'd look to a country like North Korea."[8]

"Freedom" as the definition of state strength thus appears as a paradox. To be part of the free world is to submit to rules not always of one's own design, and to disobey the rules that other countries follow—to act freely—results in ostracism from the rest of the world. The resurgence of cultural or protectionist nationalism that claims the state needs to be "free" begs an implicit question: what really makes a state strong?

In response to that question, Brexiters insisted that the state is strong when it turns inward. A scant five months later, American voters confirmed in their national elections a similar turn inward toward insularity and ethno-nationalism when they elected Donald Trump, the candidate who rose to popularity despite, or because of, his racist remarks and his insistence that the US should protect itself from "the rest" of the world. If we look at only the example of Europe or the US, we might be tempted to assume that these fears reflect a recent rejection of global flows and the changes they bring and to read cultural nationalism as the reaction to globalization and a volatile economy. But the history of Southeast Asia during the Cold War is a history of how racial tension became increasingly reified throughout the region. The openness of transnational flows and borders, perhaps unsurprisingly, has made it more difficult to subject all of human life and its complexities to state control, but at the same time, it also pushes the state toward greater social control over its people groups and the ideas they might hold about freedom, democracy, and human rights. What becomes increasingly clear in this history is how forms of social identity other than an identification with the state are allowed to flourish as long as they do not challenge the state's narratives about itself.

Read in light of the historical changes in Southeast Asia in the mid-twentieth century, cultural nationalism has a longer and broader history beyond Euro-America and the twenty-first century, and they are as traceable in fiction as in history or culture. In his short story "Thadun," the Burmese writer Ne Win Myint tells an absurd tale of a beggar who is asked to put on a play on behalf of his "corner" of the village during an important religious festival. The three elders of the impoverished community in which the story is set agree to participate in the festival, even though they have neither musicians nor funds for costumes and props. The villagers in this particular corner are too poor to take time away from farming to practice for the play, but elders could not refuse to participate in the festival because their refusal would have shamed them in front of the other elders. They find themselves saddled with obligations that are not binding by law, but that nonetheless exert an inexplicable social force over them.

When Thadun's elders return to their corner of the village, they turn the responsibility of organizing and staging the play to him because while he is a beggar he is also a musician. Thadun then comes up with a brilliant plan that allows his corner to stage a grand play with minimal resources. But at the end of the story, Thadun ultimately fails to stage his play depicting the Buddha's four encounters with suffering because none of the villagers could be persuaded to play the roles of either the old man, the sick man, or the ascetic whom the Buddha meets in his journey toward enlightenment. Thadun himself finally runs away, and the elders are shamed when their corner is the only one that fails to put on a performance.

As a parable of the modern state, "Thadun" anthropomorphizes the anxieties of the modern state as it is beholden to other states. The state's power is measured as much by its outward turn toward its neighbors as it is by its inward turn toward its own citizens. A satire of the weak, modern state that cannot stand up against "outsiders," the short story directs our attention to how the language of "shame" and "pride" is a function of nationalist fervor. This language draws the community toward a shared national goal as well as confirms the source of state power. The elders of Thadun's corner are not unaware of the suffering and poverty of those in their corner, but instead of ordering the other "hard-working" villagers to sacrifice their time, they commission Thadun, a figure of ridicule because he is from the lower classes and is therefore an "expendable" member of their community. Unlike the other villagers of their corner, Thadun can be coerced into performing this duty that no one wants. The elders, representatives of state power, perform their authority by coopting their subjects from the margins.

However, they are also leaders of their corner because they repeat other leaders' behaviors; they are leaders because they act like the other leaders. The elders' awareness of their relative position of weakness is what drives the action of the plot: Thadun's corner has to do what other corners do or risk being shamed. The state determines what is morally right or wrong, but what comes first as this tale not so subtly portrays, is the lateral relations between the elders of the corners. In other words, the moral feelings of right and wrong actions in the story are determined not merely by relations between individuals, but by the relations between the elders of the different corners. State power is formed by looking outward as much as by looking inward, as well as by the tensions between the two kinds of orientation.

"Thadun" and Brexit are thus conjoined by the same underlying narrative of anxiety. These disjunct parables of state power after WWII embody a strange overlap of cultural nationalism and its insistence that each state should act on its own and for itself, with how state structure is built out of the state's relation to its neighbors.⁹ No state can truly exist in a vacuum, and the following history of Southeast Asia in the postwar and Cold War period will demonstrate how the conditions for state power create a sense of anxiety shared across the board, and anxiety felt on the part of racial subjects in particular. The cultural nationalism that motivated Brexit is often understood as a backlash or a response to the "weakness" of the state, but a closer look at the history of the postcolonial state in Southeast Asia offers a way of understanding that race and racism play an important role in the turn to cultural nationalism.

Racial anxiety runs through what we may otherwise think of as distinct periods of cultural and political developments of the state under modernization to the state under globalization. In other words, racial anxiety does not disappear after the end of colonialism or war, and instead is symptomatic of a modern, "free" world that is composed of competing nation-states. The history of postwar, postcolonial state formation is also the history of how state interests came to shape racial discourse, and why tropes of weakness or strength have a continued hold on our cultural imaginaries. Southeast Asian postwar history demonstrates that the new postcolonial state had to keep in its sight its neighbors in the region as well as the larger states such as the US, and China or India.

The postcolonial state in the face of globalization presents itself in schizophrenic ways. On the one hand, it can position itself as weak and helpless in the face of larger and more powerful states, especially when the US, Europe, and China wield disproportionate economic or military influence in regions where size does matter. But, on the other hand, the state has to assert and perform its own power as a state in order to safeguard its "legitimacy." To be perceived as too weak is to risk being "shamed" in front of other states as well as its own subjects, and transnational comparison rather than strictly national history alone gives us a fuller picture of why anxieties over state sovereignty and racial anxiety are linked.

This history of nation-building informed by transnational concerns is neither linear nor straightforward and involved fits and starts because the region had been carved up by different European colonizers. After WWII, the anticolonial trajectories of the region took different tracks where countries such as Indonesia, Vietnam, Laos, Burma, and Cambodia experienced violent revolutions as the colonial period came to an end, but other countries such as Malaysia, Singapore, and Brunei did not.¹⁰ Despite these differences, the second half of the twentieth century was historically significant for the region as a whole because nationalisms in the various member states were formed out of a "neighborly" competition. South East Asian countries had to contend with the insecurities and uncertainties that marked anticolonial struggles and communist insurgencies across the region after experiencing the physical deprivations and poverty of WWII.

Decolonization in the region, moreover, as Ann Stoler notes, did not introduce complete freedom as it was simultaneously an entrance and integration into the world capitalist system, that is, it introduce increasingly important economic interdependence with other states in and around the region.

> Economic independence was forfeited for political sovereignty, and the initial thrust toward a social transformation of Indonesian society—glimpsed in the regional "social revolutions" of 1946—was thwarted by a nationalist leadership. . . . The political settlement that was eventually, though by no means unanimously, agreed upon rested on a protection of foreign economic interests and a cautious nonantagonistic stance toward American and Western European powers. (94)

Early nationalism in Southeast Asia was directed against colonial political rule, but not against the capitalist system or economic needs that motivated colonial conquest and rule. The continuation of capitalism and further integration into the capitalist world state system had the effect of not only maintaining colonial racial beliefs and hierarchies, especially in the former British colonies, but also entrenching them even further after decolonization.

But this integration into the world economy introduced interdependence, Southeast Asian nations nonetheless wanted to emphasize the independence of their economies and polities. Geopolitical vulnerability after decolonization accounts for this difference. Every country in Southeast Asia had significant racial groups across borders and were afraid that transnational racial loyalties would trump the new national loyalties. Racial fear and the possibility that its neighbors would become stronger either as political or economic entities was therefore an important factor in early Southeast Asian nationalisms that continue today. Each country was fearful of ceding territory to its neighbor as modern state borders and statecraft had come to be defined by integration into the international community.

Member states consequently alternated between strengthening regional ties and strengthening their own economic or political positions: "Its most striking contrast was the insistence on the sovereignty and integrity of the avowed nation-states: those principles form the very basis of the regional structures, organizations and modes of discourse that have been created" (Acharya 95). The newly decolonized Southeast Asian states were moreover too weak to defend themselves, but neither could they depend on the old colonial powers to protect them. The British, for their part, had neither a desire nor the resources to continue maintaining a military presence in the region but instead were ". . . interested in regionalism as providing, with the emergence of nation-states, for succession to empire" (109). The general consensus was that regionalism would ensure political and economic stability to the benefit of all and at no cost to the former colonizers. Concerns over domestic political and economic instabilities moreover led what is today the Association of South East Asian Nations (ASEAN) governments to subscribe to a policy of noninterference that continues to this day.

On their part, ASEAN governments neither wanted to be drawn into one power bloc or the other during the Cold War, nor did they want another ASEAN country to become dominant within the region. The ASEAN Free Trade Area (AFTA), formed in 1991, provided economic reasons to maintain regional identity and cohesion, but its inception was greeted with some measure of skepticism even within ASEAN since most member countries were not "natural trading partners" and were often in competition with one another. The reason behind creating the single regional market project then, however, was the fear that foreign direct investment (FDI) would be channeled to other emerging markets: "The growing importance of FDI-sponsored growth in the different ASEAN countries made AFTA a perceived necessity. . . . AFTA, in these accounts, is regarded as an instrument which investment diversion from the ASEAN region would be avoided, rather than as a means to trade creation as in neoclassical approaches" (Nesadurai 12).[11] Regional cohesion and integration was consequently designed to guard individual state sovereignty and to prevent "too much" economic competition within the region itself.

In 1955, Indonesia called all independent states in Asia and Africa to the Bandung Conference for several reasons: to build solidarity ties between Asia and Africa; to agree on principles for relations between the different governments in Asia; to mediate disputes between the states in question; and to work to end racism and colonialism. But it was also at this conference that the tone was set for noninterference and neutrality in the different ideologies or forms of government in the different nation-states (Christie 131–32).[12] Indonesia's effort to unite Southeast Asia to fight against communism did not gain much popularity at first, and its independence and retention of control over West New Guinea prompted the newly independent Malaya to form ties with other Southeast Asian nations in the Association of South East Asia (ASA). However, ASA was only made up of the Philippines, Malaysia, and Thailand. The Philippines and Indonesia also tried to spearhead MAPHILINDO, but that attempt failed because it was a coalition based on racial affinities.

ASEAN thus only became reality on August 8, 1967. Today, it includes Thailand, Malaysia, Singapore, Indonesia, the Philippines, Brunei, Vietnam, Cambodia, Laos, and Myanmar. At its inception, Brunei was still a British protectorate while Vietnam and Laos were not invited to join the association because of they were engaged in civil wars. Burma and Cambodia did not accept the invitation to join the association because of their proximity to China, which viewed ASEAN as a body set up by the US to contain the spread of communism in Asia despite the fact that ASEAN was based on principles of noninterference. Over the years, ASEAN accrued enough political credibility and legitimacy that the remaining countries later sought to be included under its umbrella (Than 27).

While ASEAN initially faced difficulties coming together because each Southeast Asian nation produced the same exports and competed in similar markets, the stability granted by cooperation through ASEAN brought overall political stability to the region (Tarling 214). Regionalism thus encouraged individual states to see beyond their own borders during the early years of nationalism and independence, but they did so as decidedly sovereign nation-states. Regional cooperation especially made economic sense because they were, and still are, relatively less powerful states in Asia.

> Under conditions of unequal development the efforts of societies such as the United States and Japan, themselves transregional world economies, to establish a Pacific community appear easily justifiable as efforts to reserve for themselves a Pacific domain and restrict the autonomy of other (weaker) societies in the region while preserving their own autonomy as world powers. (Dirlik 8)

Functioning as a regional bloc allows the different nation-states to act on their own, but it also gives them a large enough voice and presence with which to negotiate with other economic blocs such as the US, the EU, China, and Japan. ASEAN states shared the belief that transnational cooperation is useful insofar as it strengthens rather than weakens state power.

> The first was a "common interest [among the ASEAN regimes] in preventing radical internal political change." This, in turn, led to a common belief that political stability and continuity of leadership should assume priority over political participation in order to create the necessary climate for rapid economic growth. Secondly, ASEAN regimes shared an almost religious belief in the effects of rapid economic growth in diffusing the sources of social and political discontent within their societies. (Acharya 44)

These beliefs stem from anxieties over the legitimacy of the regimes in power, and subsequent state policies were designed especially to protect the "political stability and continuity of leadership." The strength and coherence of the state has always been perceived as central to economic power, and accounts for the turn to increasing state control during times of economic downturns or uncertainties. The focus on sovereignty and national borders is evidence that the Southeast Asian state learned to "see" transnationally in a way that enables *more*, rather than less, state control.[13] The state's desire to protect its sovereignty precedes—and guarantees—its economic survival. In other words, transnational political ties that drew the region together were successful when they strengthened national ties.

But however important political and economic ties were to securing state legitimacy on the level of international relations, those ties could only provide a limited form of cultural identity for citizens of individual countries. The state had to look elsewhere for the source of political legitimation from within, and not only outside of, its borders. The postcolonial state in Southeast Asia, like the postcolonial states in Africa and other parts of Asia, found themselves with large groups of racial and religious minorities within the arbitrary borders set in place during colonialism. There are Buddhist communities in Vietnam, Thailand, and Cambodia, for example, and these communities often share racial ties although these ties are also a hybrid, changing relation. Those countries moreover also host Muslim communities that share commonalities with Muslim communities in Malaysia, Indonesia, and the Philippines.[14]

Communities that can engender potential transnational affiliations consequently could complicate the state's categories of identity and social practices, and appear as a challenge to state power because they appear to evade state classifications and control. The conflation of race and religion in the Malaysian state's claim that all Malays are always already Muslims, for example, deliberately glosses over and ignores the hybrid and uneven notions of racial identity, practice, tradition, and place because hybrid racial and religious forms of community evade easy state categories and disrupt the narrative of the nation. Homogeneity within the state is often believed to strengthen the state, and the loyalties it might command. In other words, transnational flows and ties mediated by the state are desirable, while transnational flows and ties of race, religion, gender, or other forms of social identities that might escape state mediation seem more of a threat. The state responds to those possible threats by trying to determine what they mean as in the examples of the Malaysian state's attitudes toward Islam or "communism."

However, the actual practices of race and religion in the social life of places often fall outside of the categories of the state and complicate the Malaysian state's too-easy understandings of the relations between race and religion. The syncretism of religion in Malaysia defies obvious or normative state categories that fix either racial or religious identity as unchanging or unambiguous. For example, Mohammad Yusof's work shows that the Buddhist community in northern Malaysia, while distinctively "Malaysian"—the Muslim Malaysian king is a patron of the temple instead of a Thai Buddhist monarch—they share close links to the Buddhist community in Thailand. But the Siamese in Malaysia are not only Buddhist, they are also included in the category of *bumiputra* alongside the Malays and "other" indigenous groups such as the Orang Asli, Dayaks, Duzuns, and Kadazans. Buddhism distinguishes Siamese Malaysians from Muslim Malays in the northern Peninsula, but they are also seen as different from the Buddhist Chinese Malaysians because the roles Siamese worshipers play in temple proceedings.[15] These syncretic communities flourish so long as they do not pose a threat to the nation-state. And when Siamese Buddhists identify as "Siamese"—as opposed to the national identity of "Thai"—their transnational affiliation does not threaten their place in the nation-state because its racial undertones are less of a threat compared to the political affiliation "Thai" might call to mind.

The state therefore can react in flexible ways to transnational affiliations and consequently influence how religion is perceived within national contexts and in each historical period. Because religion can be seen as a form of liberation or a form of protest against either a repressive or failing state, the state has to be careful to divert religious criticism away from itself. The Malaysian state, for example, portrays itself as an Islamic administration that protects the rights of Muslims domestically and abroad if it is to garner support from Muslim Malays, but it must also be seen as "moderate" in international politics. It finds itself caught straddling in the tensions between tradition and modernization, and the desire to control narratives about race and religion because they form an emotional core of communities that already feel under siege by economic and political uncertainties.

> State policies toward religion in Asia have been shaped not only by modernization goals but also by the needs of states to legitimate their rule and unify their populace. Nation-building requires a very different stance toward the past than does modernization. While commitment to modernization entails rejection of those aspects of a society's past deemed impediments to a rationalized bureaucratic order, nation-building depends on the very opposite move. (Keyes 5)

The process of nation-building that harnesses religious experience and identity can be at odds with the process of modernizing.[16] Because religion often provides competing claims to that of the modern nation-state, the state then has to harness religions' claims to its own projects and goals.[17]

Racial and religious tensions are considered challenges to the state's ability to keep the peace, and countries such as Malaysia, Singapore, and China, for example, monitor religious activities as a way to maintain state "security." After the race riots of 1969, various scholars of religion in Malaysia noted an increase in religious activity in both Malay and Chinese communities. An Islamic revival began in Malaysia 1969 involving connections to the Middle East, but also to student movements (Naimah Talib). The state responded by enacting the Universities and the University Colleges Act of 1971 that prohibited students from engaging in "political activities." Religious movements, called *dakwah* movements, consequently became the "safe" way with which to voice their dissent against the state. However, this also shifted the focus of student dissent away from the state, and was redirected against secular, Western-oriented education or modernization (Shamsul 103). The Malaysian state has to present itself as "Islamic," and not as either "secular" or "Western" because it has to present itself as a protector of Malays (as a racial group) and Muslims (as a religious group) or it risks losing the support of religious voters. However, if the state presents itself as too Islamic, minority groups feel threatened or marginalized and consequently create destabilizing racial tensions within the nation-state, and in its diplomatic relations with other states.

Minority religious identity, on the other hand, can be mobilized as a form of resistance against racial assimilation and at the same time allow minority groups to claim national belonging, as the Chinese in Malaysia did.[18] Jean DeBenardi notes that after the 1969 racial riots and subsequent implementation of the New Economic Policy that instituted preferential economic treatment for the Malays, there was a rise in Chinese conversions to Islam as a way to "*masuk Melayu*" (become Malay). But surprisingly, that rise was accompanied by a revival of Chinese folk religion. Because open political dissent can sometimes be dangerous, religion becomes the vehicle through which Chinese identity and community can be safeguarded and even celebrated. The freedom to practice their religion can be seen as both a process of becoming "national" as well as a declaration of ethnic difference.

These syncretic attitudes toward religion demonstrate the cultural differences between the Chinese in Malaysia from the Chinese in China, Taiwan, Hong Kong, or other diasporic sites, and they also demonstrate how religious beliefs secure social order in a multiracial state. The practices of the Penang Hokkiens, whom DeBenardi studies, included the worship of spirits or objects—called *datuk*[19] spirits—that have identifiably "Malay" characteristics. The practice of worshiping *datuk* spirits sometimes incorporates Malay animistic beliefs, and some of the spirits are thought of literally as Malay. Aspects of both the objects worshiped and the event of such worship show a recognition and knowledge of, and respect for, Malay culture, including "costume, diet, Islamic religious practice, black magic, musical forms" (132), even as they also play a role in demarcating racial and religious differences. Worshipers of *datuk* spirits are clearly Chinese and racially different from the spirits they worship, and their customs and practices allows them to note those differences in nonconfrontational terms: "Religion provides not only a field in which community is imagined, but also a field in which one's enemies are given images—be they imperial soldiers, British colonial officers, or Malay magicians" (DeBenardi 124). These rituals set social rules and regulate proper behavior within the community, and also as each community lived and interacted with other communities. That race and religion often operate in culturally complex ways is important to note because their syncreticism resists the state's too-easy appropriation of the right to speak on behalf of, and for, Muslims as the Malaysian state often does.

These cultural histories exemplify the state's consistent and continual investment in securing public moral narratives, both religious and secular, to its own ends. Individuals and communities do not always align themselves with the state's views of the world, but their responses nonetheless register an awareness of what is important to the state. Furthermore, public moral narratives anchor the state's position in the face of global challenges.[20] These contradictions become especially apparent from the 1980s onward, as economic globalization picks up speed in Southeast Asia. The discourse of "Asian values," which emerged in the 1980s and 1990s, was part of transnational discourse that was moderately successful at further strengthening the state's role as "moral protector" in the Southeast Asian political imaginary.[21]

The idea that there are identifiable and consistent "Asian values" allows Southeast Asian states to establish affinities with other nation-states and cultures, even as they use that same rhetoric to protect their own regimes from criticism: "Ultimately, the 'anti-West' attitudes are not so much to cast doubt on the objectives of Western liberal-capitalism. Rather they are concerned with the legitimacy of an 'Asian approach' to managing internal contradiction and political dissent in the condition of capitalist modernity" (Yao 19). When criticized for human rights abuses, repression, or censorship, ASEAN countries can claim refuge under the broad label of "Asian values," that is, Asian countries should not be held to the same standards as the West because they have "their" own values.

This discourse allowed them to assert state sovereignty against the "corrupting" influence of the West but what are Asian values? The abstract category refers to diverse and sometimes contradictory religious traditions, languages, views on gender and sexuality, race, and customs. Moreover, these "values" allowed Southeast Asian leaders to ask their citizens to sacrifice "individual" rights for "state" rights (Barr 6). The idea that there is a coherent set of "Asian values" is a form of strategic Orientalism that allows the state to defend "traditional values" from "Western decadence," and that further allows the state to speak on behalf of "the people" against purported enemies in the West.

The discourse of Asian values also responds to the challenge transnational capital poses to the state and they allow the nation-state to secure its borders in the face of Western attempts to manipulate Asia's economic growth.

> In Asia, state narratives insist that Asian modernity is an alternative to the West because in their view, capitalism is a system that should strengthen state control, not undermine it. Thus, the major difference between Asian modernities and those in the West lies in the way Asian state biopolitics and economic competition are routinely recast as timeless cultural practices and values, and events generated by the breaking down of national borders are managed through institutionalizing Confucian moral economies, which are set off against Western liberal democracies. (Ong 82)

In other words, the battle for symbolic control is crucial in order for the state to retain and exert its control over the "material" structures within its reach. To do so, the discourses of culture, tradition, and religion themselves have to become a part of the state's infrastructure. But here, the alternative to capitalism's transnationalizing impulses is not a return to the "nation" per se, but to an alternative transnational form of identity, that is, by identifying with the region. This, according to Ong, has been especially successful in the case of East Asia and its claims to a generalizable Confucian culture, also taken up in Southeast Asian nations' "Look East" policy. We have yet to see if self-identified Islamic states in the region will succeed in co-opting the language of faith to protect their economic and political and power.[22]

These examples show us how the languages of culture and race, coupled with beliefs about values—religious and secular—play a large role in state formation on the level of the symbolic. The state has an investment in developing strong moral narratives about racial and cultural difference because it allows the state to reterritorialize global flow, that is, to strengthen state control against what it sees as challenges. "Asian values" enables Southeast Asian states to mobilize the twin narratives of weakness (Asians need protection from the West) and strength (Asian states will protect Asians). The narrative of victimization, ironically, has become a form of agency. The postcolonial Asian state, in other words, adopts Nietzschean *ressentiment* where political identity based on the experience of injury inculcates moral superiority in those who see themselves as victims, and those in power as evil. The state can now claim victimization vis-à-vis other more powerful states, even as it victimizes those within its borders. Competing claims of victimization—either real or imagined—perversely leads to greater and more pervasive forms of state control.

Postwar Southeast Asian history is consequently the history of how state strength grows as the different states develop cultural and institutional apparatuses to govern within its borders even as it claims to be weak in the face of its neighbors, and as Cold War tensions loomed. Moreover, this history matters because the material conditions of war, decolonization, international tensions, and the integration into the capitalist world state system shaped the social relations that produce moral tropes about national identity and belonging. As new nationalisms in Southeast Asia threw off the shackles of colonialism, decolonization increased rather than decreased the fear of racial difference because colonialism had imposed arbitrary borders that separated and distributed racial and religious groups across different countries. The newly independent states were afraid that the Chinese, Indian, Buddhist, or Muslim groups would retain racial or religious loyalties across national borders instead of forming attachments to their new nation-state. The postcolonial state learned that it had to develop a new language of shared values to secure its legitimacy. Other forms of identity such as religious, racial, gender, or sexuality were acceptable in so far as they furthered nationalist goals. Furthermore, the state has an investment in developing strong moral narratives around the symbolic significance of racial, religious, or cultural difference because it allows the state to strengthen state control—a form of reterritorialization—against what it sees as global challenges.

As a parable of the state, Sanctuaria's initial freedoms are a rejection of the state's attempts to control public moral discourse and they offered a utopian alternative to how the state posits correspondences between morality, beliefs, race, religion, and national identity. For example, Rani, Arif's Indian and Hindu wife, is under no compulsion to *masuk Melayu*, that is, to convert into Islam and adopt Malay customs, and neither is she under compulsion to follow the dietary restrictions or religious ceremonies of the Hindu faith into which she was born. However, these freedoms that Rani experiences comes at another cost; she has to submit to the bare force of the state that Arif represents in Sanctuaria.

> *"Awak jangan sekali-sekali samakan ajaran saya dengan mana mana agama pun dalam dunia ini. Ajaran saya tak kisah pun awak nak pakai tudung ke nak makan babi ke nak makan daging ke apa! Ajaran saya tak janjikan awak masuk syurga atau neraka!"*
>
> *"So sebab tu awak senang jatuhkan hukuman kat dunia ni? Bila ada orang yang membantah keputusan awak, bila ada yang menyoalkan balik ajaran awak, awak rasa tak senang? Awak mudah nak menghukum?"*

> "Don't you dare talk about my teachings in the same breath as any other religion in this world. My teachings care nothing about whether you want to cover your hair, eat pork, or beef! My teachings don't promise you heaven or hell!"
>
> "So, is that why it's easy for you to punish others in this world? Are you upset when someone disagrees with your decision or when someone questions your teaching? Is that why it's easy for you to mete out punishments?" (Translation mine, 118–19)

But the freedom from race and religion, Rani eventually found, did not translate into freedom from the state. The novel critiques the state and its control over the symbolic systems of religion and race, but it also reveals how the state's true desire is for the power to decide what consists of "right" or proper beliefs. Arif and Rani's confrontation ends quickly in a predictable male act of violence—he throws a punch to her face. Arif's Sanctuaria, stripped of the social order that race and religion provide, is unmasked as brute force; the state can only be held together by sheer power. Violence in *Sanctuaria* revolves around securing the right to determine the limits and contours of social life, and this requires control over spatial boundaries but also over symbolic life and social differences within those borders. Postracial moral vision, in other words, is untenable because the moral vision the state adopts safeguards its own interests first and foremost.

Sanctuaria is not the only recent, popular Malaysian novel to embody frustrations with and suspicions of a moralistic state. Brian Gomez's *Devil's Place*, another Malaysian novel first published in 2008 and reprinted in 2013, a year before *Sanctuaria*'s own publication, also critiques the state's views of racial determinism as moral determinism. However, it also points us to the limits of escaping the state's influence on culture and politics. Both these important contemporary Malaysian novels, which adopt utopian elements to critique how the state overdetermines the social meaning and material effects of racial identity, are nonetheless suspicious of utopian impulses.

Han Suyin's *And the Rain My Drink*, discussed in the previous chapter, forms an arc to Brian Gomez's cult hit *Devil's Place*. From the 1950s to the early 2000s, racial stereotypes continue to populate Malaysia's national imaginary; in both novels, racial anxiety is not only a feature of the decolonizing state, but also the state under globalization. The formal aspects and tone of the two novels are very different, and they have very different effects on the reader. Thematically, the two novels fall on opposite spectrums. *Devil's Place*—as the novel's title suggests—revolves around marginal and unsavory characters rather than Han's model minorities. And while Han's novel is set in the context of the communist insurgency in the mid-twentieth century, Brian Gomez's madcap caper takes place in the middle of an international Islamic terrorist plot in the early twenty-first century. The biggest difference between the two novels lies in the authors' uses of narrative perspective and how racial stereotypes are presented. Narrative perspective in Han's novel is predominantly directed toward the raced other, especially in how the moral worth of racial minorities is calculated. In contrast, *Devil's Place* tells the story mostly from the point of view of those who are usually the object of stereotypes. These differences account for why even though both authors adopt the form of satire, they have opposite effects: *And, the Rain*

My Drink while at times funny leans toward the tragic, and *Devil's Place* while at times tragic, leans toward the comic.

Both novels, however, pivot on the possibility or impossibility of seeing past stereotypes, and the state's reliance on the belief that race always determines moral behavior. Plot progression in *Devil's Place* relies entirely on how representatives of the state—detectives, politicians, journalists—cannot see past racial stereotypes to catch either the right suspects or criminals. The novel's characters evade state policing precisely because they do appear in already familiar and recognizable types. The state sees (falsely) in *Devil's Place* because the state and its representatives rely too much on preconceived notions about race, and the state's inability to truly "see" or correctly interpret racial difference is its true weakness. But this is no utopian novel with a happy ending; at the end of the novel, the misfit heroes of the novel also end up either dead or forced into exile in order to escape the state. This second Malaysian novel presents a version of postracial moral vision that is an alternative to the state, but it finally cannot be sustained outside of the state, even within its own fictional landscape. *Devil's Place*, humorous as it is, does not offer us easy answers or too hopeful resolutions about how to respond to the state's envisioning of racial difference.

The novel begins when Ning Somprasong, a Thai prostitute, bites off the penis of the client who abuses her, and he dies by accident when he slips on his own blood and falls. Her client turns out to be an international terrorist affiliated with the Jemaah Islamiyah on his way to deliver US$18 million to a local Malay Muslim terrorist, Suleiman Salleh, who acts on the orders of the Yusof Shamsuddin, the education minister.[23] Fellatio Lim, Ning's Chinese Malaysian pimp, unknowingly sends Ning to Terry's friends who have organized a bachelor's party for, Terry Fernandez, a Malayalee Indian Malaysian. Ning steals the bag after killing the international terrorist and becomes entangled with Terry after a series of mistaken identities as Suleiman, Detective Azmi Ali, and CIA agent Julio Chavez track down the money and the killers. Terry (a bar musician), Jamal Omar (a Malay bar owner), Chee Ming Chia (a Chinese Malaysian taxi driver and resident conspiracy theorist), eventually come together as an unlikely, racially mixed band of heroes who help Ning escape as the other characters pursue her and the bag of money.

What happens when the state cannot see beyond the common stereotypes of race and class? Terry, Ning, Chia, and Fellatio first appear to their pursuers as "the drunk, irresponsible Indian" and his "Asian" girlfriend of unspecified racial origin, and either as generic middle-aged Chinese men or

Chinese spies. The police and their agents repeatedly overlook these characters even when they appear right in front of them. Agent Chavez mistakenly reports that Fellatio who is ethnic Chinese Malaysian for a "Chinese"-national spy. Chavez mistakes racial identity for national identity, and his mistake leads him to a deeper misreading of the events that he sees.

> "I think the Chinese are involved somehow with bin Ahmed."
>
> "The *China* Chinese?"
>
> "I believe so."
>
> *Why the hell would the Chinese be involved?* Channing thought. [. . .]
>
> "They could have just been regular *Malaysian* Chinese."
>
> "That's what I thought at first too, sir. But there're hardly any Malaysian Chinese in government agencies here, so I don't think he was a cop or anything." [. . .] "A cab driver knows I'm with the CIA. I believe he's a Chinese agent too."

In this absurd exchange, Chinese Malaysians are not recognized as Chinese Malaysians because they have been historically underrepresented in public service, and because of how Chinese Malaysians became racialized as communist spies during the Cold War. When Chavez interrogates Fellatio, he moreover misses the linguistic cues that would have confirmed Fellatio's identity as Chinese Malaysian.

> "Of course, friend."
>
> "And stop calling me 'friend.' I'm not your fucking friend, okay?"
>
> "Okay, friend."
>
> "I said stop calling me friend, you commie fuck!"
>
> "Sorry, frie . . . uhh. . . . Sorry, boss."

> "Boss? *Boss?* Am I the head of the fucking Chinese fucking Communist fucking party?" "Uhh . . . no frie . . . uh. . . . no bo. . . . uhh. . . . uhh. . . . no." (90)

Fellatio may look Chinese, but the linguistic patterns he adopts are Chinese Malaysian; race informs Chavez's judgment even when other cultural signifiers should have alerted him to the differences between "China Chinese" and "Malaysian Chinese." Furthermore, Fellatio's lack of social skills as a result of his social class also go unnoticed in their exchanges.

Chavez mistakes Fellatio's use of the nouns "friend" and "boss" as acts of defiance or mockery because he assumes Fellatio is a Chinese spy, but in local Malaysian English, they are used either to indicate friendship, used as a form of respect, or to denote a desire to appease during conflict. Idiomatic, local forms of English in Malaysia facilitate the crossing of racial and class barriers, but Chavez misses these cues and cannot reciprocate. Chavez's ignorance of local customs and linguistic particularities in Malaysia leads to a failure to communicate and a failure to grasp the situation in which he finds himself.

However, it is not only cultural outsiders like the American CIA agent who do not see what they should see. Cultural insiders like Suleiman and Detective Azmi—who are literally partners in crime in the pay of the education minister, a supposed ally of the US state (229)—make similar mistakes because they cannot see beyond usual race and class stereotypes. But Chia the cab driver and Fellatio—a pimp, but not gay—unwittingly play key roles in the unraveling of the terrorist plot because they are the victims of racial stereotyping.

> "I don't have the fucking time to go after cab drivers, okay? He's nothing. He's not involved. He doesn't know *apa-apa*." (171)

> "Then, he had to figure out the mystery of the Chinese homo. When Suleiman had mentioned it to him again, he felt that something about the description of the man was familiar." (177)

The novel's comic effects result from how the missing connections to the crime are presented through the narrative perspectives of those most confident about their view of the world, even when they come within fingertips of the people they have to capture. The state's rigid beliefs about racial determination of moral behavior leads the agents of the state on a fruitless chase throughout the city.

The novel's plot tension is further a comment on not only local politics, but also on global concerns; local racial stereotypes exist alongside global racial stereotypes. Ning and Terry would not have had to flee if they had not been caught up in an international terrorist plot that the CIA agent stumbles on by chance. They and the other characters then find themselves fleeing from, and into, the arms of first either the Middle East Islamist terrorists (and the detective in cahoots with them), or the brash CIA agent whose hubris offends them all.

> "Look, old man, I have no fucking time for this shit. Where is the fucking girl!"
>
> "Why do you want to know?"
>
> "It's a matter of national security."
>
> "The national security of which nation?" Pak Jam asked, as he lit his cigarette.
>
> "Of . . . uh . . . the world," Chavez said.
>
> "The world isn't a nation." (148)

He states the obvious when he calls Chavez's bluff, "The world isn't a nation," and Pak Jam's droll response to Chavez further mocks the implicit US-centrism that is felt far away across the Pacific Ocean, near the equator. The anxieties felt on the part of the US require that it sees its interests as global interests, shared around the world by every country invested in the War on Terror.

But Chavez is not completely wrong. "National security" can be secured when "world" security is secured, especially when world security is conflated with a superpower's security because its anxieties can lead it to overreach. The state's need to secure its interests requires that it act not only within the state, but also outside of its borders, and as Chavez finds out from his supervisor later, it is in the US's best interests to have the terrorist plot succeed in Malaysia. As the novel climaxes, the CIA agent and the local

Muslim terrorist come face to face with one another in a symbolic clash between East and West, good and evil, Christian and Muslim.

> Suleiman watched as first Azmi and the girl, and then the old man and finally the taxi driver left the room with the money. But he knew that if he took his aim away for a minute, he would be dead. Shoot to Kill was the order for almost every law enforcement agency in the world when it came to him. But he didn't mind death. As long as it wasn't by the hands of Americans. If he was going down today, he was taking the Yank with him. (266)

In this confrontation, Suleiman's original mission of securing the US$18 million needed to purchase the bomb from the Russians falls to the sidelines in the face of what he sees as the higher goal of killing his enemy, the American. Everyone escapes the room as Chavez and Suleiman, each representing their respective countries and civilizations, see only one another and no one else. The final confrontation involves only the two characters who symbolize state power. State competition, where each state sees itself in relation to other states, is the linchpin in *Devil's Place*, that by a surprising turn of luck works in the favor of the other characters who discover that they are no longer of value either to Chavez or Suleiman.

Like *And the Rain my Drink* and *Sanctuaria*, the state's interests trumps all other kinds of interests. As a counterpoint to this narrative of state power and vision, *Devil's Place* also foregrounds a series of characters who, at the start of the novel, either did not know one another, or because of their different race and class were merely acquaintances. Pak Jam, a retired club bouncer and bar owner, like the other characters who help Terry and Ning, in contrast, refuses to be drawn in either to work for the interests of either nation or world. Instead, what takes priority is the security of the lives both the state and the world usually consider expendable: a bar owner, an unknown musician, a prostitute, and a cab driver. Neither the usual ties of race, religion, class, gender, sexuality, family, nor friendship bind this unlikely group who were brought together only by circumstance.

But unlike *Sanctuaria*, *Devil's Place* does not offer a new vision of the state, and offers instead the picture of a stateless utopia where its characters who find themselves on the margins create among themselves a new ethics of care, but who also eventually become isolated when they fall out of the state's moral vision and its surveillance. This stateless utopia ends with Ning's death, Pak Jam's secretion in an island far away from the state capital, and Terry and Chia's exile to Thailand. The state still wins at the end.

As the close readings of the two novels in this chapter illustrate, seeing outside of the state or presenting a vision of the world that escapes or elides the state's own vision of the world can be difficult to achieve. Even novels like Brian Gomez's *Devil's Place* that present an alternative to the state's own views of race and morality is finally enfolded back into the state's own delimitations of its power to define social life and the social mores within it. Terry and Ning, the prostitute, do not have a happy ever after, even if Terry chooses to live close to Ning's daughter and mother to care for them in Thailand. Neither he nor Chia are free to return to Malaysia where they remain persona non grata. Pak Jam more easily evades the state's scrutiny, as he is both Malay and Muslim, and as long as he does not espouse "deviant" Islamic beliefs, will not suffer from excessive state supervision.

But neither novel is under any illusion that culture and social life are free of state influence, even if they also contain with them the wish that we might go "beyond" the state. The postcolonial is not yet postnational. The state combusts in *Sanctuaria*, and all the characters for whom we have any real feeling in *Devil's Place* retreat to liminal spaces where they remain out of sight of the state. The desire to be beyond nation and beyond race exemplifies our collective longing and vision for a society where all is equal and able to succeed. But this vision of social progress nonetheless continues to position the state as the guarantor of wealth, property, and prosperity, and perhaps, for lack of a better social system in place, rightly so.

The literary analyses and cultural histories of the postcolonial Southeast Asian state in this chapter, however, demonstrate that the state has consistently showed an interest in regulating moral narratives, especially as it intersects with racial and religious identity because the moral narratives of the state are part of the reterritorialization of state power. In the reterritorialization of state power, the state adopts moral language to describe its actions, its relative position of weakness or strength within the world state system, and also its attitudes toward race. Racial difference and racial minorities become symbols of what the state fears under globalization, because the presence of racial difference challenges the myth that the state is unified and that it has always been unified, and that it protects and guarantees the good life for all its citizens.

The next chapter examines how the state mobilizes utopian impulses to its own ends, that is, how it mobilizes nationalist ideologies to project a future in which the state plays a large role in guaranteeing for individual citizens. The moral discourse of goodness no longer only describes the behavior expected of racial minorities, it also describes the moral goodness of the state and its ability to guarantee the good life in the form of the "American Dream." The discourse of the American Dream codifies into culture the idea that the nation-state as a whole shares common goals for the future, and that it takes a distinct capitalist form: the generation of ever-increasing profit.

Ironically, the American Dream as a trope of state strength is also part of a global vocabulary that celebrates the reterritorialization of state power. Racial narratives modeled on American forms of exceptionalism have emerged out of Asia because state power is still the axis on which global power relies; Asian versions of the American Dream allow their states to position themselves as equals and competitors for a vision of state dominance that has long been seen as unique to the American state project. For example, the new "Chinese Dream" announced in November, 2012, is Xi Jinping's answer to the American Dream, a liberal-democratic ideology of America's position as world superpower. We will see in the next chapter that global forms of the American Dream signal new, or until recently, overlooked and still emergent forms of nationalism coupled with an underlying ethnocentrism that could potentially contribute to greater global tensions. In its pursuit of power, the state deploys racial narratives of "belonging" to strengthen the state in the face of globalization's effects on changing demographics, the flight of capital, and social stability. There is nothing "post" about "postracial" ideas about race that are a product of state power and continue to be shaped and reshaped by current needs of the state.

What nation-states under globalization share is an attention to universalist, nationalist ideologies that are also utopian; these values are directed toward "uniting" the nation-state and strengthening its power. The political scientist William Norris (2016) notes that nation-states have a "grand strategy," even if they remain implicit. National visions are part of what it means to *see like a state*, to use Scott's phrase, and are an important function of nationalism in the age of globalization because they set out the state's vision in the language of "success" or "failure." The state's anxieties about its position in the world influence its attitudes toward racial minorities, and those anxieties can take the form of tropes of strength. However, the next chapter argues that the desire for power and influence under globalization is not only American, it is also global.

Chapter 4

Tropes of Security

The Global American Dream

> here, amidst
> drafts—yet
> these are not drafts
> toward a future form, but
> furious versions of the here and now. . . .
>
> —Li Young Lee, "Furious Versions"

> For Obama, Asia represents the future. . . . For years, the "pivot to Asia" has been a paramount priority of his. America's economic future lies in Asia, he believes, and the challenge posed by China's rise requires constant attention.
>
> —Jeffrey Goldberg, "The Obama Doctrine"

Toward the end of the Chinese-American author Gish Jen's third novel, *The Love Wife*, white working-class locals who trespass on a private beach attached to a house under the care of Jiabao and Lan, confront the Chinese couple in a racially charged moment; white and yellow bodies are caught in a standoff over who has the right to use the land. Jiabao and his wife are first-generation immigrants from China who run a Chinese take-out place in Portland. They live in the beach house that belongs to the Baileys, and oversee the property on behalf of the family in lieu of rent. After the initial confrontation, an unknown person sets fire to the house and Jiabao who was asleep at the time, dies in that fire. Like many other holiday homes in Maine owned by people who live outside of Maine, the property is a point of contention and a long-standing source of resentment for local Mainers. The encounter between the unnamed white characters and Jiabao, the wealthier Chinese immigrant—though he and Lan are barely "wealthy"—can be read as a parable of globalization's new chronotopes. The couple discover that class and racial inequalities cannot be easily resolved, and that their presence on the beach, ironically named Independence Island, elicits a defensive, culturalist nationalism that is partly motivated by class resentment. Published in 2004, the novel offers a prescient depiction of racial fears in response to Asia's growing economic power as a result of globalization.

In this altercation, the "foreigner" is deemed a threat because he or she now appears to be able to achieve the American Dream of home ownership. Jiabao's and Lan's apparent financial success—implicitly believed to come at the expense of white locals in town—symbolize a new kind of racial anxiety shaped by fears of the future. Financial growth in Asia pose a challenge not only to the US's economic dominance, but also to American cultural identity based on a sense of exceptionalism; American dominance may no longer be unique or attributable to anything resembling national character.

Asian American novels written at the end of the twentieth and early twenty-first centuries like Jen's *Love Wife* and Chang-rae Lee's most recent novel, *On Such a Full Sea*, depict the changes and challenges that globalization introduces, but more importantly, the critical force of their literary imaginaries also help us see the close relation between the fears that operate on symbolic and political registers informed by beliefs about the economic security of the state. These novels uncover the implicit logic that nationalism and race can no longer be imagined separately from the possibility and desirability of upward mobility, and that these opportunities are only possible if the state's own welfare is first secured. Populist nationalism in the late twentieth century can be defined by its desire for and belief in the centrality of state strength above other concerns. The belief in the importance of state strength, this chapter argues, conflates the American Dream with the state's view of its own moral goodness writ large as its ability to guarantee economic progress for the individual.

In Jen's novel especially, white anxieties over land are a synecdoche of deeper anxieties about globalization. The white locals are resentful because they can neither own nor enjoy the land on which they live. And while the very idea of a holiday home is an offence to the white local Mainers, it becomes doubly offensive when a raced body polices their access to that land. Jiabao and Lan do not drain the resources of their community and instead, their small business serves the community, hires from the community, and has generated growth in the town's depressed economy. However, the couple are still viewed as a threat by white Americans who conflate race and nation. "America" seems to have failed to guarantee success for white Americans while others have succeeded. Jiabao and Lan provoke such animosity because despite their racial difference—or perhaps, because their racial difference connotes a link to rising Asia—they have achieved the American Dream when white Americans have failed to do so.

In the confrontation, the unnamed, tattooed, white male character asserts his right to confer recognition on who he thinks is "really" American; and this belief that he has a right to do so is staked on contradictory assumptions that the American state is at once weak and strong. The specter of a Chinese man like Jiabao—naturalized citizen or not—destabilizes the tattooed man's idea of what the nation-state has become, and he responds to Jiabao's appearance by pronouncing his right to police Jiabao. He shifts the conflict over class and property rights to an argument that he believes he can win, which revolves around national identity and cultural belonging. He tells Jiabao that "Americanness" is not merely an effect of the law administered by the state, which consequently strengthens and weakens the state in the same move.

>—In any case, the fact that you're a citizen doesn't make you an American, *said the tattoo man.*
>
>—Oh really, *said Jiabao.* And how is that?
>
>—A citizen thinks this country is about law. But an American knows it is about who is really American. (341)

The tattooed man speaks on behalf of the state but his assertions also corrects the state's failure as he documents it. In his view, the state has mistakenly granted Jiabao citizenship (evidence that the state is weak), but his intervention also recalibrates Jiabao's claim to belonging, and consequently returns the state to its rightful condition (evidence that the state is strong). The tattooed man reads Jiabao's attainment of the American Dream as a failure of a weak state unable to defend itself against "outsiders." Soon after this conflict, an unknown person sets a fire that razes all the buildings on the Bailey family's plot of land, and the discovery of Jiabao's burned body among the wreckage proves to be a grisly, final statement on who does or does not belong.

But the tattooed man's confusion of race, citizenship, and rights reveals a deeper, more disturbing fear, that is, the suspicion that "America" and the American Dream no longer belong solely to white Americans. Perceptions of the state's weakness or strength underlie this tense encounter in the novel, where the characters look at not only what occurs within the nation, but also at what occurs outside the nation. Jiabao's Chinese body standing guard over the private beach symbolizes the new Yellow Peril of globalization that has arrived, literally, on American shores.

The white man's ventriloquism of the state raises curious questions. How do we learn to see like the state? Why do "patriots" or "nationalists" adopt the perspective of the state when they speak about their racial anxieties? The white, tattooed man takes up the perspective and the language of state strength in his treatment of Jiabao and Lan, but what enables this conflation of the state's interests with the individual's interests? Under globalization, the American Dream—and the upward mobility it represents—secures the national imaginary by enabling those who believe in it to adopt the state's perspective as a form of projection, especially when upward mobility is seen as fleeting and elusive. The anxiety that the American Dream is fragile or elusive is precisely what leads the individual to adopt the state's perspective as his or her own.

The confrontation is so fraught because to both Jiaobao and the tattooed man, the state's ability or inability to act is a source of anxiety but each is uneasy for different reasons. From Jiaobao's perspective, the state protects him by conferring legal recognition of his right to belong, but it cannot guarantee cultural recognition on the part of other citizens. But to the tattooed man, the presence of racial minorities signals the state's failure to protect its borders from immigration generated by global flows, and Jiaobao's raced body thus remains an object of suspicion. Jiaobao's presence is a sign that the state has become weak and compliant in the face of globalization. This weakness, however, is only temporary and mitigated as long as true patriots can step up to speak for it: ". . . an American knows it is about who is really an American." Where the state failed to protect the land from globalization's representatives—those they believe to be "wealthy" Chinese, in this case—the patriot can step up, and he adopts the perspective of the state in order to speak on behalf of it. In his policing of the foreign Other, he becomes a part of the state, and no longer merely a subject.

The raced body—either as success or failure—poses a challenge to the state, if not quite in the now, then surely in the future to come. Under globalization, racial temporality shifts from a focus on the past to a focus on the future. If yellow, brown, or black bodies symbolized backwardness under colonialism, the raced body takes on multiple and sometimes contradictory new meanings: it is both alien and backward, but it is also dangerous because it could threaten the future. Where colonial relations relegated the racial Other to "undeveloped" and barbaric spaces and times, the social and political relations now see the overachieving model minority and model nation as part of a new, threatening dystopian future. Race appears as contradictions because the state has different attitudes toward race, understood in the past tense as a relation to the past, and in the future tense, as a relation to the future. The state mobilizes racial anxiety about the past in order to preclude challenges to its legitimacy, and it mobilizes racial anxiety about the future to ensure that the state continues to play a central role in protecting its citizens against new threats.

Upward mobility is consequently both hopeful desire and a source of anxiety for both the white working-class and the Chinese American characters in Jen's *Love Wife*. More recent Asian American novels, such as Jade Chang's *The Wangs vs. the World* and Chang-rae Lee's *On Such a Full Sea*, are similarly attuned to the possibilities and anxieties of future downward mobility. The promise of the American Dream in these three novels is depicted as uncertain and out of reach, even when the characters are wealthy and upper middle class.

Individuals are interpellated as subjects of the state that plays the role of guaranteeing the good life. However, as national economies become increasingly integrated and competitive, the good life can be viable only for some, and not for all. Lucille Wong, or "Mama Wong," the Chinese-born mother of the American-born Carnegie married to Jane Bailey, or "Blondie," is diagnosed with Alzheimer's early in the novel, but her voice peppers Carnegie's train of thoughts throughout the novel, even after her illness and eventual death. Carnegie's imagination of Mama Wong's stream of consciousness presents her experiences of cultural dislocations as a new immigrant as well as her acerbic commentary on upward mobility and the American Dream. Mama Wong had raised Carnegie as a single mother without an education, and while her early successes in real estate enabled her to lift them out of a precarious life, the fear of poverty and failure never ceases to cast a shadow on her views of suitable marriage partners, adoption, family life, and even the future.

From Mama Wong's perspective, the failure to want to be upwardly mobile is dangerous because it ignores the dangers the future presents, both for the immigrant and the nonimmigrant. The failure to properly understand why ever-increasing wealth is necessary can only usher in an expedient descent to the bottom of the economic ladder.

> —You watch, she said. In ten years they are all going to need your help. They are not go up. They are go down. You know why? Not because they are stupid. They are not stupid. They are go down because they do not want to go up. They are like children who do not know what they want for Christmas, that's how spoiled they are.
>
> —They want to live in the moment, I explained. They don't believe in living for the future. It's a philosophical thing. (71)

In this argument, the novel introduces an element of certainty, and the reader is forced to choose a side. Who do we believe? The irate, rude, arrogant, and uneducated first-generation immigrant and Asian tiger mom, or her son, the assimilated, cosmopolitan protagonist?

Mama Wong's disagreement with Carnegie here—she insists that she does indeed understand the "philosophical thing"—is a disagreement not over lifestyles or cultural values, but a disagreement that comes from different experiences of anxiety that results from economic insecurity and cultural marginalization. The white, middle-class Bailey's or Carnegie himself who are like "children who do not know what they want for Christmas" do not know what it means to be in want, that is, to feel the anxieties of desire. They experience neither the dislocations of either poverty or the cultural marginalization familiar to poor, racialized immigrant workers. That is, the desire for social mobility as a necessary condition of a life with few options for success reflects how the immigrant, the racial minority, or the working class is always more attuned to the effects of unequal power relations and the precarity inherent to the social positions they inhabit.

To the poor immigrant, the American Dream is an avenue to cultural inclusion and—however tenuous—and also to economic security: "*Lan understand in this world, all kind of way to fall down. As long as you have money, you have cushion. No money, your pee-pee will be so black and blue you cannot stand up*" (232). Wealth, to the poor immigrant, can only be guaranteed by continuous accumulation. Unlike the Bailey's, Mama Wong, Jeb, and Lan either know what they want (Mama Wong), or are afraid to think about what they truly want (Jeb and Lan). From the cultural margins of both their new home in the US and the China that they left behind, racial minorities and immigrants may desire to identify with the new nation-state but find that they may be rejected. Anxiety over where they "belong," consequently, can be allayed only by economic position. Carnegie, a second-generation Asian American more accustomed to the comforts of middle-class life and to the security of his already mostly upward trajectory in his career and home life, like his wife, shares none of these fears.

White Americans like the Baileys, or middle-class Asian Americans like Carnegie, who feel protected by racial or class privilege do not always "feel," much less "understand," the anxiety of globalization, and consequently, do not look to the state for a source of dignity or identity. They discover later that they are not unaffected after Jeb's death in the fire when they come to realize that the locals' envy, anger, and resentment could have been directed at them instead.

> —It's globalization, said Gregory. Sooner or later we were bound to get caught in someone else's mess.
>
> —That trailer park, countered Peter. With no beach. Sooner or later there was going to be trouble. [. . .]
>
> —Are you suggesting, I said, that the beach should have been given to the town? [. . .]
>
> But Blondie demurred: —It was and it wasn't. The only person who could've done that, really, was Dad. [. . .]
>
> Said Peter, returning doggedly to his point: —I'm just saying maybe we didn't get caught in their mess. Maybe they got caught in ours. (351)

Peter belatedly realizes that while the conflict on Independence Island at first appears to be "someone else's mess," they could not disassociate themselves from it either. Connections formed under globalization are neither easily distinguishable nor self-evident, and their enmeshed nature is precisely what disappears from sight, even as their effects provoke ever greater rage. Published in 2004, Jen's *Love Wife* anticipated the class and race wars that propelled Donald Trump to victory twelve years later. The class inequality globalization introduces can erode—but not erase—racial privilege. The novel also anticipates a different kind of war, that is, the cultural antagonism between states.

The effects of reterritorialization, in other words, the strengthening of nationalism and state power in the age of globalization, takes place primarily as a result of the competition for economic status and cultural influence. The development of "soft power," rather than open wars over state boundaries has become increasingly important to China and other countries that have been considered insignificant or powerless on the global stage. States that desire to increase their global influence or even to secure their position do so in multiple ways including by mobilizing variations of the American Dream discourse. The American Dream enables the state to assert a common national character or identity, thus creating a homogenous cultural identity from within its borders. While this discourse first appears to be more tangentially related to racial narratives, it nonetheless reframes the state's capacities and responsibilities as part of a moral narrative to secure the "good life." And it does so by adapting civilizational discourse to new ends.

Ironically, when former postcolonial or historically marginalized states compare themselves to other states, their adoption of civilizational discourse emphasizes both their similarities to and differences from other states. Civilizational discourse in their most recognizable forms—described most famously by Samuel Huntington—emphasizes the cultural differences between one imperial power and another, or explains why one state deserves to dominate another. But in recent years, civilizational discourse also enables previously weak countries to insist that they too deserve recognition on the world stage because they are like—and sometimes unlike—those they consider to be more powerful states.

For example, when Wong-Bailey's adopted teenage daughters, Lizzy and Wendy, discuss what they hear about China from the media, school, and also from Lan, the Chinese woman who comes to live with them as their nanny, their conversations repeat popular conceptions of what global power means today. But in their repetition of popular beliefs about Chinese or American power, neither China nor the US is entirely separate or different.

> [Lizzy] went on: —Someday the Chinese are going to stand up again, and then the whole world will shake. The Chinese have five thousand years of history, after all, compared to America, which is only two hundred years old but thinks it can bully

everybody.... China is the oldest, but America is the most successful today. The CIA controls everything. Everybody has to do what America likes, because if you don't, the CIA will bomb your embassy. (215)

Because China is among the world's "oldest" civilization, in Lizzy's fifteen-year-old mind, it potentially rivals American power. Lizzy's repetition of what she has heard about world politics may be simplistic because it comes through the perspective of a youth, but it underscores how global relations is often cast as a series of conflict—especially in US-Asia relations—that pervades how we see the world. States compete with one another because they are similar and are engaged in a competition for limited resources and social capital. China's lesser position on the world stage is explained as a temporary rupture of its much longer history, as not only a "state" but also as an empire. Civilizational discourse marks as equally important both the historical fact of cultural and geopolitical difference (China is less powerful) as well as likeness (China could be just as powerful).

But China is not only more like the US; the US, conversely, is also more Chinese than it imagines: "WENDY / Lanlan says America is very Chinese, really. The Chinese invented everything and now Americans invent everything, China used to be the Middle Kingdom, and now America is the Middle Kingdom, that's why everyone has to learn English" (215). Wendy and Lizzy are taught to see China as something with which they are already familiar. They believe they understand China because they understand America, and the only difference that matters between the two states is their relative power and position in the world. Comparisons that emphasize only the similarities, as shown in the above passage, can have the unintended effect of reducing difference to a difference of relative power or status rather than of meaningful human or cultural heterogeneity. In this exchange between the teenage girls, states are depicted as at once similar and different. Their similarities are emphasized because we recognize that they are part of the world state system, but culturalist, civilizational discourse positions one state as better or more advanced than the other. Ironically, each state is always exceptional.

The similarities between states produce mutual fear, antagonism, and competition rather than cooperation or collaboration, and accounts for why globalization intensifies competition and instability on a global scale. China's eventual rise is believed to herald the US's possible decline as the world's superpower, as if the success of one country depends on the failure of the other. Nationalist narratives are based on a sense of exceptionalism and deployed in a global political system where their similarities encourage a competitiveness that can lead to antagonism. The anxiety produced out of competition revolves not only around real and present dangers, but also around how competitor states can become future threats. American exceptionalism based on the cultural narrative that the US is the land of opportunity is challenged by other similar cultural narratives that insist the US is no longer the only place where upward mobility is open to all: "Still America, [Lan] said. Just not the only one" (291). The American Dream no longer belongs to the US alone. However, this sense of hypercompetitiveness is not an effect generated by individual states, but because each individual state operates within a system of states.

Upward mobility as part of nationalist narratives of state strength—the US as not the "only" land of opportunity, in other words—both generates and manages anxiety under globalization when the success or failure of the state's ability to guarantee social mobility acts as a cultural bellwether of state power. Mama Wong, Lan, and the working class Mainers are far more attuned to these future insecurities than Carnegie or the Baileys because they are always attuned to the need to be upwardly mobile. In their contradictory feelings about the upward mobility of racial minorities, the successful Asian immigrant and the white working class are ironically similar in how they adopt the state's own attitudes on the precarity of the future, especially as the US becomes increasingly threatened by other states with growing economic and political clout. The rise of the global American Dream is seen as a threat to the US's own ability to guarantee the American Dream for its own citizens, but it is a cultural effect that reflects changes already underway in global history.

The American Dream Goes Global

Asia's economic growth in the twenty-first century has been remarkable to even the most casual observer. In January 2016, Forbes's list of the twenty wealthiest people in the world included its first Chinese billionaire.[1] This list of the world's most privileged and financially successful people on the planet has been historically dominated by the US; the list is still mostly North American but it also records an astonishing number of ultrawealthy Chinese: 400 billionaires and billionaire families reside in China alone. For perspective, while there are 95 billionaires in New York City—on its own, this is an astounding number—Beijing surpassed New York City by an additional 5 billionaires, to bring their total to 100 billionaires.[2] India is not far behind in the race between China and the US for greater wealth.[3]

Globalization's accelerated economic development and industrialization have introduced seismic changes to class and culture in Asia itself: new money and new social privileges now appear as important themes in much of the region's popular culture, as well as in Asian communities in North America. Recent popular films and television across Asia and the Pacific, for example, feature the fictionalized lives of the sons and daughters of new business elites and old political dynasties: "Noble Bride: Regretless Love" (China); "Ice and Fire of Youth" (China); "Fated to Love You" (Taiwan); "Ultra Rich Asian Girls of Vancouver" (Canada); "The Heirs" (Korea); "Secret Garden" (Korea); "Ola Bola" (Malaysia); "Moonlight Resonance" (Hong Kong); "The Millionaire's Wife" (Philippines); "Pan Rai Phai Puk" (Thailand), and so on. Often consumed and spread across national borders all around Asia, they have become profitable and best embody recent cultural assumptions about wealth, work, race, kinship ties, cultural norms, and gender roles. Similarly, Kelvin Kwan, the Singaporean American writer, has published two best sellers on ultrarich Asians and Asian Americans, *Crazy Rich Asians* and *China Rich Girlfriend*, and a movie franchise based on the books is in production, the first of which was shown in theaters in Fall 2018.

Asia's rapid economic growth is often read as a sign of its coming power, as well as an uncertain political future where the balance of global power remains in question. Class tensions in popular literature and media listed above are often represented as romances between the wealthy and those who aspire to be wealthy, where celluloid romances resolve the problem of economic inequality through the trope of marriage, but romantic fantasy is only a symptom of the kinds of anxieties that have accompanied the economic boom in twenty-first century. The fuller picture of globalization's effects in Asia is far grimmer, and while Asian economic growth and development have been welcome they are accompanied by new challenges in a region often differentiated by racial hierarchies and geographic locations. A 2013 report by the United Nations Department of Economic and Social Affairs notes that Asia and the Pacific sends over 95 million economic migrants to the rest of the world, while it also hosts 59.3 million migrants.[4] Migration, war, and uneven economic development as well as instabilities in the world's financial markets have created great demographic shifts.[5] Globalization produces deep social and economic inequalities as much as it produces new wealth, and income inequality poses new challenges to the states in the region.

Despite, or perhaps because of, the dizzying gaps between immense wealth and debilitating poverty, global variations of the American Dream have emerged in Asia as an important narrative that brings together the sometimes contradictory discourses on state power, state responsibility, and race. The narrative of upward mobility in popular culture may become even more culturally significant as income gaps grow ever greater. In Asia, state legitimacy is already conflated with its ability to guarantee increasing wealth to its citizens where global versions of the American Dream perform state strength by setting out the state's future goals in economic and moral terms. Xi's "Chinese Dream," touted as part of his vision for China moving forward in the twenty-first century, is the most prominent but by no means the only example of such discourse at work around the world. Political sovereignty no longer provides any guarantee against foreign influence or interferences; each state must now be wealthy enough to safeguard its sovereignty.

The "Chinese Dream" refers to general ideals surrounding the work ethics of the common man and woman that will return China to greatness and prosperity. Individuals labor and strive, in other words, so that the nation can be great. Nationalism in the form of a global version of the American Dream possesses emotive force because it makes statements about the role the state can play in guaranteeing the future, even if it has disciplinary effects in the present. Even in examples where national vision does not exist as an official statement, cultural narratives of national identity are essentially built on "national values" that reinforce social cohesion and a collective identity. The American Dream or its global forms help the state to project itself as the advocate, and even author, of new wealth, and consequently, of human freedom and well-being. The state's views on race are enfolded into the range of goals encoded in these national visions for economic and moral uplift. Consequently, the state mobilizes utopian narratives that conflate individual economic security and state power in international relations not only because it wants to secure its status as an ascending world power—as in the case of China—but also to secure its status as a state itself. Because states compete for resources and status, economic power guarantees state legitimacy.

Globalization and capitalism's challenge to the state thus rewrite ideas of the good life where upward mobility and economic independence—two core ideals of the American Dream—influence our conceptions of race and global relations. The global American Dream describes individual uplift as a part of national uplift in a catachresis that strengthens state legitimacy by conditioning how we see as part of how the state sees, that is, by conflating individual good and the state's good. This narrative justifies—and makes appealing—state control in the face of transnational flows of money, people, and power. It further allows the state to project itself as an important actor in the age of globalization, where economic competitiveness in the world, read as economic independence in the world system, is an important form of state legitimacy today in the US and in Asia.[6]

The belief in upward mobility that is central to the global American Dream, moreover, is the belief that we will not only become richer, but that we *must* become richer. To fail is to be left out of the world, and to be poor is to be less than human. The global American Dream condenses beliefs about what makes human life meaningful because it tells stories about what is good under globalization, but also presents globalization as a threat that only the state can prevent. Consequently, the American Dream and other narratives like it give us insight into how states see their roles today, but in the process, it also renews the idea of the nation—a form of reterritorialization—in a period of history where global connections affect everything from demographic changes, politics, the economy, and the environment. The growth of capital, the emergence of new owners of production in new parts of the world, and the opening up of new markets accompanied by an increasing militarization of Asia has the capacity to mobilize nationalism and patriotic fervor in Asia—and outside of it—in the twenty-first century because it increases state competition.[7]

The American Dream provokes patriotic fervor in the nation because it simultaneously claims that its nation-states are like other nation-states, but that it is also superior to other states. Ironically, each nation-state adopts a similar rhetoric that ties the state's well-being to individual action, work ethics, and eventual prosperity; each claims its own national vision as a form of exceptionalism.[8] Finally, these national visions put into service ethnocentrism and racial insularity by claiming that these values are narrowly "American," "Chinese," or "Malaysian," as if the national body is always homogenous.

Global "national" visions—an oxymoron if there ever was one—of the American Dream are moreover moral narratives about what counts as success and how to achieve it. They create and sustain belief in the imagined community by creating a narrative of not only opportunity and economic growth, but also of moral character and a calculus of who deserves what and why. The American Dream as nationalist ideology is the secular form of the prosperity gospel where wealth is the evidence of the moral worthiness of the state, and also of the individual.[9] The American Dream of freedom, equal opportunity, and the pursuit of happiness epitomizes not only beliefs about the nature and scope of what constitutes "national culture" but also the capitalist ideology of ever-increasing economic growth as a form of social good.[10]

Moral good has a long history of being intimately tied to economic concerns in the cultural history of the American Dream. The phrase "The American Dream" itself was not widely used or known until the 1930s after WWI, and the historian Jim Cullen attributes its origin to James Truslow Adams. The ideals now associated with the American national motto goes back to the Puritans' arrival in New England in the early and mid-seventeenth century, but many of the ideals that incorporated what we might now consider to be common sense, which make up the American Dream, are in fact the product of hundreds of years of deliberation, change, and refinement in the courts, media, schools, and public debates. "Freedom," for example, meant economic freedom as well as religious freedom. During this time, freedom was also popularly conceived as referring to the freedom of white men to own slaves and the freedom to engage in commerce.[11] Abraham Lincoln fought slavery not only because he believed black slaves to be the equals of white people, but also because slavery made it harder for poorer European Americans to compete with those who could afford slaves. Freedom for slaves was a social good because it would ensure more equitable economic growth and development for *white* people in general.

Today, the American Dream remains closely associated to the Protestant ethic in a capitalist economy and its cultures that link hard work and moral worth (Sherman 182). Recent sociological studies of poor, working-class Americans like these record how the American Dream gives them the language and ideology with which to understand their experience of economic instability and marginalization. Economic instability, unsurprisingly, increases racial tensions, and the capaciousness of the American Dream as a concept moreover helps the working poor to negotiate those differences. In Michéle Lamont's study of black and white working-class men, racial tensions rise between workers of different racial groups because of job insecurities, increased competition, and the perception that workers from other racial groups may have an easier time under the new economy.[12]

But because the American Dream and the moral values associated with it are capacious and fluid, even those who feel left out of the race for wealth nonetheless emphasize and identify with the different values represented by the American Dream to understand and explain their position in the world.

This, however, results in what Lamont calls "new forms of racism that are moral in character" (71). Rather than signify biological difference, race is now perceived to be about moral differences, where individuals value "self-reliance," "work ethics," and "discipline," or what they see as "key American values," and use them to describe their cultures and communities even in the face of economic hardship.[13] To working class white men, "American identity" remains important to their sense of self. The poor see themselves as a part of American success stories not because of their net worth, but because they work hard; the American Dream belongs to them because there is moral worth inherent to working hard. Moral values and moral narratives of hard work serve as a placeholder for actual economic success, because they provide meaning and psychological comfort in the face of economic and political vulnerabilities or changes.

Ironically, the American Dream as cultural identity becomes more and not less important as its promise and the possibility of achieving it can appear to recede in uncertain times. The American Dream is consequently relevant not because it affirms net economic worth as something already achieved, but because it provides the working class with access to a narrative of moral worth in the present and possible upward mobility, even if it is one that is projected into the future. In this formulation, state strength becomes ever more important as a guarantor of social stability. Stories about what counts as "success" and who should succeed are moral narratives about culture, nation, and identity in the US in a global economy. Their beliefs about success, wealth, and cultural identity are based on what the state will do for them in the future. The state thus positions itself as the guarantor of social mobility and uplift in the age of globalization. Its use of utopian language about the future good life—as symbolized by its formulation of the American Dream in the US, and elsewhere—can offer us alternatives to the status quo, but they can also be used to create new narratives or repurpose old ones that justify state control and state power.

As a conceit of what the nation-state is, or can be, the American Dream represents the desires and longings of many, but it also creates "the many" through its assertions of the good life. When subjects identify with the anxieties and hopes that the American Dream promises, they also identify as the communal "we" of the nation, and in so doing, reaffirm the belief that the nation-state secures for Americans freedom and equal opportunity. Upward mobility and equal opportunity, both important ideals to the American Dream, secure the state's legitimacy in the face of globalization's challenges.

The American Dream is therefore central to the lives of the working poor because of the possibilities it represents, and the underdog narrative that scripts the poor as victorious as long as they remain "American," and as long as "America" remains strong.[14] And because depictions of new Asian wealth or power in popular culture, media, and state narratives usher in a (re)turn to civilizational discourse that relies on and intensifies new fears of rising competitor states, the American Dream and its global variants are furthermore tied to a rising, dangerous ethnocentrism in the US and in Asia. Anxieties around race and state power have intensified because the state now confronts anxieties around the precarity of wealth in the face of shared global concerns around economic, political, technological, and demographic changes. Upward mobility is taken to be evidence of national success attributable to the state in question, but it is itself partly a drive responding to global political and economic exigencies.

The specific forms that national visions of upward mobility and state strength take may vary in particular contexts, but in general they make abstract claims about national identity, culture, values, and the state's ability to guarantee the future.[15] However, these visions of state success include one important caveat: that their citizens contribute to the moral project of state success. Malaysia's national plan, *Wawasan 2020*, for example, emphasizes economic development as an important form of self-determination in the wake of Western colonialism, economic imperialism, and military dominance.[16] National economic growth to the postcolonial state is evidence of the state's ability to act in the world: ". . . *Wawasan 2020 (W2020) telah diperkenalkan dengan objektif untuk menjadi negara maju mengelang tahun 2020 dengan acuan sendiri.*"[17] The phrase "*dengan acuan sendiri,*" that is, "by our own design" (translation mine), insists that economic growth and development has to be achieved on the state's own terms, implicitly for the benefits of its citizens, and emphasizes that economic flourishing by the year 2020 is both a promise and a claim that it is the state's responsibility, and right, to take actions that will guarantee national economic flourishing.[18] The slip from "promise" to "right" is a slip from accountability to despotism; the state reserves to right to take any kind of action it deems necessary to protecting its economic and political growth.[19]

This insistence on sovereignty is moreover an insistence on the good behavior of the citizenry and provides national vision based on a policing of individual behavior. *Wawasan 2020* identifies nine major challenges to achieving *Wawasan 2020*, and the first two challenges address the internal, and external, challenges to state power.

1. Mewujudkan negara Malaysia bersatu yang menpunyai matlamat yang serupa dan dikongsi bersama. Ia mesti menjadi negara yang aman, berintegrasi di peringkat wilayah dan kaum, hidup dalam harmony, berkerjasama sepenuhnya, secara adil dan didokong oleh satu bangsa Malaysia yang mempunyai kesetiaan politik dan dedikasi kepada negara;

   Create a Malaysia that is *united*, and that shares the same goals. It must become a country that is peaceful, integrated at the federal and communal levels, lives in harmony, *cooperative to the very best of their abilities*, live in fairness, and supported by one *nation* that possesses national loyalty and dedication to the country.

2. Wewujudkan masyarakat yang berjiwa bebas, tenteram dan maju dengan keyakinan terhadap diri sendiri, bangga dengan apa yang dicapai serta gagah menghadapi pelbagai masalah. Masyarakat Malaysia ini mesti dapat dikenali melalui usaha mencapai kecermelangan, sedar semua kemampuannya, tidak mengalah kepada sesiapa, dan dihormati oleh rakyat negara lain. . . .

   Create a citizenry that lives in freedom, peace, and development, and that has self-confidence, pride in achievement and courage in facing trouble. *Malaysian citizens must be known for their hard work in attaining excellence, be aware of all their abilities, lose to no one, and be respected by citizens of other countries.* . . . (translation and emphasis mine)

In this vision of a developed Malaysia at peace with itself and its neighbors, the emphasis on political unity and economic growth comes at the cost of difference and diversity of human experiences, visions, and will. I translate the word *bangsa* in the first point of the manifesto as *nation*: ". . . supported by one *nation* that possesses national loyalty and dedication to the country." But the word *bangsa* in Malay can also be translated as *race*, as in "bangsa Melayu," "bangsa Cina," "bangsa India," and so on. In this equivocal choice of the Malay word, the tensions between race and nation are unconsciously sublimated in the document.

The manifesto identifies and emphasizes how the state needs to be prepared to respond to global challenges directed at the state, and assumes that Malaysia's economic and political development can be realized only if the state's citizens are *well-behaved*.[20] Rather than a state that acts in the service of the people, the state now calls the people to serve the well-being of the state as part of its moral duty. The definition of what is meaningful human life is concatenated to the definition of a "successful" state.

Citizens of the state are seen as moral actors whose responsibilities are to support the growth of the state. Point number 4 makes this even more explicit: "*Mewujudkan masyarakat yang sepenuhnya bermoral dan beretika, yang mana warganegaranya kukuh dalam nilai agama, dan kejiwaan dan didorong oleh tahap etika paling tinggi,*" or "Create a citizenry that is most moral and ethical, in which their citizenship is strongly based in religion, and full of life and encouraged by the highest levels of ethics." The people's moralities need to be monitored and controlled because it could stand in the way of the state's vision of a better life. The underlying claim of this document is the unstated reference of "unity," "harmony," and "religion" as "Malay unity," "Malay harmony," and "Muslim religion."

The state thus positions itself as the guarantor of social mobility and uplift in the age of globalization—although some countries may do so in less overt and codified ways than the Malaysian state—and it does so by mobilizing the utopian claim that it possesses a vision or a dream for the good of its people. In the cultural logic of the postcolonial state under globalization, state subjects *should* act to serve the purposes of the state because the state has a moral vision that in turn protects their interests. But, in the process, the state effectively defines "the good life" for all. The next section offers an overview of how utopian thought as a critical voice has an ambiguous history, and how it can be both critical, and absorbed into the state's own vocabulary.

Utopian Language and Race

Utopia reimagines the world by reimagining other, more perfect institutional structures, social hierarchies, kinship ties, gender roles, and more.[21] To the twentieth-century philosopher Ernst Bloch, utopian thought was necessary to cultural life because it gives voice to the people's desires, challenged common beliefs about what was possible, and consequently sets those changes into motion. For Bloch, thinking about the future is not a form of escapism but the precursor to action because fiction articulates who we are as human beings and how we relate to the world. Art and literature, traditionally considered part of the superstructure and thus subject to material forces and the means of production, has a transformative role to play because they reveal lack or absence in the present world. The humanities and intellectual work perform a utopian function through contemplation, and in contemplation engage the world precisely because they direct us to see what does not yet exist but could exist.

Hope is not merely an emotion; it is not a happy or pleasant feeling devoid of material consequences, nor is it irrational. Often experienced as an emotion and grounded in ideal forms of social life that exists only in the abstract, hope nevertheless moves us forward and outward: "The anticipatory thus operates in the field of hope; so this hope is not taken *only as emotion*, as the opposite of fear (because fear too can anticipate), *but more essentially as a directing act of the cognitive kind* (and here the opposite is then not fear, but memory)" (*Utopian Function* 12). Utopian hope, or what Bloch calls "anticipatory illumination," is not set in opposition to the emotion of fear but rather to "memory," because hope is a desire that moves us toward a new reality. Hope appears vague and amorphous because this desire to change or to move beyond the limits of our present vision is necessarily subject to historical change, and consequently, our freedom lies in the very lack of a programmatic vision or function.

This conception of utopia, as José Esteban Muñoz argues, reminds us that if hope is to capture our collective imagination, it has to remain open to all possibilities because descriptions of utopia run the risk of becoming a prescription of what human life and human freedoms should look like: "Utopia is not prescriptive; it renders potential blueprints of a world not quite here, a horizon of possibility, not a fixed schema. It is productive to think of utopia as a flux, a temporal disorganization, as a moment when the here and the now is transcended by a *then* and a *there* that could be and indeed should be" (97). Instead, the continual reevaluation of our political desires and present realities offers the hope that we can move forward and outward to something more than what already exists. In its insistence on the ambiguous and the not quite fully formed, Bloch's utopian possibility is a drastic contrast to the modern state's insistence on legibility and certainty.

Unlike Bloch, fiction to Paul Ricoeur (1986) can become a form of escapism or flight of fancy. For Ricoeur, a utopia that presents an alternate vision of society has to grapple with the question of power and revise actual relations of power, or run the risk of escaping from what it wants to critique. He is more interested in "practical" utopias that attempt to dismantle existing power relations, and to do so, state power and the state itself has to be made completely irrelevant: "Fourier's utopia does not provide a political answer but rather denies that politics is the ultimate question. The problem is not how to create the good political state but how either to exist without the state or to create a passion-infused state" (309). Utopia can change existing forms of social and political relations only when it introduces a radically new discourse that goes outside the limitations of the state. It cannot be limited by the forms of thought and boundaries on which our existing realities already depend. Utopia must displace power's narrative about itself, and present to us different questions about what makes up our beliefs about life and self. For critics such as Ricouer and Wallerstein, the state poses the greatest limits to utopia because the state has the capacity to exert power over physical and intellectual life.[22]

But the problem of the state remains crucial to our considerations of utopia because the world state system has been the basis of our political and social structures since the modern era. Wallerstein argues that the modern world has never experienced true revolution because all revolutions that have occurred between the sixteenth and twentieth centuries have only taken place within the structure of the state.[23] True revolution can only occur when the underlying structures of the world changes and the world state system no longer organizes social and political life. In the second half of the twentieth century, decolonization and the claim to sovereignty has appeared as a form of "liberation" for many in the third world in the mid-twentieth century only to enlarge and bolster the existing state system rather than introduce new political systems (28). All states, including communist or socialist states, exist as part of the capitalist world state system.

The representation of race in utopia, moreover, poses its own particular kind of challenge in the state and the world is imagined.[24] How should we conceive of race in a perfect world? Edward Chan argues that writers such as Dorothy Bryant, Margy Pierce, and Samuel Delany reimagine utopias that include racial Others as their subjects, and do so by disrupting how racial identity works at the level of semiotics. The reader is confronted by racial signifiers, but the reader is also forced to relearn what these signifiers mean and in the process reconsiders the hierarchies that underlie social life. Chan goes on to argue that we cannot imagine race in the future because we depend too much on liberal democracy and the abstract subject on which political rights reside. We cannot imagine race in what is essentially a "postrace" future because we cannot imagine a new kind of subject position beyond the ones that already exist now (480). Race can only be rethought and reconfigured if the political structures of the state on which our societies depend are also transformed.

Falling somewhat between the two positions on the state's relation to utopia—Bloch and Muñoz on one end, and Ricouer, Wallerstein, and Chan on the other—Lisa Lowe takes a different tack to argue that utopian ideals lie between and mediate the abstractions of freedom and the actual realities of modern life, and that they do so by revising the scope and nature of our social relations. The state continues to overdetermine our social relations, but utopian possibilities can also create new forms of social relations outside of and apart from what is determined by the state even when our lives have to be lived within its cultural and institutional parameters. For Lowe, utopia opens up new opportunities for acting and intervening in the present world because it already exists as a provisional space under capitalist conditions where some forms of agency can still thrive.

> In imagining utopia, we figure another totality with its own system, laws, and beliefs, and in this imagination we perform a fiction of community, whether socialist, democratic, national, or religious, that is another space outside our present history. Socialist utopia figures a world with different social relations: with no labor or private property; with social relations that are humane, not commodified; a society that is just, egalitarian. ("Utopia" 11–12)

Utopia reimagines how the formal and informal rules that govern our conduct can exist in the now insofar as it exists in the space created by our performance of that "fiction of community." Here, utopia not only exists in the future or as something intangible that has yet to happen, but also in the present in small pockets of space and time where new forms of community can be created because the state cannot mediate all forms of social relations. Utopia, in other words, can exist outside of the state, but it has yet to fully escape the state.

However, utopian language is also crucial to the state's project especially as a response to the challenges globalization brings. The state's "grand visions" of the future—in its invocation of the American Dream or a variant thereof—enlivens national sentiments as a desire for utopia in a world that is destabilized by globalization, war, migration, or transnational affiliations such as religion, language, or tribalism. Under these historic conditions, race has a renewed significance, but the language used to describe race can be contradictory and conflicting. As we have already seen, there is a return to ethnocentric, civilizational discourse that ties the state to dominant racial groups. However, race under globalization is also described as being "postrace," and in popular culture language around race shifts between the two modes. Asian and Asian American success now proves that we are now "beyond race," except their success is also perceived as negative and unwanted.

Given these conditions, the way we understand why race continues to matter has to take into account the desire for hope, and how hopes for the future can be used by the state, and also against the state. Racial stereotypes of the Asian/Asian American as threat persist in these descriptions of economic and social progress where utopian narratives about the nation cast race at once as no longer relevant, as well as fixed and natural, because both modes of seeing race prioritize not epistemic concerns about the true meaning of race, but because how we think of race can strengthen state power or destabilize it.[25] Not every individual or every state will attain the utopian goal of accruing ever-increasing wealth and prosperity. The state harnesses the emotions of hope and anxiety to redirect anxieties about upward or downward mobility against the "enemies" of the state identified as the "foreign" competitor states outside its borders and the "foreign" racial minorities inside its borders.

However, the utopian view that we are already postrace is important to the state because it enables the state to present the body politic as whole and stable, and also simultaneously threatened by racial minorities who potentially disrupt the unity and harmony of the nation. Postracial discourse claims that the utopian political reality of color blindness already exists, and this claim is important because it confirms the state's success in managing racial difference. But the notion that race has negative social effects is now turned into a threat to state legitimacy when racial prejudice and inequality is identified as a problem. Appadurai argues that under high globalization, levels of racial violence have actually increased on a global scale rather than diminished because the world state system inadvertently institutes mechanisms that are the prior condition of racial violence. The racial anxiety of globalization is actually a fear of racialized masses, and more specifically, of being "overwhelmed" by those who have historically been considered racial minorities.[26]

Modern state-craft creates the very concepts of "majority" and "minority" that divide the nation; the census organizes its population by creating a symbolic register that counts who belongs and who does not. The categories of majority and minority are now put under stress because of the intensity of transnational global flows of peoples, goods, and money across borders. As such, the abstract categories by which we designate who belongs and who does not are particularly subject to change, either legally or illegally, and even legal means that contribute to the changing of these numbers could be viewed with suspicion.

> As abstractions produced by census techniques and liberal proceduralism, majorities can always be mobilized to think that they are in danger of becoming *minor* (culturally or numerically) and to fear that minorities, conversely, can easily become *major* (through brute accelerated reproduction or subtler legal or political means). These linked fears are a peculiarly modern product of the inner reciprocity of these categories, which also sets the conditions for the fear that they might morph into one another. (83)

Our demographic and legal categories seem to provide order in a time of chaos, but they are fungible categories. Majority groups such as Malays in Malaysia and white people in the US feel threatened by racial minorities whom they outnumber because minorities could—and probably will—outnumber those who see themselves as part of the majority today. Race thus poses a threat to the state because it represents future uncertainties. "Postrace," in other words, is a utopian discourse about the future and the threat racial minorities might pose to the American Dream, and it has the effect of returning us to a political triage that minimizes the racial pain of Others in a zero-sum game.

The presence of minorities generates uncertainties about the national self and culture regardless of whether or not they succeed or fail. If minorities are wealthy and successful (model minorities), they are the ones who enable globalization's excesses and who succeed at the expense of "local" citizens. If minorities are poor and dangerous (terrorists, traitors, thugs), they symbolize the failures of the state to protect its "own" citizens, thus undermining its legitimacy. Consequently, race is still an important term because it can be made to signify and explain how the state needs to be vigilant against potential threats.

Under globalization, race is described or figured in economic terms and in the future perfect tense: they will have become the new masters of the universe. For example, the narrative voice of the Kwan's novels—narrative perspective and narrative voice are often incongruent or sometimes overlap—presents Singapore and the different branches of various wealthy Chinese families in Hong Kong, Malaysia, and China as objects to be viewed by the reader who is simultaneously a tourist, that is, the reader is taught to see the wealthy Asian as an outsider would. In this rarefied atmosphere of unimaginable riches where shopping trips to Paris are a private jet ride away, the reader gawks at the crass ostentation of Asia's millionaires and billionaires who come from old fortunes as well as new money. The new, successful Asian is still mostly unsavory, unlikable, and always on the "outside," regardless of whether their bodies circulate in Asia or Asian America.[27]

These new model minorities also stand in for the model postcolonial nation-states that have grown under globalization and whose own versions of the American Dream reveal how the American Dream, finally, is a synecdoche of world power. From model minorities to model nations, racial tropes are moral terms grounded in a belief in and desire for the exemplariness of the state. The state's "success" unequivocally defines the value of human life, both in the present as well as future tenses. The American Dream and its global variants are narratives of anxiety as well as hope because globalization introduces new wealth but cannot guarantee equal access to that wealth, and race elicits contradictory emotions because it embodies the state's contradictory responses to globalization's changes.[28] Asians stereotyped as model minorities and success stories in Asia and Asian America are a catachresis of powerful stories about globalization, citizenship, race, economic progress, and social uplift. But they can still be a threat because they are minorities who, because of their success, can potentially shift relations of power. Consequently, the model minority of globalization heralds not an end of race as a socially meaningful category of human race, but it does signal how its meanings are changing.

This other kind of "Asian" of the future—the model minority from model nations outside the US—symbolize new threats to the American Dream because they are harbingers of how wealthy Asian countries may pose a threat to US global power. If Asians and Asian Americans are not a threat now, they "might" be in the future to come. New Asian wealth and the size of their economies mean that they may also have the power to affect and destabilize a fragile global economy and/or a fragile US economy. The old figure of the communist has been replaced by the new figure of the capitalist extraordinaire, poised to benefit from the new global economies. This new model minority, however, continues to generate racial anxiety, especially because race now figures our relation to the good life as it might exist in the future.

Chang-rae Lee's fifth novel, *On Such a Full Sea*, revises the model minority that first appeared fifteen years ago in *A Gesture Life*, and the comparison of his novels draw our attention to how the new model minority, while similar to the old one, nonetheless reflects significant changes in contemporary culture's orientation toward race, especially in response to increasing precarity under globalization. If *A Gesture Life* locates the model minority in relation to the past relations of colonialism and WWII, then *On Such a Full Sea* locates the model minority in relation to the future and the state's anxieties about how labor, immigration, and global politics will affect its own power and status in the future.

Set in an indeterminable future where the US and China have experienced total social reorganization and repopulation after an environmental disaster, *On Such a Full Sea* was written and inspired after Lee's visits to Asia, including to the sweatshops of Shenzhen, China, where globalization's effects are on full display. In the novel's diegesis, China and many parts of the US have been rendered dangerous and barely hospitable to human life as a result of overindustrialization, and its technology protects a delicate ecosystem simultaneously sustained by a new social system that is as robust as its natural environment is fragile. Fan, the protagonist, is a descendent of immigrants from what used to be southern China, and whose ancestors were subsequently forced to relocate to the reengineered B-Mor, formerly known as the city of Baltimore, which has been turned into a "facility" where its ethnic Chinese inhabitants live self-contained lives literally sealed off from other cities. The novel begins as a kind of postracial utopia, where racial and class differences at first sight seem to have no negative effects. The state that administers the upper-class "charter" cities and the working-class facilities like B-mor runs with the efficiency of a well-oiled machine, and every citizen knows their place. The economic and social stability of the two spaces—predominantly organized by class but effectively maintaining racial segregation—are contrasted to the "open counties" where anarchy and violence rule.

We soon discover that race has few social effects, only because no one challenges their allotted roles in the postapocalyptic state and the ecosystem it has created. Upward mobility remains highly valued and sought after, but it is available only for the best and brightest children in the facilities. In the postracial world of the novel's diegesis, race seems nonexistent because to disrupt the racial segregation of the charters and the facilities would be to risk another apocalypse. "Social harmony" justifies racial and economic segregation, and they are just as marked in *On Such a Full Sea* as they were in *A Gesture Life*. Order, safety, and wealth of the state come at the expense of the racial minority and others unlucky enough to be excluded from the charters.

If *On Such a Full Sea* depicts a postracial utopia, it is the state's utopia rather than a Blochian utopia of new possibilities. Life in the facilities, we are told, guarantees safety, security, and work, and its education system offers the workers' children the option to "test" up and qualify to move out into the upper-class charter cities. The American Dream in this social system guarantees a minimal middle-class life with the possibility of more for the select few who qualify. In exchange, everyone submits to state control. No one can choose to enter the facilities because they are always at capacity, but anyone can opt to leave for the anarchy and violence of the open counties where individual dictators or others who have managed to accrue sufficient military might rule over small fiefdoms.

Racial anxiety is subsumed under a more generalized anxiety around physical survival and wealth. The unequal relationship between the charter and the facilities is maintained in exchange for the good life that the state promises. In other words, the novel's depiction of a postapocalyptic New World offers a morality tale about globalization, but it is a morality tale told from the perspective of the state. The novel's New World is at once dystopian and utopian, and this contradiction is an effect of narrative perspective: what is dystopian to the state's subjects is utopian to the state.

The dystopian elements of the novel are in fact central to securing the state's vision of utopia where every single body is legible and consequently "useful" to the state. The novel's descriptions of globalization's model worker focalize how the control over human bodies is a displaced form of control over disease, and anything that might destabilize the collective wealth in the state. The bodies of the facilities' workers are surveilled and controlled because they produce food for everyone in their social system. Like the fish they raise, the workers' bodies are objects to be seen, evaluated, and chosen. Bodies are supervised because they pose a possible threat—a condition of the future tense—to the state's delicate balance of economic, natural, and security needs.

In this fantasy tale of biopolitical power, Fan first appears to be its quintessential model minority because she is the state's model worker. She excels at swimming and diving in the fish tanks that supply the elites of the charter cities with their choice protein, and her comfort and ease in the water where she works daily almost seems biologically engineered. Model workers like Fan secure society's health—and consequently its wealth and stability—in a fragile world that has already undergone destruction. However, as the novel continues, the near identical perfections of the bodies on display are cause not for celebration but further cause for anxiety.

The narrative slows down in the descriptions of bodies—animal and human—forces us to see how bodily perfection is the result of fear and anxiety surrounding what exceeds state control: that the human body is frail and susceptible to disease. The body's limits, as it turns out, incites the state to enact even more stringent forms of control over the human body.

> . . . it doesn't matter if our fish are of unsurpassed quality, virtually identical in size and composition, and raised in such a way as to make it almost impossible, if not ridiculous, to try and choose among them. And yet they do, studying the displays like they were buying gemstones, and while there are no jostling scrums like at a special clearance or sale in B-mor, when someone else picks the very one they've identified as theirs, the one they'd determined was destined to best nourish and block any rogue unknittings in their cells, they can't help but get there just a bit earlier the next time. (406)

The perfect fish can be successfully reproduced over and over again, but their perfection serves as an ominous reminder of the precarity of human life. Exemplariness becomes a source of unease, revulsion, and distress, and the uniformity of the bodies symbolize how human excesses have led to ever greater forms of human control over nature, including animal as well as human life.

The passage describes the fish that Fan and her people raise in their "facility," but the fish are also a synecdoche of the workers who produce those fish in the climate-controlled fisheries. The exemplariness of the workers acts as a fetish where human bodies disappear; Fan and her fellow laborers would not be valued, or even allowed to live out their lives, in the charter's facilities if they were not model workers. The exemplariness of the bodies under scrutiny becomes grotesque when narrative time slows down so that we see what that exemplariness actually constitutes.

> Our best B-Mor primes. Look at the eyes, luminous and clear. Even on ice, the scales are tiled tight to one another, the points of the fins unbroken, unclipped. Peel forward the gills and see

the darkest cherry red, as if there's blood hotly pushing through its robust, meaty body. The mouth is closed but not clamped in any grimace, saying instead this with a tranquil set of jaw:

We are in good order.
Take us up.
We are ready to be chosen. (405)

The passage arrests narrative time as the consumer—a word that takes on a monstrous meaning when Fan later narrowly escapes capture by a cannibalistic family—inspects human beings the way they would animals, either dead or alive. The workers in the facilities, and the human beings "kept" in lieu of pet animals in the charters, experience different levels of comfort but similar kinds of surveillance.

If we compare Lee's two novels, Fan shares so much with Hata, the model minority in *A Gesture Life*. It is easy to focus on how the two characters are alike: both are model workers, both are kind and well-liked in their communities, and both eventually leave their communities in a form of self-exile. Hata leaves his town as a kind of recompense to his adopted daughter, and Fan leaves the facilities and the charters to continue her search for her "disappeared" lover. Both characters leave the safety and security the state provides in order to keep the state intact. Their exiles at the denouement of both plot resolutions have as their goal the social harmony of the body politic rather than true justice for the victims of social violence.

But *On Such a Full Sea* shares a more important overlap with *A Gesture Life*, and also with the other novels examined in this book: all these novels retain some measure of unreliability throughout, especially with regard to the raced subjects central to their narrative worlds. The raced subjects surprise us in these ethnic novels, not merely because they destabilize popular racial stereotypes or beliefs about race. Narrative surprises such as this do the valuable work of revealing how minorities cannot be reduced to typology. But the element of unreliability in these novels does more than just that. Unreliability in these novels produce as a narrative effect the very experience of racial anxiety. What do we see when we see a racial subject? And when can we trust what we see? The readers are forced into an uneasiness that they may not want, but the questions raised in the process of reading these novels are symptomatic of broader historical and cultural trends, especially as the state responds to globalization's challenges. Who is the stranger on our shores?

In *A Gesture Life*, we discover that Hata, the model minority protagonist, is not who he seems to be even to himself, while in *On Such a Full Sea*, we discover that we cannot trust our own judgment as to who is the real model minority in the novel. To our surprise, the true model minority in *On Such a Full Sea* is not Fan but the unknown, omniscient narrator whose narrative perspective focalizes the effects the state has on Fan's journey through the facilities, the open counties, and the charters. *On Such a Full Sea* rewrites John Bunyan's *Pilgrim's Progress* as a journey of globalization's physical and moral challenges, but unlike the *Pilgrim's Progress*, the narrator displaces Fan as the moral center of the novel. Fan turns out to be not the model minority but the transgressor in this tale; she suffers precisely because she rejects the role assigned to her. Had she stayed in the facilities after Reg was disappeared, she would not have risked injury, multiple kidnappings, near rapes, and even possible death.

And while the narrator sympathizes with Fan throughout the novel, he or she nonetheless describes the challenges Fan faces in her journeys as opportunities to return to the securities provided by the state-system. The narrator's apparent sympathy for Fan's quiet revolt is wistful and even hopeful, but the voice dismisses as romantic fantasy any hope of utopian change.

> B-mor works because we work, our sense of purpose driving us that extra measure, that extra hour, and then, of course, the knowledge of what's out in the counties and what it used to be like here before the originals landed refueling us whenever we flag. . . . There are times we need to remind everyone of those conditions, especially people like Fan's boosters who even now would be *so misguided* as to believe they can follow her example and simply step outside the gates and embark on some journey that will write itself on our houses and walls, like the murals our originals found splashed all over the deserted neighborhoods. . . . For aren't all such murals as bounteous in their hopes as in their scale? Aren't they expressions of the grandest wishes, which by definition will never come true? (14–15, emphasis mine)

The omniscient narrator is the quintessential model minority not merely because he or she is the model worker, but because he or she willingly submits to state ideology. Like Hata, the narrator rewrites notions of morality not as ethical obligation to another human being, but as traits of self-control ("because we work") and self-discipline ("our sense of purpose") that are themselves part of the American Dream as a narrative of individual uplift. The narrator may sympathize with Fan's hope to find Reg, but ultimately recognizes her goals are impossible: "Aren't they the expressions of the grandest wishes, which by definition will never come true?" The moral worth of individual actions cannot exist outside and apart from the moral goals of the state.

If Hata was an unreflective model minority who never fully understood his own commitments, the narrator represents the new model minorities of *On Such a Full Sea* who are now as fully committed to the state's safeguarding of its own interests as their own. Their interests as individuals cannot be untangled from the state's own interests precisely because they see like the state, and seem unaware that they do so. Anxiety about the future—and the losses that could be incurred—is a crucial part of the utopian project of the state, and as individuals adopt these anxieties, they also adopt the state's views and interests.

At the beginning of the novel, Fan is recognizable as the quintessential model minority, but by the end of the novel, she disappears because she ceases to be legible or profitable to the state project. The significance of bodies—what they look like, what they are capable of, and what they mean in social life—are important to both *A Gesture Life* and *On Such a Full Sea*, but in both novels, Fan's and Hata's lives fall out of narration when they cease to be useful, that is, when they stop being "model minorities." The endings of both novels are wistful, hopeful, and even celebrate the moment when they step outside of the state's view of exemplariness. But both novels also leave the state intact by ejecting the model minority who refuses to remain exemplary: "You need not come back for us" (*Full Sea* 352).

Under globalization, race is seen in relation to the future and not only the past, and it appears as a contradiction: it is obsolete because we are already postrace, but it is also a present threat because global migration could potentially change majorities into minorities. Under globalization, the American Dream as a form of utopian nationalist ideology facilitates cultural inclusion but it also produces a general, prevailing anxiety that facilitates a confusion of state interests for individual interests. The model minority of globalization is incorporated into the national imaginary not only to secure the cohesion of the state, but also state strength on a global level.

The American Dream and its global variants mobilize postrace discourse as an example of the state's strength, and in the process, concatenates fears around racial difference to the state's own goals. How the state invokes moral language either explicitly (racial stereotypes) or implicitly (state strength) to organize social life matters not only within the nation but also as part of global politics because they produce a culture of anxiety. Novels such as *On Such a Full Sea* remind us that the state's use of utopian narratives subjects racial minorities to the state's own moral projects—projects that have as their goal not individual happiness and well-being, but moral projects that secure the state's own power in the face of new global relations and often unstable economic realities.

Epilogue

The global life of racial tropes, surprisingly, turns out to be a story about the state. Far from being merely a representational regime, common stereotypes used to describe race reveal racial anxiety to be the condition of being a subject of the state under globalization. The state's anxieties about its relative position in the world causes it to keep all subjects, but especially racial subjects, under moral surveillance. *The State of Race* consequently locates the social meaning of race in a nexus of language about "good" or "bad," "moral" or "immoral," and "desirable" or "undesirable" behaviors that when taken together, describe the good life as the state defines it.

Fiction helps us see that the state has material and cultural effects on our lives because it mobilizes the language of ethics. The cultural histories of the state first brought to the forefront the political questions that *The State of Race* asks in its chapters. But it is the fiction—rather than history or politics—that most clearly directs our attention to the emotional responses racial tropes can engender. Fiction documents and embodies as text how racial subjects experience anxiety when the state views them with suspicion, and also with absolute certainty that it has the right to monitor racial behavior for the common good. As the novels examined in the book demonstrate, racial anxiety is produced out of the social expectations placed on minor subjects who find themselves represented as threat, or possible future threats, in the eyes of the state. Fiction is the canary in the coal mine when it points us to how the return of civilizational discourse threatens our collective imaginaries in the US, and also in Asia. It also points us to how we share a cultural imaginary grounded on racial anxiety because the state developed and expanded on a global scale in the twentieth century.

Literature's most important contribution—as far as *The State of Race* is concerned, at least—lies in its disruptions of racist discourse and imagery embedded in either popular culture, or in the myths about the state and the roles it plays today. Racist imageries embody ways of feeling and thinking that reflect a view of the world belonging not necessarily to individuals, but to the state. But if we come to the conclusion that our good is bound up with the state's own welfare, we risk surrendering our ability to define ethics and culture for ourselves. And to adumbrate human life and freedom to the state's own interests is a surrender of which we should be suspicious. As Han's novel forces its readers to ask, who is the fool? The answer is not that some are fools and others are not. In their uses of unreliability, the novels treated in the book cause us to wonder with some discomfort if we could all be willing fools.

If we are fools, perhaps it is because our hopes, and not only our anxieties, for the good life continue to revolve around the state and its abilities to guarantee wealth and prosperity in the age of globalization. Precolonial and even most of the divergences in the histories of Malaysia and the US throughout the twentieth-century might predispose us to believe that the two different countries are on separate trajectories with little to unite them. But the otherwise very different states are both motivated to take similar attitudes toward issues around security, wealth, and upward mobility, and these shared motivations have led them to use very similar languages to justify why race continues to matter.

The problems that globalization poses to a world superpower like the US and to a smaller, weaker state like Malaysia are the same challenges that globalization poses to other states: economic inequality, diminishing and limited natural resources, climate change, migration, and even the threat of war. This list of shared challenges illustrates how states around the world are confronted with the same problems that lead the US and Malaysia to take antagonistic or resentful stances toward those they consider "outsiders." No state remains unaffected by the concerns of other states. These are not always new challenges, but they have intensified in recent years. What these states share is also an anxiety directed at racial minorities, possibly of a magnitude that might increase rather than decrease. The desire to secure state sovereignty in the face of global challenges is far too often accompanied by a fear of the Other.

Literature causes us to pause, however, because even if it diagnoses how racial anxiety is now symptomatic of shared global conditions, its interventions can obscure as much as they help us see global connections. To place novels taken from the different national canons alongside one another can sometimes seem reductive because fiction has been assumed to reflect, celebrate, or critique the specific histories and cultures out of which they have emerged. But this book does not argue that novels in different national or linguistic traditions are "the same." Art and creative works read within national canons are singular and unique, and even when individual literary works share certain features they retain a trace of difference.

Instead, comparison in this book advances the possibility that minor literatures share more than we first suspect because we all participate in a global culture not necessarily of our own choosing. This global culture is fluid and adaptable across history and geography, but it issues from the state as a primary institution that regulates social life everywhere. And because the state continues to play an overdetermined role in mediating human and institutional exchanges across borders, it cannot but help shape our cultural imaginaries.

And because the minor literatures in *The State of Race* are also politically engaged art, they return our attention to the state. The novels' use of similar racial tropes reveal a shared sensitivity to the state's use of racial language and its influence over our visions of the good life, and hopes for the future. The literary examples included in this book show us that our societies, unconsciously or otherwise, adopt the state's view of things because we too often share in the state's anxieties about its power and position. State-centered logic would have us believe that individuals cannot flourish if the polis suffers because individual good is tied to the larger social good as the state defines it. We need to recognize, however, that the state's use of moral language can ask racial subjects to sacrifice either their freedoms or well-being to guarantee the wholeness of the state in its drive toward more and ever greater power. Nationalism is particularly insidious when it is presented as an ethical or moral good. *The State of Race* posits that the demands on racial subjects to always be fully legible—and always good—are neither isolated to one culture nor exceptional to one state, but are built into the ideologies and structures of the modern nation-state as it exists in the world.

Notes

Introduction

1. During the final stages of the writing of this book, Najib Razak and the parties in his coalition that have been in power since national independence were voted out, to the surprise even of the opposition parties. While I share in the early euphoria of the unexpected and rapid political changes that have taken place in Malaysia's fourteenth General Elections in 2018, I believe that the state will continue to be strengthened even after the change of government. Race relations in the country may improve, and the worst of racist language in political discourse may be minimized. I certainly hope that a book like this one will become irrelevant in the future. But the fundamental interrelation of state machinery and racial formation shows little evidence of becoming decoupled, at least at the time of publication.

2. In this limited study, I am unable to catalog all racial tropes, and instead I offer readings of a few of the more ubiquitous ones that appear in both sites of comparison. In this limited study, I am unable to catalog all racial tropes, and instead offer readings of the more common ones that appear in both sites of comparison. These racial tropes include recognizable stereotypes such as the model minority or the terrorist spy, as well as broader cultural narratives such as exceptionalism, civilizational difference, and the American Dream or its global variants of culturalist-nationalist concepts that influence our ideas about race and nation.

3. I want to also note here that the argument of *The State of Race* considers similarity to be a feature of racial thinking rather than of the novels in which they appear. The novels themselves have a much more complex relation to racial representation, as the chapters themselves elucidate. Furthermore, while language has been central to the making of colonial subjects, the process of subject formation may not always be strictly limited by language itself. For example, David Pomfret's comparison of British and French colonial history indicates overlaps in social conditions not necessarily demarcated by language or empire. Transnational events in history may have broader implications than previously thought.

4. The Martinique philosopher Frantz Fanon's *Wretched of the World*, published in French in 1961 and in English two years later, offers a trenchant analysis of how postcolonial elites take on the mantle of former colonizers, and I hope to extend this analysis in my focus on postcolonial states under globalization, especially as they are manifested in lesser-known postcolonial states outside of Africa, East Asia, and South Asia.

5. James C. Scott's seminal work on the modern state, *Seeing Like a State: How Certain Schemes to Improve the Human Condition Have Failed*, lists race as part of what the state tracks in its project of creating and governing its citizens, but the focus of the book does not track this in a sustained way.

6. *The State of Race* does not represent national canons and their linguistic diversities. Malaysian literature includes literature in Malay, English, Mandarin, Tamil, and to a lesser degree, in one of the fourteen languages of the *Orang Asal* or indigenous communities. Moreover, Malaysian literature written in Mandarin, while an important area within Malaysian literary studies, is not on its own representative of "Chineseness" in Malaysia, which also includes groups from other Sinitic languages such as Hokkien, Cantonese, Hakka, and Teochew, among others. Finally, Malaysian fiction address a wide variety of themes including the divide between the urban and the rural, local spiritual cosmologies, traditional mythologies, gender difference, traditional customs, modernity and alienation, and so on.

7. For reasons of space, this book does not address Anglophone world writing in detail, but recent novels in that tradition could also be read under the theoretical aims that *The State of Race* proposes.

8. In her essay "Between Nationalism and Transnationalism," Ien Ang makes the pointed and necessary observation that "multiculturalism" in Southeast Asia and the putative West is not always the same, and for that very reason we need to pay closer attention to how racial discourse operates in different national contexts. While I cannot adequately engage with her comparison of Australia and Malaysia here, Ang's observation that Australia insists on "absolute sameness" in their expectance of assimilation while Malaysia insists on "absolute difference" in its approach to multiculturalism exemplifies how racial thought is often reduced to either strict similarity or difference. This conversation requires more space than I have, and I raise this point only to suggest that instead of adopting the state's default position on race that tends to understand race only in terms of either similarity or difference, we need comparative methodologies that pay greater attention to the fluidity and dynamics of similarity and difference in cultural life.

9. Jade Ferguson pointed me to this volume of essays very early on in the project, before I fully understood the implications of the study.

10. Prasenjit Duara draws on the Marxist historian Giovanni Arrighi's work on the world state system to argue that state legitimacy continues to be a problem not only because it is a relatively late social construction often set in opposition to primordial ties such as blood, religion, and language, but also because the world state system is based on an endless competition for resources and power. The world

state system founded on the Westphalian model of the interstate system established in the mid-seventeenth century is an inherently competitive system where its various members jostle for dominance.

11. Following Ann Stoler and others, *The State of Race* posits that national independence creates the very conditions for racial thinking because while the former colonies may have achieved political freedom in the second half of the twentieth century, decolonization led to greater global economic dependence on the world state system itself.

12. When the British installed one candidate for the throne as sultan over another, they ignored Malays royal customs and ceremonies, and the rest of the court would have thought the installation an illegitimate farce (Chai 6).

13. The first resident, J. W. W. Birch disregarded Malay customs, alienated of local chiefs, appropriated indigenous taxation systems, attempted to abolish debt-slavery, and imposed British penal codes; these acts finally led to a Malay insurrection, and he was speared to death on Nov 2, 1875, while taking a bath in the river (Chai 11).

14. William Roff points out that the British conceived of themselves as holding the balance between Malaya's plural communities, a variation of the white man's burden (106).

15. Much of Malay customary law in the nineteenth century was derived from the sixteenth-century Malacca Code based on the *Hukum Shera* (religious law), *Hukum Akl* (principles of natural justice), *Hukum Faal* (principles of right conduct), and the *Hukum Adat* (custom and customary law); but myths and legends from and about this period still play an important role in Malay literature (Roff 6).

16. The Malay Annals (*Sejarah Melayu*) expound the divine responsibility and authority of the Malay rulers, and the mythical genealogy of the kingdom's sultans are traced back to Raja Iskandar Zulkarnain, that is, Alexander the Great (Andaya 2001, 44). Also see Khoo Kay Khim (1991), chapter 1, for an overview of the royal and aristocratic structures of the Malaccan sultanate.

17. According to T. N. Harper, the rulers of Johore and Selangor were awarded the titles of "Sultan" by Queen Victoria in exchange for signing treaties with the British in 1885 and 1887.

18. In recent years, the debate over who is or is not a Malay has resurfaced, but it is beyond the scope of this summary to offer an extended overview of these debates. See for example news reports such as http://www.malaysia-today.net/constitutionally-mamak-are-not-malays/ and http://www.freemalaysiatoday.com/category/nation/2017/07/21/bumi-status-for-indian-muslims-najib-accused-of-ignorance/; accessed September 30, 2017. I include these recent examples as illustrations of how race is a function of state power.

19. In the 1920s and 1930s, Muslims of Arab origin first resisted identification as Malays but eventually capitulated (Nagata 104).

20. Minangkabau custom differs from other Malay customs; for example, they are a matrilineal community.

21. Victor Purcell also tells a story of how Munshi Abdullah during a river trip up to a Chinese village in Pahang, arrived to find "hundreds of Malays and Chinese, armed to teeth, awaiting him on the bank. [. . .] The Chinese at Kampong China were Hakkas and they intermarried with Malay women or Balinese slaves [. . .]" (7). These Chinese remained "Chinese," and the two communities seemed to have cooperated amicably enough.

22. However, foreigners who marry Malays, especially Malay women, are not always able to obtain permanent resident status or citizenship as a result of stringent and gender-biased immigration laws.

23. The Kapitan mediated disputes, but he did not always succeed in quelling the different factions. For example, requests for help from the contending Malay elites fueled the dispute between the Ghee Hin and Hai San secret societies in the Larut tin mines.

24. Similarly, *South East Asia Under Japanese Occupation*, a collection of essays edited by Alfred McCoy in 1980, presents new research on how the Japanese enabled political elites to continue accumulating political power in ways that helped entrench them in positions of power during decolonization.

25. However, Yoji Akashi argues that the Japanese encouraged Malay women to become educated and politically active. The Indian community in Malaya also became more politically active during this time and this momentum was carried over into postwar labor and trade movements (62).

26. Indian and Arab communities were brought to Southeast Asia because of trade, and they settled in the coastal areas of the region as early as the fifteenth century. Religion and trade were interlinked for the native Indonesian and Arab communities, especially with the founding of Sarekat Islam (Islamic Association) in 1912: "While much of the rhetoric of the emergent Arab identity turned on Islam, the driving force at this time was their business interest. Arab and native leaders drew closer through the organizations in the name of Islam that were established in the face of Chinese competition; typically, these were educational institutions" (Mandal 166). Religion and trade drew the two ethnic communities—Arab and Malay—into public life together in ways that the Chinese community could never enter. In other parts of Southeast Asia, Chinese immigrants were racialized—in similar but sometimes different ways—based on their economic participation in their adopted homelands. These processes caused Anthony Reid to pronounce of Southeast Asian social formation that "Ethnicity was probably as much a consequence of entrepreneurial minority status as its cause" (2: 126). In other words, identification with a particular "race" as we have come to understand it today was in part created out of the economic activities of different communities that previously identified with other, ties stronger than race.

27. Few Malays could read the Quran because they did not know Arabic, and the "nationalization" of religious activity started to take place around the mid-twentieth century (Peletz 61).

28. Karen Kurotsuchi Inkelas (2006) posits that the myth of the model minority is due in large part to post-1965 changes in immigration law where preferences

were given to professionally trained immigrants. Immigrants with higher education and training are more likely to influence their children to be high achievers in schools (13). While this conjecture might explain high-achieving Asian American students, it does not completely explain the model minority myth that David Palumbo-Liu identifies as emerging in 1966, in reference to Japanese Americans (*Asian/American* 174).

29. In this context, "Asian" symbolizes supposedly primordial values and traits that are desirable, but "Asia" in the early twentieth century is also portrayed as that which is decayed and in need of revitalization through American ideals and systems. At the same time, Asian immigrants were seen to bring with them the capital needed to revive the stagnant US economy. State and popular narratives then had to explain and downplay Asian success in order to preserve narratives of US liberalism and progress. The construction of "Asia" in the US at this time referred mostly to East Asia, particularly Japan and China even if both countries were assigned different kinds of racial qualities.

30. Individual agency is possible and necessary, but they can take new forms of cultural resistance that are outside of the bounds of the state. For example, see Marcela Fuentes's work on transnational activism mediated by changes in digital media.

31. See also Appadurai, page 145.

32. I want to be careful to note here that not all ethnic literatures are national allegories. Some of the novels I have chosen to interpret, for example, Shaz Johar's *Sanctuaria*, are deliberately allegorical, but the others are not. Rather, I am interested in how racial language itself reflects the state's interests, and the form of the ethnic novel in general is more wide-ranging than I am able to devote attention to in this book.

33. Each novel may teach us about Malaysian or Asian American cultural formations and increase our understanding of their literary traditions, but this book does not claim to provide full representation of either canon.

34. Other important critiques in the fields of comparative literature and cultural studies include a linguistic approach that destabilizes the nation-state and the institutions it develops in order to secure national identity and culture. Shu-mei Shih's notion of the Sinophone has played an especially large role in reconfiguring the field of Chinese Studies. Her essay "Does Language Determine Identity?" addresses the Malaysian case most directly, and offers a trenchant overview of how Chinese Malaysians are caught in the middle of national and transnational political pressures after the rise of Chinese global power.

35. Richard Kim's *The Martyred* might have made a more obvious pairing because it was published closer to Han's novel, but I chose instead to focus on Lee's more recent novel to show first that racial minorities have continued to feel the pressures of performing moral goodness even after the Cold War. But second, and more importantly, Lee's deft depiction of the model minority as an unreliable narrator showcases the narrative effect of racial anxiety much more clearly. Readers interested in Kim's novel should instead turn to Josephine Park's attentive analysis

of *The Martyred*, which draws our attention to how the novel takes the form of a "moral struggle" (49), and identifies its cultural politics as arising out of necessity in response to Cold War alliance politics between Korea and the US. In Kim's novel, Christianity plays a much larger role in the language of morality and citizenship in ways that are important but to devote space to that theme would have pushed the scope of this book beyond its current focus and configuration.

36. The arbitrary threat of exclusion is not random; rather, it is arbitrary because it is global or all-encompassing.

37. A single book study cannot successfully represent all racial groups or languages. In my choice of literary examples, I decided to examine novels from a variety of racial groups including authors who are Korean American (Chang-rae Lee), Chinese American (Gish Jen), Malay Malaysian (Shaz Johar), and Indian Malaysian (Brian Gomez). Han Suyin might be described to be a more "cosmopolitan" kind of Chinese, but her novel remains one of the best-known novels written on Malaysia about the communist insurgence during the period itself. Mahua literature receives broader attention within Sinophone studies especially in the US, and I chose instead to highlight other Malaysian novels that remain relatively understudied outside Malaysia. Unfortunately, literature from the Indian Malaysian community written in Tamil or other South Asian languages remain inaccessible to me for reasons of linguistic incompetence, and I chose instead to include a novel written in English by an author of Tamil descent.

38. In a manuscript about the literary and cultural conjunctions between Asia and Asian America, Lee is one of the most acclaimed living Asian American writers who keeps the US and Asia in his vision simultaneously. Novels such as Ruth Ozeki's *Tale of a Time Being*, Catherine Chung's *Forgotten Country*, or Preeta Samarasan's *Evening Is the Day*, and memoirs such as Shirley Lim's *Among the White Moon Faces* could have added to the richness of this study if not for the constraints of space.

Chapter 1

1. I do not mean to argue that literature can never contribute to our well-being, or that the relationship between literature and ethics is always suspect. For one example of how literature and philosophical ethics can be thought of together in productive ways, see Timothy O'Leary's essay, "Foucault, Dewey, and the Experience of Literature."

2. Asian Americans do not benefit from affirmative action policies but because so much of race relations in the US are read through the rubric of black-white relations, the racialization of Asian Americans is related to, even if it is independent from, the claims of rights that are more usually associated with groups such as African Americans or American Indians (De Genova 8). Work such as *Racial Transformations: Latinos and Asians Remaking the United States* emerging from comparative race studies

also provide new ways for talking about racial formations across different contexts where critical foci fall on the ways in which social categories such as "Latino" and "Asian" have been produced historically in the US.

3. David Palumbo-Liu notes in *Asian/American* that the state's power to exclude is itself constitutive of the state's powers.

4. Rey Chow prioritizes the term *ethnic* and its association with myth making and forms of socialization, and also to avoid the biologism that taints "race." As her book focuses on "Chineseness" where "ethnic" can be more expansive and opens up inclusion to those who identify as "Chinese" by way of linguistic identity, this term functions in her schema. However, I have taken the opposite approach and use "race" because the states in the contexts that I have chosen to focus on in this book—the US and Malaysia—continue to use the term *race*, and racial groups are still defined by biology or phenotype, moral values, and religion. Furthermore, Chow reads the systemic function of racism as different from scapegoating (15), while I read scapegoating as an important part of how society holds itself together.

5. See pages 152–67 of *Residues of Justice* for more on the cognitive affinities between capitalism and humanitarianism in the US in the nineteenth century.

6. The term only first appeared in a *New York Times Magazine* article published in 1966, and was then used retroactively. Asian Americans were held up as examples that minorities could excel without the help of the state, thus proving that the poverty African Americans experienced was not a result of institutional racism (Palumbo-Liu *Asian/American* 172). However, Hsu's history of immigration laws also demonstrate that the US practiced selective immigration with Asian immigrants and allowed only the most highly educated or successful professionals to enter the US, thus creating disproportionately well-educated or driven Asian immigrant community.

7. Benedict Anderson's seminal work on early nationalism, *Imagined Communities*, argues that nationalism was created as a result of print capitalism where the market produced a shared sense of belonging where none existed before. The act of reading provided a material dimension to the experience of interpellation in the nationalist imaginary, but this process of interpellation also requires moral justification. Control over the symbolic "we" continues to be important to nation-states under late capitalism, where religion and its deployment of moral or ethical language provides one of the more powerful forms of national identity especially in the cases of the US and Malaysia.

8. The Derridean notion of the supplement could work here as well, but it seems less central to the novel.

9. These histories become flattened out and made the same in the model minority where all Asian Americans are the same, regardless of the economic and political histories behind their communities' immigration to the United States.

10. Simultaneously, as Colleen Lye demonstrates in *America's Asia: Racial Form and American Literature, 1893–1945*, the racialization of Asia depended on U.S. national identity and U.S. relations with the nation-state in question.

11. For Omi and Winant, "race" does not refer to phenotypical difference but to how one is treated because of those differences (1986, 55).

Chapter 2

1. See Boon Kheng Cheah's "The Communist Insurgency in Malaysia" for an explanation of the controversy around the start of the war. Both the British and the communists accuse the other of beginning the war (135).

2. Malaya became "Malaysia" in 1963 and expanded from Peninsular to include the states of Sabah and Sarawak, but not Singapore.

3. "Screening of the New Village Suspended," Yiswaree Palansamy, July 28, 2013. http://www.themalaysianinsider.com/malaysia/article/screening-of-the-new-village-suspended; accessed August 16, 2013.

4. Kek Huat Lau's documentary, "Absent without Leave," was deliberately filmed without overt attention to political history and took a personal tone but was nonetheless banned from being shown in Malaysia in March 2017.

5. Because I read this novel as being a modern, feminist Malay novel, I will not develop my reading of it here in this chapter, which is primarily focused on racial stereotypes. However, I include this novel as an example because it provides a distinct counterpoint to other novels more focused on racial divide influenced by the colonial state's on understanding of race.

6. Most communists were Chinese, but there were significant numbers of Malay communist soldiers and leaders.

7. Racial politics and state censorship control and direct the kinds of literature and films that can be published or screened in Malaysia, and they define which films or books are "national" films or literature. Not all fiction is coopted by the state, but they are also not recognized as "national literature." Nami Cob Nobbler's *Main Kotor* and Shaz Johar's *Sancturia* are two recent examples of independent Malay fiction that parodies the state's use of racial language in order to critique it.

8. *Samfoo* literally means "shirt and pants" in Cantonese, and sometimes both the top and bottom were cut from the same fabric.

9. Andrew Wilford offers a brief account of how the different races were affected by the Japanese occupation, especially the lesser known history of how Tamils were treated by the Japanese (23).

10. The perpetrators of the Batang Kali massacre were never brought to justice, for example.

11. This characterization of colonial powers as "good" or "bad" is self-serving as Anne Stoler's and Karen Strassler's essay on Javanese oral histories of Dutch and Japanese colonialism demonstrates. The narrative of "good" or "bad" colonialism, they argue, scripts Javanese WWII survivors into the (nationalist) tale of deprivation and heroism, thus enabling both the Dutch and the Javanese to reframe their wartime

experiences into narratives of agency. Colonialism was remembered as "benign," because it sustained the narrative the interviewees wanted to tell in present-day Java.

12. The British Military Administration (BMA) after the Japanese surrender was remarkable for its inflation, corruption, and a very active black market.

13. The different racial groups had different early responses to Japan's invasion. Chinese in Malaya already harbored anti-Japanese sentiments prior to the Japanese Occupation of Malaya because they were aware of how the Japanese had treated the Chinese during the second Sino-Japanese War. Malay collaborators, however, guided the Japanese in Malaya during the early part of the invasion because they were promised independence from the British. Under the Japanese, Malay collaborators displaced the Malay aristocracy and native elites who had worked closely with the British and became the new ruling native elites. The early Malay collaborators who came into power under the Japanese were from the Kesatuan Melayu Muda (KMM) and they were resented and feared not only by the Chinese, but also other Malays, especially the aristocracy, because these new Malay elites took on the responsibility of arresting and interrogating both suspected communist members as well as the old cohort of Malay elites who did not cooperate with the Japanese (Cheah 104).

14. The Malayan Communist Party (MCP) and the MPAJA were not the only resistance groups in Malaya, but they played the largest role. However, not all who called themselves communist were truly communist either. Bandits, vindictive locals, and Kuomintang soldiers sometimes passed themselves off as communist as well.

15. Chin Peng was recognized for his distinguished service during WWII with an Order of the British Empire (OBE), and ironically, was notified of his honors immediately after the communists unintentionally assassinated Lai Te, the former head of the CPM who was also a spy for Britain (Chin 191).

16. When the British returned to Malaya after WWII, they returned as "heroes" and the natives who were left behind in the war were examined for their conduct and loyalties during the war in what P. G. Lim, a prominent Chinese Malayan lawyer of the time, calls "hypocritical." She maintains that many locals remained silent for fear of being branded traitors or communists (119).

17. While the communists mainly consisted of Chinese Malayans, they also included Malays and Malay leaders in the central committee.

18. See other instances when they received reports of other communist military actions on pages 227 and 239.

19. Even today, politicians can be hauled into court for having supported communists in the past: http://www.themalaysianinsider.com/malaysia/article/news-on-mat-sabu-pro-communist-based-on-video-reporter-tells-court; accessed September 22, 2014.

20. Today, relatives of those killed in the Batang Kali massacre continue to press the UK for justice. "Relatives of Malaysians Killed by British Troops in the Batang Kali Massacre Vow to Take Their Fight to the Supreme Court." http://www.independent.co.uk/news/uk/home-news/relatives-of-malaysians-killed-by-british-

troops-in-the-batang-kali-massacre-vow-to-take-their-fight-to-the-supreme-court-9202912.html; accessed March 20, 2014. 21. For all intents and purposes, each platoon worked independently of the others while they awaited communications through the communists' courier network.

22. This does not excuse the brutality of communist soldiers, but rather recognizes the measures to which the communists had to resort to in order to survive harrowing and uncertain conditions. Communists were portrayed as the embodiment of evil rather than as human beings, and recovering these histories is as much about recognizing their humanity as it is about understanding how nationalist culture works the way it does today.

23. The lack of accurate historical documentation of the communist movement and Communist Party means that an important area of national history has been lost, and for this, we can thank the British colonial government. Colonial files from this period have been destroyed or are still kept secret today, for example, the Batang Kali massacre (Chin 243).

24. This is remarkable given the depth of Chinese anger and resentment against the Japanese who massacred the Chinese by the tens of thousands.

25. Yong also details on pages 642–45 the involvement of Indonesian and Malay leaders and members of the Communist Party in Malaya.

26. Many of the early anarcho-communists who arrived to Malaya after WWI, and were deported back to China for their views and political activities; the British continued to deport communists and suspected communists as a form of social control post-WWII.

27. The MCP was never successful at broadening their support and movement to the Malay community even if some of their key leaders were Malay. The party was defending Chinese interests rather than Malayan interests, but this, perhaps, was due to how closely Malays identified nationalism with communalism (Short 1083, 1088).

28. The CPM was disbanded on December, 2, 1989, and the Socialist Party of Malaysia, or Parti Sosialis Malaysia (PSM), faced a difficult time registering as an official party because most laws set in place during the emergency have not been lifted or amended. Consequently, the Malaysian government continues to possess the authority to arrest and detain people without trial.

29. Indian Malaysians are subject to similar rhetoric, to "balik India," but as this chapter focuses on the demonization of communists in Malaysia who were seen as Chinese, this section focuses primarily on Malay-Chinese tensions. The anthropologist Andrew Willford provides a compelling account of contemporary resentments in the Indian Malaysian community, especially among those whose families and ancestors have long worked in the plantation system.

30. Among other "benign" colonial policies that have been continued by the postcolonial state are Britain's emergency laws that allow for detention without trial, which reappeared first as the Internal Security Act (ISA) and now the Security Offences (Special Measures) Act 2012 (SOSMA).

31. Judith Strauch puts the number of villagers resettled as one in four Chinese, and one in ten Malayans.

32. Sir Henry Gurney envisioned these camps as a form of "protection" for the Chinese Malayan peasantry (Barber 67), but even the staunchly patriotic Barber records that the implementation of Gurney's vision was a form of incarceration and punishment (105).

33. Fiona Lee offers a nuanced reading of the novel where she reads literature as a "translation" of history, and where the narrator is a translator who is under suspicion because the act of translation contains the possibility of betrayal. This essay, on the other hand, focuses instead on the novel as satire and how satire focuses our attention on the moral dimension of the raced subject, and how the raced subject cannot escape policing, not even when they perform exemplarity.

34. Ironically, it was Chinese Malayans' commitments to transnational political struggles that allowed them to later argue for their right to belong to the new national polity.

35. Barbara and Leonard Andaya estimate the number of Chinese massacred during this time to fall between 5,000 and 25,000. See also T. N. Harper, page 88. Akashi puts this figure at "tens of thousands" (67), while Cheah puts this figure "between 6,000 and 40,000" (80).

36. Aihwa Ong points out that ethnicity often influences immigration policies in contemporary Southeast Asia. For example, the aftermath of the Indochina war brought ethnic Chinese, Vietnamese, Cambodians, and Laotian refugees to the shores of Malaysia, but they were rejected for asylum because that could have led to eventual citizenship. However, Malaysia did accept Cham refugees from Cambodia whom they considered to be a part of the Malay-Muslim diaspora (220). Fernando Zialcita also points out that during the Balkan Wars in the 1990s, Malaysia offered asylum to Bosnians because they were part of the Islamic *umma* (21). In these two cases, religious affiliation trumps regional associations, mostly because ethnic identity continues to be a source of anxiety within the national body.

37. This identification is due in part to British efforts to steer Malay politics away from Islamicization. In order to counter this movement toward Islam at the unifying principle during this period, as Anthony Milner argues, the British encouraged a mythmaking based especially on the Malaccan Sultanate—itself a result of transnational flows—from which the term *Malay* was derived: "Valorizing the pre-colonial sultanates, the origins and ceremonies of which were as much Hindu-Buddhist as Islamic, seems to have been one aspect of a strategy of promoting Malay 'tradition' as a bulwark against what the British saw as the expansion of 'pan-Islamic' influence among the Malays. The British, at the same time, probably also expected the study of pre-colonial sultanate history would be to the ideological benefit of their royal 'allies'" (Andaya 273).

38. This is set against the colonial myth of the "lazy Malay." This narrative is taken up and perpetuated by Malay politicians as a justification for Malay preferential treatment.

39. Preeta Samarasan's, Rani Manicka's, and K. S. Maniam's fictions offer beguiling examples of how Indian Malaysians are racialized. K. S. Maniam's short story, "Kling," is a heart-rending piece on the hypersexualization of Indian women in particular.

40. See also Anthony Short's *In Pursuit of Mountain Rats* and Anton Gill's *The Journey Back from Hell*.

41. Ironically, the work of independent, Malay filmmakers such as Amir Muhammad and Fahmi Reza provide a fuller picture of race relations during the communist period ("Filling in the Gaps" 255–57).

42. In both the novel and Barber's account, General Templer was fond of sticking his feet into the bottom drawer of his desk (Barber 153).

43. A. J. Stockwell argues that in their anxiety to protect Malay rights in a fight that was seen as a zero-sum game vis-à-vis other racial groups, the United Malays National Organization (UMNO) often collaborated with the British to oppose radical elements within the Malay community (481). But the history of Malay politics within the Malay community is beyond the scope of this book.

44. Especially in countries that have a history of arresting or imprisoning publishers, booksellers, artists, and writers, such as China, Hong Kong, and Malaysia.

Chapter 3

1. *Pak* is used informally to address older men in a respectful manner.

2. A *surau* can be described as a small building for prayer that provides the same functions as a mosque. Additionally, Malays are always assumed to be Muslim in Malaysia, as conversion out of Islam for Malays is controversial and conducted through the *syariah* courts rather than by civil law. See, for example, Mohd. Al Adib Samuri and Muzammil Quraishi.

3. Shaz Johar is not the only contemporary Malaysian writer interested in allegories of the state. Given Malaysia's struggle with corruption and intellectual freedom, this interest in allegory is not surprising, but I chose to focus on Shaz's and Brian Gomez's novels because of their popularity and because these particular novels are more nuanced compared to other novels of the same period such as Roslan Mohd. Noor's *The GODs* or Saat Omar's *Sejadah*. However, contemporary novels published in Malaysia in recent years also include novels of other genres outside of the allegory including detective novels, the bildungsroman, romance and gothic novels, poetry, science fiction, experimental fiction, and so forth. The limited scope of this manuscript—focused especially on racial forms and their relationship to the state—does not permit adequate explanations or even descriptions that compose the breadth of Malaysian literature, or to explain how these literatures fall in or out of the genres and forms that are already more familiarly known in American and Asian American literature.

4. The Ministry of Islam in the State of Selangor.

5. The National Ministry for the Development of Islam.

6. http://www.thestar.com.my/news/nation/2017/10/10/jakim-preacher-to-be-probed-for-insulting-johor-sultan/; accessed October 19, 2017.

7. The "postnational" or "transnational" turn in history and cultural studies is important not because the state has been weakened, but because global capital flows and international political tensions have deterritorialized state power only to reterritorialize it. For me, the "postnational" does not mean that the state acts in service of capital as some scholars argue. See. for example, John Rowe (2000). In my view, if the state acts in service of capital, it does so only to strengthen itself. Following Deleuze and Guattari, Prasenjit Duara (2005) observes that the nation-state undergoes deterritorialization during globalization, where the relationship between place and culture becomes decentered. The nation-state is not weakened in the process of reterritorialization; rather, the relationship between culture and politics now goes beyond their borders because territorial sovereignty is no longer the sole determinant of political identity or cultural experience.

8. http://www.nytimes.com/2016/06/24/business/britains-dreams-of-a-swiss-miracle-look-more-like-fantasy.html?hp&action=click&pgtype=Homepage&clickSource=story-heading&module=span-ab-lede-package-region&region=top-news&WT.nav=top-news&_r=0; accessed June 24, 2016.

9. However, as the previous chapter argues, the anticommunist insurgencies, especially in Malaysia and Singapore, were in fact violent even if independence eventually entailed a peaceful transfer of power.

10. However, Nesadurai also postulates that AFTA's success also depends on the political significance of domestic capital within the ASEAN nations.

11. ASEAN's policy of noninterference also meant that member countries would not seek to change—or hold accountable—another country's political or economic regimes or programs. Protests within contemporary ASEAN nations are liable to find themselves shut down if they attempt to criticize human rights abuses in other ASEAN countries (Ong 231).

12. In the Cold War, Southeast Asian nations argued that ASEAN would ensure "Asian defense by Asians themselves" (Acharya123).

13. When the nation-state cannot provide a stable enough framework through which individuals understand or make meaning of their lives, we see a search for and return to other ideologies that offer a more coherent narrative of the present and the future: "So personal and communal identities become centrally important as sources of meaning, either—in Castell's account—proactively pulling toward a better future—feminism, environmentalism—or reactively harking back to a preferred past, related to God, family, ethnicity, locality" (Lyon 38). Religion, especially when it is tied to racial identity, the way it often is in the case of either Malay Muslims in Malaysia and white Christians in the US, becomes part of how we read the nation-state as well as the world and our position within it.

14. Most of the monks who lead the Buddhist temples in the northern region of Malaysia are ethnically Siamese, and many travel back to Thailand to receive further training while Thai monks are also brought to Kelantan to conduct rituals. As part of their ordination, the Kelantan Siamese monks travel to Thailand and other parts of the country as part of their training and religious duties, thus creating and maintaining identifications not bound either by place or locality.

15. Shamsul AB also comes to the same conclusion in his study on the effects of Islamic revivalism and the *dakwah* movements on Malaysian non-Malay communities (see especially pages 111–14).

16. In 1930, the French founded the Buddhist Institute and put in place other educational reforms in Cambodia to lessen the influence of Thai Buddhism and politics in Cambodia (Keyes 48, Anderson *Imagined* 125).

17. In the recent elections on March 8, 2008, the ruling coalition's loss of a long-held two-thirds majority is partly a sign of protest against the state's refusal to protect the rights to religious freedom, among others things.

18. *Datuk* can be translated as "grandfather," or a general term of respect for older men in this context.

19. Interestingly enough, the idea that states can be "injured" is not only a postwar, twentieth-century phenomenon and in fact, has legal precedence as the colonial relations between Britain and China demonstrate. Lydia Liu argues in a short essay on war that the language of victimization on the part of states can be traced back to nineteenth-century European colonialism in Asia. Liu looks at a nineteenth-century example of how James Matheson, a British opium dealer, translated a Chinese word, *yi*, meaning "foreign principal," into "barbarian," and the Chinese word was given meaning outside its own linguistic system. In this example of unequal power relations, one party is able to rewrite another's lexicon. Ultimately, the Chinese were forbidden to use a word in their own language that was mistranslated and used as pretext for taking legal action against the Chinese themselves. The experience of injury on the part of the British colonial powers was not merely an emotion but had legal effects. Britain made the claim that a state—in this case, the British state—could experience insult or injury that requires redress and recognition. Ironically, in the present moment, China continues to identify as victim as a result of the trauma it experienced in the nineteenth century even as its influence has grown and as its relations to the autonomous regions of Xinjiang, Tibet, and Hong Kong, and to Taiwan, the Republic of China (ROC), have grown more confrontational.

20. Michael Barr argues that Southeast Asian leaders—with Singapore's Lee Kuan Yew and Malaysia's Dr. Mahathir Mohammad, both prime ministers at that time—can, and often did, use the argument for "Asian values" to legitimate existing power structures within their societies.

21. The previous Prime Minister Abdullah Badawi's failed efforts to resurrect and deploy *Islam Hadhari*, translated as "Civilizational Islam," can be read as an attempt to replicate the success of the Asian values discourse.

22. In Malaysia, the Education minister is informally next in line to become the prime minister.

Chapter 4

1. http://www.forbes.com/sites/liyanchen/2016/01/05/billionaire-wang-jianlin-becomes-the-first-mainland-chinese-to-crack-the-worlds-top-20-richest/#2715e4857a0b1426b5e635f7; accessed January 20, 2016.

2. http://www.scmp.com/print/news/china/economy/article/1916518/china-accounts-90-cent-worlds-new-billionaires-number-super-rich; accessed February 26, 2016.

3. http://blogs.wsj.com/indiarealtime/2015/02/04/india-has-worlds-third-largest-number-of-billionaires/; accessed January 20, 2016.

4. http://www.unescap.org/sites/default/files/SDD%20AP%20Migration%20Report%20report%20v6-1-E.pdf; accessed January 20, 2016, page 16.

5. During the last decade, Malaysia has become an important educational hub for students across Africa, and new kinds of racial tensions have risen between locals and African students.

6. Governments dependent on international aid, or on foreign remittances by its own people, for example, are seen as sick or unhealthy.

7. Donald Trump's candidacy and subsequent election was accompanied by alarmed commentaries on the rise of tribal nationalisms in the US and around the world. See, for example, these news reports: http://www.economist.com/news/leaders/21710249-his-call-put-america-first-donald-trump-latest-recruit-dangerous, accessed November 21, 2016; http://www.businessinsider.com/what-happens-after-trump-is-president-2016-11; accessed November 21, 2016; https://www.washingtonpost.com/national/the-white-flight-of-derek-black/2016/10/15/ed5f906a-8f3b-11e6-a6a3-d50061aa9fae_story.html?postshare=6771480263825131&tid=ss_fb-bottom; accessed November 28, 2016.

8. Among a minority, the Cultural Revolution provides an alternative utopia to the current Chinese status quo. See, for example, http://www.scmp.com/news/china/society/article/1970331/why-are-so-many-chinese-nostalgic-cultural-revolution; accessed June 9, 2016.

9. Rey Chow argues in *The Protestant Ethnic and the Spirit of Capitalism* that within the context of US-China relations, "ethnic protest" takes place as part of global circulation of cultural visibility and currency. For Chow, "Chineseness" is produced out of capitalist relations that commodify humanity, and to mobilize victimization as critique of the West is to reinscribe humanity as commodity within the same circulations of cultural power capitalism always already sets into motion. Xi Jinping's *Chinese Dream*, however, avoids the route of what Chow calls ethnic protest, even as it remains within the limitations of capitalist form in its valorization of the state as economic actor.

10. Despite greater economic inequalities, the belief that upward mobility is the norm continues to be popular. See for example http://www.newyorker.com/science/maria-konnikova/americas-surprising-views-on-income-inequality; accessed November 21, 2016.

11. In the nineteenth century, freedom meant the freedom to own slaves in (*Dred Scott v. Sanford*, 1857). In the early twentieth century, employers fought for the right to enforce labor contracts that take precedence over government provisions for the protection of workers (*Lochner v. New York*, 1905). The freedom of the state to protect "the people" meant the right to prosecute those whose speech it considered dangerous (*Schenk v. US*, 1919). Franklin Roosevelt thought that in addition to freedom of speech and worship, the people should be free from want and fear as well. However, his successor, Harry Truman was quick to replace "want" and "fear" with the "freedom of enterprise" (Cullen 58 and 107).

12. Poor white men often do not feel privileged and, in fact, feel "cheated" out of what is theirs because they cannot do for their families what their fathers and grandfathers' could do (Williams 2010, 160). In this historical moment, his feeling of precarity and fear of falling out of one's class, however, might afflict all but the wealthiest in the world.

13. Lamont also suggests that antiracism efforts might want to deploy market-based values or language to counter these racist positions rather than emphasize multiculturalism or the celebration of racial difference. Her study continues from David Roediger's earlier study on how nineteenth-century white workers used black stereotypes to reinforce beliefs about "capitalist work discipline" in order to cope with the fears of job insecurity.

14. Francisco Duina's *Broke and Patriotic: Why Poor Americans Love Their Country* extends this analysis beyond workers to other sectors of society including senior citizens and the homeless, that is, those who are no longer in the work force or actively seeking work.

15. Cullen points out that while the phrase "American Dream" was not in use and popularized until the 1940s, it has played an important role in America's history.

16. In contrast, Singapore may not have an official national vision, but the Singaporean story is also grounded on the belief that Singaporeans as a nation share the values of hard work, self-sufficiency, and meritocracy.

17. http://www.epu.gov.my/wawasan-2020-1991-2020; accessed May 16, 2016.

18. Tun Dr. Mahathir Mohammad, the prime minister who introduced this initiative, was famously anti-Western and anticolonial in rhetoric, and equally famously authoritarian. Growth and national development in Malaysia and China can be attributed to postwar nation-building and state social engineering, but critics have argued that it comes at the expense of individual freedom and human rights. Malaysia and China share a common orientation toward economic growth as a form of cultural nationalism.

19. As the manuscript goes through its final revisions, Malaysia has recently witnessed a historic election where the ruling coalition that has been in place for over sixty years since the founding of the nation suffered a shock defeat and was replaced by the opposition that presents itself as less corrupt and less racist. While the effects of this new change remains to be seen, the state is now viewed with more optimism, and nationalist feelings have grown.

20. Ben Sasse, a Republican senator from Nebraska, published a book in 2017 that deploys much of the same rhetoric of hard work and individual contribution to the nation's greatness, *The Vanishing American Adult: Our Coming-of-Age Crisis—and How to Rebuild a Culture of Self-Reliance*. While not formally adopted as a national statement, his book points to how conflations of the American Dream as a cultural narrative of the self and of the state is part of mainstream discourse.

21. Utopia has a long presence in philosophy and fiction, of which dystopian fiction is often regarded as an offshoot, that is, as rendering utopia as a failed project. During the Cold War, totalitarianism came to be imagined as a destructive form of utopianism, and the Cold War saw a rise in dystopian fiction and a growing suspicion that utopias were inherently dystopian especially in the twentieth century (Claey 108).

22. Wallerstein coins the neologism "utopistics" a politics that does not promise idealist, utopian goals and that instead insists on a scientific understanding of revolution and change, draws on rationality and rigorous historical research to identify how real change can take place.

23. This is not to say, however, that there has been no change, or that revolutions have had no effects on cultural life. Revolutions and mass protest do introduce new ideas and new political vocabularies, and in times of transition and volatility, ". . . small fluctuations can have great effects" (Wallerstein 64).

24. Minority writers have found utopia and dystopia particularly useful in challenging our ideas about racial formation, especially in the second half of the twentieth century. The growth of utopian and dystopian fiction began in the 1960s, when women and ethnic minority writers began making significant contributions to the genre, starting with science fiction writers such as Joanna Russ, Marge Piercy, Margaret Atwood, and Samuel Delaney, who wove themes on race, gender, and sexuality into their depictions of other imaginary worlds and the alternative human societies and human interactions possible within them. Minority writers who did not start out writing science fiction began adopting the genre in the 1980s and 1990s: Nadine Gordimer, *July's People* (1981); Buchi Emecheta, *The Rape of Shavi* (1983); Ben Okri, *Astonishing the Gods* (1995); and Amitav Ghosh, *The Calcutta Chromosome* (1995). More recent work includes Karen Tei Yamashita's *Tropic of Orange*, set in a fiery, dystopic Los Angeles almost at war; Ted Chiang's short stories on knowledge, technology, and the body; Katie Kitamura's *Gone to the Forest*, a portrayal of a violent settler colonial society; Chang-rae Lee's satire on American

life and social hierarchies in *On Such a Full Sea*; and even Ruth Ozeki's *A Tale of the Time Being* includes utopian language in its use of the trope of time travel. Ho Anh Thai's *Apocalypse Hotel*, cyberpunk fiction from Singapore and Malaysia, Shaz Johari's *Sancturia*, and even Brian Gomez's madcap caper about a multiracial group of misfits depict utopian or dystopian communities enabled by either new scientific knowledge, or by crime.

25. Wendy Chun describes the imagining of a dystopian future as part of "high tech Orientalism," that is an interrogation of Orientalism not grounded in colonial forms of control but in nationalist anxiety and directed against other countries seen to be authors of US felt "helplessness." The context for Chun's remarks is US fear of Japanese domination in technological innovation in the 1980s. The "global American Dream," however, is a sign that this felt helplessness as global phenomenon could lead to greater racial tensions.

26. Our fears, and hopes, about the future organize all our social experiences under high globalization. The popularity of a film like Danny Boyle's *Slumdog Millionaire* in 2008 offers an example of how the spectacle of bodies of color embodies how we imagine the "rest" of the world as exotic, but also precarious. The utopian narrative based on the belief that wealth and riches are within reach of the poor through hard work and luck helps viewers negotiate the fear and anxiety produced by the site of brown bodies, alien in their culture, values, and language.

27. Books and films like Kwan's, however, ignore the generations of wealth and privilege that racial majorities in Asia have accrued.

28. Mohsin Hamid's *How to Get Filthy Rich in Rising Asia* is a grim meditation on hard work, new wealth, and success in Asia's new economies. The novel's rags-to-riches plot satirizes even as it uses the American Dream as a frame to give a haunting, bittersweet account of the life of a young boy born in a rural South Asian village. The protagonist's dreams of success and wealth is interrupted by his failures in both, and eventually he resorts to fraud and lies to gather the capital he needs to become a legitimate businessman who oversees a growing empire. The global American Dream is a source of anxiety as much as it is inspirational.

Works Cited

Abdullah, C. D. *The Memoirs of Abdullah C. D.: The Movement until 1948*. Petaling Jaya, Malaysia: SIRD, 2009.
Acharya, Amitav. *Regionalism and Multilateralism: Essays on Cooperative Security in the Asia-Pacific*. Singapore: Times Academic Press, 2002.
Ahmad, Mohsin. *How to Get Filthy Rich in Rising Asia*. New York: Riverhead Books, 2013.
Aijaz Ahmad. "Islam, Islamisms and the West." *Socialist Register* (2008): 1–37.
Akashi, Yoji. *New Perspectives of the Japanese Occupation of Malaysia and Singapore, 1941–45*. Singapore: Singapore University Press, 2008.
Akeel Bilgrami. "What Is a Muslim? Fundamental Commitment and Cultural Identity." *Critical Inquiry*, vol. 18, no. 4 (Summer 1992): 821–42.
Andaya, Barbara, and Leonard. *A History of Malaysia*. New York: Palgrave Macmillan, 2001.
Anderson, Benedict. *Imagined Communities*. New York: Verso, 1991.
Ang, Ien. "Between Nationalism and Transnationalism: Multiculturalism in a Globalising World." ICS Occasional Paper Series, vol. 1, no. 1, 2010, pp 1–14. Penrith, UK: Institute for Culture and Society.
Anuar, Mustafa K. "Defining Democratic Discourses: The Mainstream Press." Loh and Khoo, 138–64.
Appadurai, Arjun. *Fear of Small Numbers: An Essay on the Geography of Anger*. Durham, NC: Duke University Press, 2006.
A. Samad Said. *Salina*. Selangor, Malaysia: Wira Bukit Sdn Bhd., 2012.
"Asia-Pacific Migration Report 2015: Migrants' Contributions to Development." *Asia-Pacific RCM Thematic Working Group on International Migration*, 2015. unescap.org/sites/default/files/SDD%20AP%20Migration%20Report%20report%20v6-1-E.pdf. Accessed January 20, 2016.
Augustin, Robin. "Bumi Status for Indian Muslims: Najib Accused of Ignorance." *Free Malaysia Today*, July 21, 2017. http://www.freemalaysiatoday.com/category/nation/2017/07/21/bumi-status-for-indian-muslims-najib-accused-of-ignorance/.

Aw, Tash. *Harmony Silk Factory*. New York: Riverhead Press, 2005.
Barnard, Timothy, ed. *Contesting Malayness: Malay Identity across Boundaries*. Singapore: Singapore University Press, 2004.
Barr, Michael. *Cultural Politics and Asian Values: The Tepid War*. New York: Routledge, 2002.
Bascara, Victor. *Model Minority Imperialism*. Minneapolis: University of Minnesota Press, 2006.
Barraclough, Simon. "The Dynamics of Coercion in the Malaysian Political Process." *Modern Asian Studies* 19, no. 4 (1985): 797–822.
Barber, Noel. *War of the Running Dogs: How Malaya Defeated the Communist Guerrillas, 1948–60*. London: Collins, 1961.
Bloch, Ernst. *The Principle of Hope*. Translated by Neville Plaice, Stephen Plaice, and Paul Knight. Cambridge, MA: MIT Press, 1986.
———. Transl. Jack Zipes, and Frank Meclenburg. *The Utopian Function of Art and Literature: Selected Essays*. Cambridge, MA: MIT Press, 1988.
Brooks, Peter. *The Melodramatic Imagination: Balzac, Henry James, Melodrama, and the Mode of Excess*. New Haven, CT: Yale University Press, 1995.
Brown, Wendy. "Wounded Attachments." *Political Theory* 21, no. 3 (1993): 390–410.
———. *States of Injury: Power and Freedom in Late Modernity*. Princeton, NJ: Princeton University Press, 1995.
Carroll, Hamilton. "Traumatic Patriarchy: Reading Gendered Nationalisms in Chang-rae Lee's *A Gesture Life*." *MFS: Modern Fiction Studies* 51, no. 3 (2005): 592–614.
Chai, Hon-Chan. *The Development of British Malaya, 1896–1909*. Kuala Lumpur, Malaysia: Oxford University Press, 1964.
Chan, Edward. "Utopia and the Problem of Race: Accounting for the Remainder in the Imagination of the 1970s Utopian Subject." *Utopian Studies* 17, no. 3 (2006): 465–90.
Chakrabarty, Dipesh. "The Time of History and the Times of Gods." Lowe and Lloyd, 35–60.
Cheah, Boon Kheng. *Malaysia: The Making of a Nation*. Singapore: Institute of Southeast Asian Studies, 2002.
———. *Red Star over Malaya: Resistance and Social Conflict during and after the Japanese Occupation over Malaya, 1941–1946*. Singapore: Singapore University Press, 2003.
———. The Communist Insurgency in Malaysia, 1948–1990: Contesting the Nation-State and Social Change. *New Zealand Journal of Asian Studies* 11, no. 1 (2009): 132–52.
Chen, Liyan. "Billionaire Wang Jianlin Becomes the First Mainland Chinese to Crack the World's Top 20 Richest," *Forbes*, 15 January 2016, https://www.forbes.com/sites/liyanchen/2016/01/05/billionaire-wang-jianlin-becomes-the-first-mainland-chinese-to-crack-the-worlds-top-20-richest/#6656841c9258.

Chin, Peng. As Told to Ian Ward and Norma Miraflor. *My Side of History*. Ipoh, Malaysia: Media Masters Publishing Sdn. Bhd., 2003.

Cheever, John. *The Stories of John Cheever*. New York: Knopf, 1978.

Cheng, Anne Anlin. "Passing, Natural Selection, and Love's Failure: Ethics of Survival from Chang-rae Lee to Jacques Lacan." *American Literary History* 17, no. 3 (2005): 553–74.

Cheu, Hock Tong, ed. *Chinese Beliefs and Practices in Southeast Asia: Studies on the Chinese Religion in Singapore, Malaysia, and Indonesia*. Petaling Jaya, Malaysia: Pelanduk Publications, 1993.

Christie, Clive. *A Modern History of Southeast Asia: Decolonization, Nationalism, and Separatism*. New York: Tauris Academic Studies, 1996.

———. *Ideology and Revolution in Southeast Asia, 1900–1980: Political Ideas of the Anti-Colonial Era*. Surrey, UK: Curzon Press, 2001.

Chow, Rey. *The Protestant Ethnic and the Spirit of Capitalism*. New York: Columbia University. 2002.

———. Toward and Ethics of Postvisuality: Some Thoughts on the Recent Work of Zhang Yimou. *Poetics Today* 25, no. 4 (2004): 673–88.

———. *Not Like a Native Speaker*. New York: Columbia University Press, 2014.

Chuh, Kandice, and Karen Shimakawa. *Orientations: Mapping Studies in the Asian Diaspora*. Durham, NC: Duke University Press, 2001.

Chun, Wendy. "Othering Space." Mirzoeff, 241–54.

Chung, Catherine. *Forgotten Country*. New York: Riverhead Books, 2013.

Claeys, Gregory, ed. *The Cambridge Companion to Utopian Literature*. Cambridge, UK: Cambridge University Press, 2010.

———. "The Origins of Dystopia: Wells, Huxley and Orwell," 107–34.

"Constitutionally, Mamaks Are Not Malays." *Malaysia Today*, 15 December 2015, http://www.malaysia-today.net/2015/12/15/constitutionally-mamak-are-not-malays/.

Cullen, Jim. *The American Dream: A Short History of an Idea That Shaped a Nation*. New York: Oxford University Press, 2003.

Day, Tony, and Maya H. T. Liem, eds. *Cultures at War: The Cold War and Cultural Expression in Southeast Asia*. Ithaca, NY: Southeast Asia Program Publications, 2010.

DeBenardi, Jean. "The God of War and the Vagabond Buddha." Cheu, 143–64.

De Genova, Nicholas, ed. *Racial Transformations: Latinos and Asians Remaking the United States*. Durham, NC: Duke University Press, 2006.

Derrida, Jacques. *The Gift of Death*, Translated by David Wills. Chicago, IL: University of Chicago Press, 1995.

Dirlik, Arif. *What's in a Rim? Critical Perspectives on the Pacific Region Idea*, 2nd ed. New York: Rowman & Littlefield Publishers, 1998.

Dimock, Waichee. *Residues of Justice: Literature, Law, and Philosophy*. Berkeley: University of California Press, 1997.

Duara, Prasenjit. "The Legacy of Empires and Nations in East Asia." Nyíri and Breidenbach, 35–54.

Duino, Francisco. *Broke and Patriotic: Why Poor Americans Love Their Country*. Stanford, CA: Stanford University Press, 2017.

Eaglestone, Robert. "One and the Same? Ethics, Aesthetics, and Truth." *Poetics Today* 25, no. 4 (2004): 595–608.

Eskin, Michael. "Introduction: the Double 'Turn' to Ethics and Literature?" *Poetics Today* 25, no. 4 (2004): 573–94.

Esperitu, Yen Le. *Asian American Panethnicity: Bridging Institutions and Identities*. Philadelphia, PA: Temple University Press, 1992.

Fuentes, Marcela. "Performance Constellations: Memory and Event in Digitally Enabled Protests in the Americas." *Text and Performance Quarterly* 35, no. 1 (2015): 24–42.

Girard, René. *Violence and the Sacred*, translated by Patrick Gregory. Baltimore: Johns Hopkins University Press, 1977.

———. *Job: The Victim of His People*, translated by Yvonne Freccero. Stanford, CA: Stanford University Press, 1987.

Gladney, Dru, ed. *Making Majorities*. Stanford, CA: Stanford University Press, 1998.

Gomez, Brian. *Devil's Place*. Kuala Lumpur, Malaysia: Fixi Novo, 2013.

Gordan, Avery, and Christopher Newfield, eds. *Mapping Multiculturalism*. Minneapolis: University of Minnesota Press, 1996.

Gullick, J. M. *Malaysia*. London: Ernest Benn Limited, 1969.

———. *Rulers and Residents: Influence and Power in the Malay States, 1870–1920*. New York: Oxford University Press, 1992.

Gunew, Sneja. *Haunted Nations: The Colonial Dimensions of Multiculturalisms*. New York: Routledge, 2004.

Handler, Richard. "On Dialogue and Destructive Analysis: Problems in Narrating Nationalism and Ethnicity." *Journal of Anthropological Research* 41, no. 2 (1985): 171–82.

Han, Suyin. *And the Rain My Drink*. London: Jonathan Cape, 1956.

Harper, T. N. *The End of Empire and the Making of Malaya*. Cambridge, UK: Cambridge University Press, 1999.

Harper, Tim, and Sunil S. Amrith. "Sites of Interaction: An Introduction." *Modern Asian Studies* 46, no. 2 (2012): 249–57.

Harpham, Geoffrey. *Getting It Right: Language, Literature, and Ethics*. Chicago, IL: University of Chicago Press, 1992.

———. *Shadows of Ethics: Criticism and the Just Society*. Durham, NC: Duke University Press, 1999.

Honig, Bonnie. *Democracy and the Foreigner*. Princeton, NJ: Princeton University Press, 2001.

Hollinger, David. "The Concept of Post-Racial: How Its Easy Dismissal Obscures Important Questions." *Daedalus* 140, no. 1 (2011): 174–82.

Hunt, Arnold. "Moral Panic and Moral Language in the Media." *British Journal of Sociology* 48, no. 4 (1997): 629–48.
Inkelas, Karen Kurotsuchi. *Racial Attitudes and Asian Pacific Americans: Demystifying the Model Minority.* New York: Routledge, 2006.
Ismail, Mohamed Yusoff. *Buddhism and Ethnicity: Social Organization of a Buddhist Temple in Kelantan.* Singapore: Institute of Southeast Asian Studies, 1993.
"Jakim Preacher to be Probed for Insulting Johor Sultan," *The Star*, October 10, 2017, https://www.thestar.com.my/news/nation/2017/10/10/jakim-preacher-to-be-probed-for-insulting-johor-sultan/.
Jameson, Frederic. *Archaeologies of the Future: The Desire Called Utopia and Other Science Fictions.* London: Verso, 2005.
Jen, Gish. *The Love Wife.* New York: Alfred Knopf, 2005.
Jerng, Mark C. "Recognizing the Transracial Adoptee: Adoption Life Stories and Chang-rae Lee's *A Gesture Life*." *MELUS* 31, no. 2 (2006): 41–67.
Kambourelli, Smaro. "The Limits of the Ethical Turn: Troping towards the Other, Yann Martel, and Self." *University of Toronto Quarterly* 76, no. 3 (2007): 937–61.
Kessler, Clive. *Islam and Politics in a Malay State.* Ithaca, NY: Cornell University Press, 1978.
Kahn, Joel, and Francis Loh, eds. 1992. *Fragmented Vision.* Honolulu: University of Hawai'i Press, 1992.
Kaplan, Amy, and Donald Pease, eds. *Cultures of United States Imperialism.* Durham, NC: Duke University Press, 1993.
Keyes, Charles, ed. *Ethnic Change.* Seattle: University of Washington Press, 1981.
Khoo, Gaik Cheng. *Reclaiming Adat: Contemporary Malaysian Film and Literature.* Vancouver: University of British Columbia Press, 2006.
———. "Filling in the Gaps of History." Day and Liem, 247–64.
Khoo, Kay Khim. *Malay Society: Transformation and Democratization.* Petaling Jaya, Malaysia: Pelanduk Publications, 1991.
Konnikova, Maria. "America's Surprising Views on Income Inequality," *The New Yorker*, November 17, 2016, http://www.newyorker.com/science/maria-konnikova/americas-surprising-views-on-income-inequality.
Kow, Shih-li. *Ripples and Other Stories.* Kuala Lumpur, Malaysia: Silverfish, 2008.
Kwan, Kevin. *Crazy Rich Asians.* New York: Doubleday, 2013.
———. *China Rich Girlfriend.* New York: Doubleday, 2015.
Kwong, Man-ki. "China Accounts for 90 per cent of World's New Billionaires as the Number of Super-Rich Swells Globally," February 24, 2016, http://www.scmp.com/print/news/china/economy/article/1916518/china-accounts-90-cent-worlds-new-billionaires-number-super-rich.
Lamont, Michéle. *The Dignity of Working Men: Morality and the Boundaries of Race, Class, and Immigration.* Cambridge, MA: Harvard University Press, 2000.
Lee, Chang-rae. *A Gesture Life.* New York: Riverhead Books, 1999.
———. *On Such a Full Sea.* New York: Riverhead Books, 2014.

Lee, Fiona. "Spectral History: Unsettling Nation Time in 'The Last Communist.'" *Concentric: Literary and Cultural Studies* 39, no. 1 (2013): 77–95.
Lee, Rachel C. *The Americas of Asian American Literature*. Princeton, NJ: Princeton University Press, 1999.
Lee, Young-Oak. "Transcending Ethnicity: Diasporicity in *A Gesture Life*." *Journal of Asian American Studies* 12, no. 1 (2009): 65–81.
Lim, Phaik Gan. *Kaleidoscope: The Memoirs of PG Lim*. Petaling Jaya, Malaysia: Strategic Information and Research Development Centre (SIRD), 2012.
Lim, Shirley Geok-Lin, Stephen Sohn, and Gina Valentino, eds. *Transnational Asian American Literature: Sites and Transits*. Philadelphia, PA: Temple University Press, 2006.
———. *Among the White Moon Faces: An Asian American Memoir of Homelands*. New York, NY: The Feminist Press at CUNY, 1997.
Lionnet, Françoise. "Continents and Archipelagoes: From *E Pluribus Unum* to Creolized Solidarities." *PMLA Special Topic: Comparative Racialization* 123, no. 5 (2008): 1503–15.
Liu, Lydia. "The Thug, the Barbarian, and the Work of Injury in Imperial Warfare." *PMLA* 124, no. 5 (2009): 1859–63.
Loh, Francis, and Boo Teik Khoo, eds. *Democracy in Malaysia: Discourses and Practices*." Surrey, UK: Curzon Press, 1992.
Loughran, Trish. "Transcendental Islam: The Worlding of Our America: A Response to Wai Chee Dimock." *American Literary History* 21, no. 1 (2009): 53–66.
Lowe, Lisa, and David Lloyd. *The Politics of Culture in the Shadow of Capital*. Durham, NC: Duke University Press, 1997.
———. "Utopia and Modernity: Some Observations from the Border." *Rethinking Marxism* 13, no. 2 (Summer 2001): 10–18.
———. *The Intimacies of Four Continents*. Durham, NC: Duke University Press, 2015.
Lyon, David. *Jesus in Disneyland: Religion in Postmodern Times*. Malden, MA: Blackwell Publishers, 2000.
Lye, Colleen. *America's Asia: Racial Form and American Literature, 1893–1945*. Princeton, NJ: Princeton University Press, 2004.
Machart, Regis, Choon Bee Lim, Sep Neo Lim, and Eriko Yamato, eds. *Intersecting Identities and Interculturality: Discourse and Practice*. Newcastle Upon Tyne, UK: Cambridge Scholars Publishing, 2013.
Mai, Jun. "Why Are So Many Chinese Nostalgic for the Cultural Revolution?" *South China Morning Post*, June 9, 2010, http://www.scmp.com/news/china/society/article/1970331/why-are-so-many-chinese-nostalgic-cultural-revolution.
Marr, Timothy. "'Out of This World': Islamic Irruptions in the Literary Americas." *American Literary History* 18, no. 3 (2006): 521–49.
Mauss, Marcel. *The Gift: The Form and Reason for Exchange in Archaic Societies*. New York: W. W. Norton, 1990.

McCoy, Alfred, ed. *Southeast Asia under Japanese Colonization*. New Haven, CT: Yale University Southeast Asia Studies, 1980.
Melas, Natalie. *All the Difference in the World: Postcoloniality and the Ends of Comparison*. Stanford, CA: Stanford University Press, 2007.
Mills, Charles. *The Racial Contract*. Ithaca, NY: Cornell University Press, 1999.
Milmo, Cahal. "Relatives of Malaysians Killed by British Troops in the Batang Kali Massacre Vow to Take Their Fight to the Supreme Court," *The Independent*, March 19, 2014, https://www.independent.co.uk/news/uk/home-news/relatives-of-malaysians-killed-by-british-troops-in-the-batang-kali-massacre-vow-to-take-their-fight-9202912.html.
Milner, Anthony. *The Invention of Politics in Colonial Malaya*. Cambridge, UK: Cambridge University Press, 1994.
Mirzoeff, Nicholas, ed. *The Visual Culture Reader, 2nd ed*. London: Routledge, 2003.
Mohd. Al Adib Samuri, and Muzammil Quraishi. "Negotiating Apostasy: Applying to 'Leave Islam' in Malaysia." *Islam and Christian-Muslim Relations* 25, no. 4 (2014): 507–23.
Mohsin, Hamid. *How to Get Filthy Rich in Rising Asia*. New York: Riverhead Books, 2013.
Mullen, Bill, and Cathryn Watson, eds. *WEB Du Bois on Asia: Crossing the World Color Line*. Jackson: University of Mississippi Press, 2005.
Muñoz, José Esteban. *Cruising Utopia: The Then and There of Queer Futurity*. New York: New York University Press, 2009.
Mying, Ne Win. "Thadun." Yamada 4–10.
Nagata, Judith. "In Defense of Ethnic Boundaries: The Changing Myths and Charters of Malay Identity." Charles Keyes, 87–116.
Nelson, Cary, and Lawrence Grossberg, eds. *Marxism and the Interpretation of Culture*. Chicago: University of Illinois Press, 1988.
Nesadurai, Helen. *Globalization, Domestic Politics and Regionalism: The ASEAN Free Trade Area*. London: Routledge, 2003.
"News on Mat Sabu's pro-communism." *The Malaysian Insider*, September 22, 2014, https://www.themalaysianinsider.com/malaysia/article/news-on-mat-sabu-pro-communist-based-on-video-reporter-tells-court.
Nyíri, Pál, and Joana Breidenbach, eds. *China Inside Out: Contemporary Chinese Nationalism and Transnationalism*. Budapest, Hungary: Central European University Press, 2005.
O'Leary, Timothy. "Foucault, Dewey, and the Experience of Literature." *New Literary History* 36, no. 4 (2005): 543–57.
Omi, Michael, and Howard Winant. *Racial Formation in the United States: From the 1960s to the 1980s*. New York: Routledge, 1986.
Ong, Aihwa, and Michael Peletz, eds. *Bewitching Women, Pious Men: Gender and Body Politics in Southeast Asia*. Berkeley: University of California Press, 1995.

Ong, Aihwa. "State versus Islam." Ong and Peletz, 159–94.
Ozeki, Ruth. *A Tale for the Time Being*. New York: Penguin, 2013.
Palumbo-Liu, David. *Asian/American: Crossings of a Racial Frontier*. Stanford, CA: Stanford University Press, 1999.
———. Rational and Irrational Choices: Form, Affect, and Ethics. Shih and Lionnet, 41–72.
Park, Josephine Nock-Hee. *Cold War Friendships: Korea, Vietnam, and Asian American Literature*. New York: Oxford University Press, 2016.
Patel, Atish. "India Has World's Third Largest Number of Billionaires," February 4, 2015, http://blogs.wsj.com/indiarealtime/2015/02/04/india-has-worlds-third-largest-number-of-billionaires/.
Peletz, Michael. *Islamic Modern: Religious Courts and Cultural Politics in Malaysia*. Princeton, NJ: Princeton University Press, 2002.
———. *Reinscribing "Asian (Family) Values": Nation Building, Subject Making, and Judicial Process in Malaysia's Islamic Courts*. Notre Dame: Occasional papers of the Erasmus Institute, 2003.
Pomfret, David. *Youth and Empire: Trans-colonial Childhoods in British and French Asia*. Stanford, CA: Stanford University Press, 2016.
Purcell, Victor. *The Chinese in Southeast Asia*. London: Oxford University Press, 1951.
———. *The Chinese in Modern Malaya*. Singapore: Eastern Universities Press, 1960.
———. *The Memoirs of a Malayan Official*. London: Cassell, 1965.
Qader, Nasrin. *Narratives of Catastrophe: Boris Diop, ben Jelloun, Khatibi*. New York: Fordham University Press, 2009.
Rafael, Vicente. *White Love and Other Events in Filipino History*. Durham, NC: Duke University Press, 2000.
Rashid Maidin. *The Memoirs of Rashid Maidin: From Armed Struggle to Peace*. Petaling Jaya, Malaysia: SIRD, 2009.
Rani Manicka. *The Japanese Lover*. London: Hodder and Stoughton, 2010.
Reid, Anthony. *Southeast Asia in the Age of Commerce, 1450–1680: Volume One, The Land Below the Winds*. New Haven, CT: Yale University Press, 1988.
———. *Southeast Asia in the Age of Commerce, 1450–1680: Volume Two, Expansion and Crisis*. New Haven, CT: Yale University Press, 1993.
Ricci, Ronit. Citing as a Site: Translation and circulation in Muslim South and Southeast Asia. *Modern Asian Studies* 46, no. 2 (2012): 331–53.
Ricoeur, Paul, and George H. Taylor, eds. *Lectures on Ideology and Utopia*. New York: Columbia University, 1986.
Roff, William. *The Origins of Malay Nationalism*. New Haven, CT: Yale University Press, 1967.
Rowe, John Carlos. *Post-nationalist American Studies*. Berkeley: University of California Press, 2000.
Sadanand Dhume, "The Myth of a Moderate Malaysia," *Forbes*, August 30, 2009.
Samrasan, Preeta. *Evening Is the Whole Day*. New York: Houghton-Mifflin, 2008.

Sanjeev Khagram, and Peggy Levitt, eds. *The Transnational Studies Reader: Intersections and Innovations.* New York: Routledge, 2008.

Scott, James. *Seeing Like a State: How Certain Schemes to Improve the Human Condition Have Failed.* New Haven, CT: Yale University Press, 1999.

Shamsul, A. B. "Bureaucratic Management of Identity in a Modern State: 'Malayness' in Postwar Malaysia." Dru Gladney, 135–50.

———. "Idea and the Practice of 'Malayness' in Malaysia." Timothy Barnard, 135–48.

Shaz, Johar. *Sancturia.* Petaling Jaya, Malaysia: Buku Fixi, 2014.

Sherman, Jennifer. *Those Who Work, Those Who Don't: Poverty, Morality, and Family in Rural America.* Minneapolis: University of Minnesota Press, 2009.

Shih, Shu-mei. "Comparative Racialization: An Introduction." *PMLA* 123, no. 5 (2008): 1347–62.

———. "Does Language Determine Identity? Thoughts on Sinophone Malaysian Literature." Machart, Lim, Lim, and Yamato, 57–69.

Shih, Shu-mei, and Françoise Lionnet, eds. *Minor Transnationalism.* Durham, NC: Duke University Press, 2005.

Stewart, James. "Britain's Dreams of a Swiss Miracle Look Like Fantasy," *New York Times,* June 23, 2016, https://www.nytimes.com/2016/06/24/business/britains-dreams-of-a-swiss-miracle-look-more-like-fantasy.html?hp&action=click&pgtype=Homepage&clickSource=story-heading&module=span-ab-lede-package-region&region=top-news&WT.nav=top-news&_r=0.

Squires, Catherine. *The Post-Racial Mystique: Media and Race in the Twenty-First Century.* New York: New York University, 2014.

Sumit, K. Mandal. "Popular Sites of Prayer, Transoceanic Migration, and Cultural Diversity: Exploring the Significance of *Keramat* in Southeast Asia." *Modern Asian Studies* 46, no. 2 (March 2014): 355–72.

Stoler, Ann. *Capitalism and Confrontation in Sumatra's Plantation Belt, 1870–1979.* New Haven, CT: Yale University Press, 1985.

Syed Ahmad Hussein. "Muslim Politics and the Discourse on Democracy." Loh and Khoo 74–110.

Tarling, Nicholas. *Regionalism in Southeast Asia: To Foster Political Will.* New York: Routledge, 2006.

Than, Mya, and Carolyn Gates, eds. *ASEAN Enlargement: Impacts and Implications.* Singapore: Institute of Southeast Asian Studies, 2001.

Tan, Twan Eng. *The Garden of Evening Mists.* New York: Weinstein Books, 2012.

Tsing, Anna Lowenhaupt. *Friction: An Ethnography of Global Connection.* Princeton, NJ: Princeton University Press, 2005.

Yong, C. F. Origins and Development of the Malayan Communist Movement: 1919–1930. *Modern Asian Studies* 25, no. 4 (1991): 625–48.

Wallerstein, Immanuel. *Utopistics: or Historical Choices of the Twenty-First Century.* New York: New Press, 1998.

"Wawasan 2020," *Economic Planning Unit of the Prime Minister's Department, Malaysia.* epu.gov.my/wawasan-2020-1991-2020. Accessed May 16, 2016.

Willford, Andrew. *Tamils and the Haunting of Justice: History and Recognition in Malaysia's Plantations.* Singapore: NUS Press, 2014.

Williams, Joan C. *Reshaping the Work-Family Debate: Why Men and Class Matter.* Cambridge, MA: Harvard University Press, 2010.

Williams, Linda. *Playing the Race Card: Melodramas of Black and White from Uncle Tom to O. J. Simpson.* Princeton, NJ: Princeton University Press, 2002.

Winant, Howard. "Race and Race Theory." *Annual Review of Sociology* 26 (2001): 169–85.

Yamada, Teri Shaffer, ed. *Virtual Lotus: Modern Fiction of Southeast Asia.* Ann Arbor: University of Michigan Press, 2002.

Yao, Souchou. *Confucian Capitalism: Discourse, Practice, and the Myth of Chinese Enterprise.* London: RoutledgeCurzon, 2002.

Yiswaree, Palansamy. "Screening of the New Village Suspended." 2013. *Malaysian Insider.* https://www.themalaysianinsider.com/malaysia/article/screening-of-the-new-village-suspended. Accessed August 16, 2013.

Filmography

Lelaki Komunis Terakhir. Dir. Amir Muhammad, 2006. https://www.youtube.com/watch?v=sTM0BwgDXn8.

The Big Durian. Dir. Amir Muhammad. Videocassette. Doghouse 73 Pictures, 2003.

Sepet. Dir. Yasmin Ahmad. Videocassette. MHz Film, 2004.

Index

1Malaysia Development Berhad (1MDB), 92

adat, 7, 157, 177. See also Malay
Abdullah Badawi, 168
Abdullah, C. D., 74–75 See also *Memoirs of Abdullah C. D., The*
Absent Without Leave. See Kek Huat Lau
Africa, 7, 11, 18, 102, 104, 156, 169
African American, 31, 41, 44, 160, 161. See also American
alienation, 10, 35, 36, 46, 54, 156
All the Difference in the World. See Melas, Natalie
American: Dream, 4, 24, 29, 31, 32, 41, 45, 46, 57, 118, 119, 120, 122, 123, 124, 126, 128, 130, 131, 132, 133, 134, 141, 142, 144, 148, 155, 171, 172; state, 6, 43, 118, 121; values, 36, 133
America's Asia. See Lye, Colleen
Amir Muhammad, 67, 166. See also *Lelaki Komunis Terakhir; Big Durian, The; Sepet*
amok, 6. See also Malay
Among the White Moon Faces. See Shirley Lim
Andaya, Barbara, 165. See also *A History of Malaysia*

Anderson, Benedict, 161, 168. See also *Imagined Communities*
anticommunist, 58, 167
Appadurai, Arjun, 21–22, 140, 159. See also *Fear of Small Numbers*
apocalypse, 29, 143, 172
apocalyptical, 10
Arab, 17, 157–158
army, 12, 41, 50–52, 73, 75, 82
Arrighi, Giovanni, 156
ASEAN Free Trade Area (AFTA), 102
A. Samad Said, 65. See also *Salina*
Asia Pacific, 1, 17
Asian: American, 6, 10, 17–19, 24–25, 29, 32, 34, 39–40, 46, 57, 120, 123, 125, 140, 159–160, 166; Values, 108, 109, 168
Asian/American. See Palumbo-Liu, David
assimilate, 43, 84
assimilation, 27–28, 32, 40, 42–44, 47, 57, 106
Association of South East Asia (ASA), 103
Association of South East Asian Nations (ASEAN), 101–104, 108, 167
Aw, Tash, 79. See also *Harmony Silk Factory*
authoritarian, 74, 89, 91, 93, 170

Baba and *Nyonya* Chinese, 14. See also *Peranakan*
Baling Talks, 76
Bandung Conference, 102
Barber, Noel, 72, 75, 79, 165. See also *War of the Running Dogs*
Buddhist, 104–105, 109, 165, 168
Big Durian, The. See Amir Muhammad
binary, 4, 41, 95
biology, 11, 12, 64, 161
biological difference, 11–12, 36, 133
biopower, 37
Birch, J. W. W., 157
Bloch, Ernst, 136, 137, 139, 144. See also *Principle of Hope, The*
Brexit, 4, 97, 99–100
British: Malaya, 12–13; Military Administration, 65–66, 71, 163; war propaganda, 73
Brunei, 100, 103
bumiputra, 105
Bunyan, John, 147
Burma, 12, 41, 50, 100, 103
Burmese, 51, 97, 98

censorship, 60, 67, 78–79, 108, 162
census, 140–141
Cambodia, 1, 100, 103–104, 165, 168
Cantonese, 15, 156, 162
Capitalism and Confrontation in Sumatra's Plantation Belt. See Stoler, Ann
Cheah, Boon Kheng, 70–71, 162–163, 165. See also *Malaysia; Red Star over Malaysia*
Cheever, John, 45. See also *The Swimmer*
Chiang, Ted, 171
Chinese: Americans, 5, 29, 123, 160; communist, 60, 62–63, 67, 74; Dream, 118, 130, 169; Exclusion Act, 20; imperial court, 14. See also Malayan; Malaysian
Chineseness, 67, 71, 156, 161, 169
Chin, Peng, 72, 74–76, 163. See also *My Side of History*
Chinese in Southeast Asia, The. See Purcell, Victor
Christie, Clive, 16, 102. See also *Modern History of Southeast Asia, A; Ideology and Revolution in Southeast Asia, 1900–1980*
Chow, Rey, 20, 37, 161. See also *Protestant Ethic and the Spirit of Capitalism, The*
Chung, Catherine, 160. See also *Forgotten Country*
Chun, Wendy, 172
Cina: babi, 6, 8; *balik*, 8, 76, 81; Kapitan, 15
civilization, 13–14, 86, 127
civilizational discourse, 126–127, 134, 140, 151
Cold War, 4–5, 8, 10, 17, 19–20, 58, 64, 85–86, 95, 97–98, 100, 102, 109, 113, 159, 167, 171
Cold War Friendships. See Park, Josephine Nock-Hee
colonial: economy, 5; logic, 8, 16, 25; regime, 8, 59, 73, 83
colonialism, 3, 15, 71
color-line, 6
comfort woman, 32, 41, 50
comic, 83, 112, 114
commodity, 25, 41, 57, 169
commonwealth, 7
competitors, 69, 95–96, 118
communist: camp, 62, 73, 82; informer, 81, 84; insurgency, 12, 59, 65, 67, 69, 71–72, 78–79, 86, 111, 162; rehabilitated, 62, 80–81, 83; spy, 51, 81, 85; terrorists, 60, 70.

See also Malayan Communist Party (MCP)
Conference of the Rulers. *See* Federal Council
Confucian, 19, 108–109
coolie, 11, 18
cosmopolitan, 21, 63, 124, 160
Crazy Rich Asians. See Kwan, Kevin
culture: anxiety of, 8, 29, 149; global, 3, 5, 8, 22, 24, 30; globalization, of, 21; popular, 3–4, 23, 129–130, 134, 140, 152
cultural: difference, 1, 6–7, 86, 107, 109–110, 126; life, 3, 16, 22, 85, 136, 156–171; nationalism, 22, 39, 97–98, 99–100, 170

democracy, 60, 74–77, 83, 98, 138
Democracy and the Foreigner. See Honig, Bonnie
demographic, 17–18, 118, 129, 134, 141
deport/deportation, 6, 8, 24, 67, 76, 78, 164. *See also* expulsion
deterritorialization, 21, 28, 167
Devil's Place. See Gomez, Brian
disposition, 12, 74
divide and rule, 11
Duara, Prasenjit, 156, 167. See also *Legacy of Empires and Nations in East Asia, The*
Dubois, W. E. B., 6–7
Dutch, 12, 16, 162
Duterte, Rodrigo, 1
dystopia/dystopian, 29, 89, 93, 123, 144, 171–172

economic: actor, 9, 169; growth, 29, 104, 108, 128–129, 131–132, 134–135, 170; imperialism, 134; insecurity, 124; migrants, 129; position, 125; security, 120, 124, 130; success, 17, 41, 133
emotion, 39, 137, 168
empire, 80, 102, 127, 155, 167, 172
End of Empire and the Making of Malaya, The. See also Harper, T. N.
ethics, 34–35, 37–38, 44, 52–53, 55, 116, 130–131, 134, 136, 160
ethical, 29, 34–35, 37–38, 44, 51–52, 55–56, 136, 147, 161
ethnic: conflict, 23; groups; identity, 23, 165; literature, 28, 35 159; studies, 26; unrest, 96
ethnocentric, 8, 13, 131, 140
European: colonialism, 9–10, 35, 168; Union, 97
Evening is the Day. See Preeta Samarasan
exception/exceptional/exceptionalism, 6–7, 29, 39, 85, 118, 120, 128, 131
exchange value, 68
exclusion, 3, 8, 20, 27, 36, 57, 77, 160
exile, 24, 31, 42, 46, 53, 56–57, 81, 112, 117, 146
expulsion, 6, 27, 55–56, 85. *See also* deportation

Fanon, Frantz, 155
Federal Council, 16. *See also* Conference of the Rulers
Fear of Small Numbers. See Appadurai, Arjun
flexible, 2, 105
Forgotten Country. See Catherine Chung
Force 136, 72–74

Garden of Evening Mists, The. See also Tan, Twan Eng

gender: norms, 6; roles, 90, 129, 136
geopolitical, 5, 9, 17–18, 29, 101, 127
Gesture Life, A. See Lee, Chang-rae
Girard, René, 53–55. See also *Violence and the Sacred; Job*
Glissant, Éduoard, 2, 25
global: culture, 3, 5, 8, 22, 24, 29, 30; flows, 3, 5, 9, 26, 97–98, 122, 141; encounters, 3, 5; history, 1, 128; politics, 11, 143, 149; racial tropes, 3, 69, 115
Gomez, Brian, 28, 111, 117, 160, 167, 172. See also *Devil's Place*
Gone to the Forest. See Kitamura, Katie
good life, 117–118, 123, 126, 130, 133, 136, 142, 144, 151–152
governmentality, 96–97
guerrilla, 60, 75
Gullick, J. M., 14. See also *Malaysia; Rulers and Residents*

Hakka, 50, 156, 158
Hamid, Mohsin, 172. See also *How to Get Filthy Rich in Rising Asia*
Han, Suyin, 59, 61, 64, 66, 77, 80, 83–85, 111, 160. See also *Rain My Drink, And the*
harmony, 44, 53–54, 56, 91, 135–136, 143, 146
Harmony Silk Factory. See Aw, Tash
Harper, T. N., 13, 157, 165. See also *End of Empire and the Making of Malaya, The*
Hindu, 14, 90, 110; Buddhist, 165
History of Malaysia, A. See Andaya, Barbara
historical-materialist, 5, 64, 151
Hokkien, 6, 15, 107, 156
Honig, Bonnie, 53. See also *Democracy and the Foreigner*
Huntington, Samuel, 126
hybrid, 104–105

hypernationalist, 10

ideology, 29, 41, 69, 118, 131–132, 147–148, 152
Ideology and Revolution in Southeast Asia, 1900–1980. See Christie, Clive
illegal, 85, 141
Imagined Communities. See Anderson, Benedict
immigrant: first-generation, 119–124; second-generation, 125
imperial: center, 29; gaze, 5; relations, 11
imperialism, 25, 40, 48, 50, 74, 134
inclusion, 3, 8, 18, 21, 55, 57, 72, 77–78, 84, 124, 148, 161
incommensurability, 25, 38
indentured labor, 9, 15, 70
informer, 63, 80–81, 84
internal enemy, 60
internalized racism, 12
interpellated, 44, 57, 81, 123
interrogation, 81–82, 172
Intimacies of Four Continents, The. See Lowe, Lisa
India, 1, 6–7, 11–13, 129, 135, 164
Indian Malaysian, 112, 160, 164. See also Malaysian
indigeneity, 7
indigenous, 7, 16, 105, 156–157
internalized racism, 12
internment, 62, 77, 80, 83–83
Indonesia, 5, 100, 102–104
industrialization, 9, 129
Internal Security Act (ISA), 164. See also Security Offenses (Special Measures) Act 2012 (SOSMA)
Invention of Politics in Colonial Malaya, The. See Milner, Anthony
Islam, 7, 14, 92, 105, 107, 110, 158, 165–168
Islamic, 17, 74, 78, 105–107, 109, 111, 117, 158, 165, 168

Islam and Politics in a Malay State. See also Kessler, Clive

Jabatan Agama Islam Selangor (JAIS), 92
Jabatan Kemajuan Islam Malaysia (JAKIM), 92, 167, 177
Japan, 7, 18, 20–21, 33, 40, 41–43, 49, 52, 82, 103, 159
Javanese, 14, 162
Jemaah Islamiyah, 112
Jen, Gish, 29, 119–120, 123, 125, 160. See also *Love Wife, The*
Job. See Girard, René

Kapitan Cina, 15, 158. See also Kapitan system
Kapitan system, 15. See also *Kapitan Cina*
kerajaan, 15
Kesatuan Melayu Muda (KMM), 75, 163
Kessler, Clive. See also *Islam and Politics in a Malay State*
Khoo, Kay Khim, 157. See also *Malay Society*
kiasu, 6
Kim, Richard, 159. See also *The Martyred*
Kitamura, Katie, 171. See also *Gone to the Forest*
Kow, Shih-li, 67. See also *Ripples and Other Stories*
Kwan, Kevin, 129, 141, 172. See also *Crazy Rich Asians*

Lai Tek, 72, 163
Laos, 5, 100, 103
Lau, Kek Huat, 162. See also *Absent Without Leave*
Lee, Chang-rae, 29, 31–33, 40–57, 120, 143–149, 160. See also *Gesture Life, A; On Such a Full Sea*

left behind, 6, 10, 36, 125, 163
Legacy of Empires and Nations in East Asia, The. See Duara, Prasenjit
Lelaki Komunis Terakhir. See Amir Muhammad
Lim, P. G., 163
Lim, Shirley, 160. See also *Among the White Moon Faces*
linguistic, 2, 5, 12, 14–15, 23–24, 26–48, 113–114, 153, 156, 159–161
Lionnet, Françoise, 2, 40
Lectures on Ideology and Utopia. See Ricoeur, Paul
Loomba, Ania, 7
Love Wife, The. See Jen, Gish
Low, Hugh, 13
Lowe, Lisa, 17, 139. See also *Politics of Culture in the Shadow of Capital, The; Intimacies of Four Continents, The*
Lye, Colleen, 18–19. See also *America's Asia*

Maidin, Rashid, 74. See also *Memoirs of Rashid Maidin, The*
Malaccan: Kingdom, 13; Sultanate, 13, 157, 165. See also Melaka
Malay: *adat*, 7; amok, 6; language, 6; nationalism, 10; supremacy, 8. See also amok, Melayu, Muslim
Malaya, 11–13, 16, 59–60, 62, 65, 69, 72–74, 76, 78–79, 103, 158, 162–164
Malay Annals. See *Sejarah Melayu*
Malayan: Emergency, 60, 76, 78–81, 85, 164; People's Anti-Japanese Army (MPAJA), 72, 163; Union, 78
Malaysia. See Cheah, Boon Kheng
Malaysia. See Gullick, J. M.
Malaysian Chinese Association (MCA), 76

Malay Society. See Khoo, Kay Khim
marginalization, 27, 48, 124, 132
masuk melayu, 14, 107, 110
Megat Iskandar Shah, 14
Melaka, 12, 67. See also Malaccan
Melas, Natalie, 24–26. See also *All the Difference in the World*
Melayu, 13, 135
Memoirs of Abdullah C. D., The. See Abdullah, C. D.
Memoirs of Rashid Maidin, The. See Maidin, Rashid
Middle East, 106, 115
migrant, 13
migration, 3, 37, 129, 139, 148, 152
Milner, Anthony, 14–15, 165; *Invention of Politics in Colonial Malaya, The*
model nation, 27–28, 123
modern, 3, 8
modernity, 108, 156
modernizing, 15, 22, 106
modernization, 66, 100, 106
Modern History of Southeast Asia, A. See Christie, Clive
modes of racial thought, 1–2
moral: degeneration, 59, 66; difference, 8, 36, 86, 133; duty, 136; fear, 70; force, 5, 57; goodness, 27, 46, 56–57, 82, 85, 118, 120, 159; judgment, 12, 71; narrative, 10, 69–70, 86, 107, 109–110, 117, 126, 131, 136; outrage, 6; threat, 63; trope, 17, 30, 83, 109. See also exemplarity
multiculturalism, 156, 170
Munshi Abdullah, 157
My Side of History. See Chin, Peng

Najib Razak, 1
Narendran Modi, 1

national: history, 1, 6, 33, 41, 60, 65, 79, 100; imaginary, 11, 33, 39, 41, 52, 55, 56, 78, 111, 122, 148; security, 60, 115; uplift, 29, 130
native elite, 16, 70, 163
New Village, 60, 77, 162. See also internment camps
nonwhite, 6, 41, 70

On Such a Full Sea. See also Lee, Chang-rae
Orang Asal, 7, 156. See also *Orang Asli*
Orang Asli. See *Orang Asal*
Order of the British Empire (OBE), 163
Oriental/Orientalist, 3, 18, 79
Origins of Malay Nationalism, The. See Roff, William
Ozeki, Ruth, 160. See also *Tale of a Time Being*

Palumbo-Liu, David, 18, 37–38, 159. See also *Asian/American*
Pan-Asian prosperity, 48–49
Pan-Islamic, 17
Parameswara, 13
Park, Josephine Nock-Hee, 159. See also *Cold War Friendships*
Parti Kebangsaan Melayu Malaya (PKMM), 74
Parti Sosialis Malaysia (PSM), 164. See also Socialist Party of Malaysia
Penang, 12, 107
Perak, 13, 16
Peranakan, 14. See also *Baba* and *Nyonya* Chinese
Philippines, 1, 5, 103–104, 129
Pilgrim's Progress. See Bunyan, John
poetics of relations, 25
policy, 11, 76, 102, 107, 109, 167
political identity, 12, 15, 109
Politics of Culture in the Shadow of Capital, The. See Lowe, Lisa

populist, 1, 9, 10, 120
Portuguese, 12
postapocalyptic, 143–144
postcolonial elites, 8, 115
postnational, 117, 167
postracial, 90–91, 111–112, 118, 140, 143–144
power relations, 3, 52, 72, 124, 137, 168
precarious, 3, 9, 24, 49, 56, 77, 84, 123, 172
precarity, 124, 128, 134, 143, 145, 170
precolonial, 10, 14–15, 91, 152
Preeta Samarasan, 160. See also *Evening is the Day*
primordial, 22, 91, 156
Principle of Hope, The. See Bloch, Ernst
prosperity gospel, 131
Protestant Ethic and the Spirit of Capitalism, The. See Chow, Rey
propaganda, 20, 72–73, 75, 78, 82
protectorate, 103
Purcell, Victor, 157. See also *Chinese in Southeast Asia, The*
pursuit of happiness, 10, 131

Queen Victoria, 157

race: informal system of, 11; matters, 3, 43; relations, 14, 22, 29, 34–35, 40–41, 47, 49, 57, 60, 155, 166; riots, 59, 106; social meaning of, 1–2, 111, 151
raced subjects, 12, 25, 27, 35, 57, 77, 82, 146, 165
racial: assimilation, 28, 106; behavior, 8, 11, 24, 57, 84–85, 90, 151; categories, 11–12; community, 13, 26; discourse, 3, 100, 140, 156; figuration, 2, 20, 23; formation, 4, 17, 27, 33, 40, 56, 69, 79, 155, 171; group, 3, 12, 14, 53, 106; hierarchy, 7, 35, 49, 64; identity, 3, 9, 15, 16, 23, 64, 68, 72, 82, 105, 111, 113, 138, 167; language, 2, 5, 10, 12, 153, 159; management, 11; subject, 28, 30, 96, 146; subjection, 11, 34, 85. See also modes of racial thought
racialization, 17–19, 21, 25, 43, 54, 61, 82, 160–161
racist discourse, 8, 20, 152; imagery, 6
Rain My Drink, And the. See Han, Suyin
raja, 15–16
Red Star over Malaysia. See Cheah, Boon Kheng
Reid, Anthony, 158. See also *Southeast Asia in the Age of Commerce*
reliable, 62, 77, 90, 93
regionalism, 96, 102–103
rehabilitated: communist, 80, 83; informant, 81; terrorist, 62
Resident, 13, 16, 157. See also Residential System
Residential System. See Resident
ressentiment, 109
reterritorialization, 21, 28, 110, 117–118, 126, 131, 161
Ricoeur, Paul, 137–139. See also *Lectures on Ideology and Utopia*
rights of the majority, 6
Ripples and Other Stories. See Kow, Shih-li
rising Asia, 89, 121, 172
rituals, 107, 168
Roff, William, 157. See also *Origins of Malay Nationalism, The*
rubber plantation, 11, 62, 75
Rulers and Residents. See Gullick, J. M.

Salina. See A. Samad Said

Sancturia. See Johar, Shaz
Sarekat Islam (Islamic Association), 158
Sasse, Ben, 171. *See also The Vanishing American Adult*
satire/satirical, 23, 59, 61, 64, 84, 91, 111, 165, 171
scapegoat, 53–54, 56
Scott, James, 95–96, 118, 156. See also *Seeing Like a State*
secret: identity, 57; society, 15, 158
Security Offenses (Special Measures) Act 2012 (SOSMA), 164. *See also* Internal Security Act (ISA)
Seeing like a state. See Scott, James
segregation, 7, 11, 13, 77, 143, 144
Sejarah Melayu, 157. See also *Malay Annals*
sepet, 6. *See also* Amir Muhammad; slit-eyed
Shamsul AB, 168
Shaz, Johar, 28, 89–91, 159–160, 162. See also *Sancturia*
Shih, Shu-mei, 2, 25–26
Siamese, 105, 168. *See also* Malaysian
Singapore, 12, 62, 65, 100, 103, 106, 129, 142, 167
sinicized, 67
sinitic, 156
slit-eyed, 6. See also *sepet*
social: change, 4; conflict, 55; discipline, 34; experience, 4, 10, 33, 172; identity, 12, 36, 98; organization, 11, 27; problem, 3, 7; violence, 33–34, 40, 52–54, 57, 146
Socialist Party of Malaysia (PSM). *See* Parti Sosialis Malaysia
soft diplomacy, 20
soft power, 126
South Asia/South Asian, 46, 156, 160, 172
Southeast Asia in the Age of Commerce. See Reid, Anthony

South China Seas, 12
state: apparatus, 8; borders, 5, 101; development, 17, 22; growth, 2, 3; ideology, 147, 152; legitimacy, 3, 8, 22, 96, 104, 130–131, 156. *See also* nation-state, ideology
stereotype, 2, 6, 26, 39–40, 58, 61, 68, 78, 83, 93
Stoler, Ann, 101, 157. See also *Capitalism and Confrontation in Sumatra's Plantation Belt*
Straits Settlement, 12
social contract, 69
Swettenham, Frank, 13, 16
sultan, 14–15, 71, 91, 157
sultanate, 13, 15, 90, 157, 165
surau, 89, 166
surrendered, 29, 84
syariah, 166
synecdoche, 20–21, 28, 142, 145
syncretic/syncretism, 13, 105, 107

Tan Cheng Lock, 76
Tan Malaka, 16
Tan, Twan Eng, 79. See also *Garden of Evening Mists, The*
Tarling, Nicholas, 103. See also *Regionalism in Southeast Asia*
Thailand, 67, 103–105, 117, 129, 168
The Martyred. See Kim, Richard
The Swimmer. *See* Cheever, John
The Vanishing American Adult. See Sasse, Ben
tin mines, 11, 13, 15, 75, 158
Teochew, 15, 156
Tongsan, 8. *See also* China
translation, 5, 38, 165
transhistorical, 33
Treaty of Pangkor, 12
Takezawa, Yasuka, 7
Tale of a Time Being. See Ozeki, Ruth
tragic, 112

tribalism, 22, 139
Tropic of Orange. See Yamashita, Karen Tei
Trump, Donald, 1, 98, 126, 169
Tsing, Anna Lowenhaupt, 5
tuberculosis, 68
Tun Dr. Mahathir Mohammad, 74, 168, 170
Tunku Abdul Rahman, 76

undercover, 73, 79, 82, 84
unequal, 3
United Malays National Organization (UMNO), 76, 166
unreliable/unreliability, 3, 10, 24, 27, 33, 42, 45, 48, 90, 146, 152, 159
uplift, 29, 130, 133, 136, 142, 148
upward mobility, 24, 120, 122–123, 128, 130–131, 133–134, 143, 152, 170
US. *See* America
US-Asia relations, 19, 127
Universities and the University Colleges Act of 1971, 106
use value, 41, 53, 57
utopia: nationalist, 118, 130, 133, 136, 144, 148; postracial, 90–91, 143–144; socialist, 139; stateless, 116
utopian: community, 172; fiction, 23; future, 130–140; hope, 137; language, 133, 136, 139, 172; novel, 94, 112; possibility, 137, 139, 144; state, 90
Utopistics. See Wallerstein, Immanuel

victim narratives, 29
victimization, 10, 40, 54, 56, 78, 86, 109, 168–169
Vietnam, 5, 100, 103, 104
villagers, 77, 94, 98–99, 165
Violence and the Sacred. See Girard, René

virtue, 12, 37–38
visible, 5, 39, 42, 89
vision: national, 130–131, 134; postracial, 91, 111–112; state, 116–117, 136, 144; social progress, of, 117

Wallerstein, Immanuel, 22–23, 138–139, 171. *See also Utopistics*
war propaganda, 73
War of the Running Dogs. See Barber, Noel
war on terror, 97, 115
wartime, 33, 41, 64, 162; ally, 60, 71
Wawasan 2020, 134
West, 11–12, 18, 70, 78, 108–109, 116, 156, 169
Westphalian, 156
white: Americans, 36, 41, 119, 122, 125; colonizer/colonialist, 16, 62, 72, 82–83; man's burden, 157; nationalism, 6, 10; rage, 6; US culture, 6; working class, 119, 123, 128, 132–133, 170
world: economy, 17, 101; history, 4, 30; stage, 9, 126–127; state system, 2–3, 5, 9, 22, 26, 28, 86, 97, 101, 109, 117, 127, 138, 140, 156; superpower, 118, 152
Wretched of the Earth. See Fanon, Franz
World War II (WWII), 2, 4–5, 10, 20, 23–24, 33, 41, 58, 60, 64, 68, 70–72, 77, 86–87, 97, 99–101, 143, 162–163

Xi Jinping, 1, 118, 130

Yamashita, Karen Tei, 171. *See also Tropic of Orange*
yellow: body, 12, 46, 81, 119, 123; peril, 1, 6, 18, 20, 122

www.ingramcontent.com/pod-product-compliance
Lightning Source LLC
Chambersburg PA
CBHW030654230426
43665CB00011B/1093